The Nixon Guaranteed Income Proposal

Substance and Process in Policy Change

M. Kenneth Bowler

Ballinger Publishing Company ● **Cambridge, Mass.**
A Subsidiary of J.B. Lippincott Company

International Standard Book Number: 0–88410–011–1

Library of Congress Catalog Card Number: 74–3093

Printed in the United States of America

Library of Congress Cataloging in Publication Data

Bowler, M   Kenneth
      The Nixon guaranteed income proposal.

        1. Public welfare—United States.   2.   Guaranteed annual income—
United States. I. Title.
HV95.B66   362.5   74–3093
ISBN   0–88410–011–1

For
Marion H. and Jennie W. Bowler

Contents

List of Tables

Acknowledgments

My largest debt is to John F. Manley, who, more than anyone, has helped me to appreciate and understand Congressional politics and political science research. I am grateful for the general guidance, specific suggestions, and words of encouragement he provided throughout this study.

Theodore R. Marmor provided needed encouragement and insight into the substance and politics of U.S. welfare policy, and Lewis Anthony Dexter helped me to understand the process of policy change. I am grateful to both of them. Others who read parts of the book at various stages of completion and offered helpful suggestions include: Kenneth W. Allen, Barbara Hinckley, Richard Nathan, Geoffrey Peterson, Austin Ranney, and Ira Sharkansky.

The cooperation of Nixon Administration officials, House Ways and Means Committee members, and Senate and House professional staff members kind enough to consent to my request for interviews made this book possible. My special thanks are due to several people who went out of their way to assist me, including Congressman James C. Corman; Alice Gordon, Legislative Assistant to Congressman Corman; Richard Nathan, former Deputy Undersecretary of HEW; Geoffrey Peterson, Legislative Assistant to Senator Abraham Ribicoff; and Robert Ruben, Administrative Assistant to Congressman Corman.

Special acknowledgment and appreciation are also due to Nancy Lloyd for her excellent research and editorial assistance, and Margaret Pladna for her cheerful and professional job of typing the manuscript. A financial grant for computer time was provided by the University of Maryland Baltimore County Computer Center.

The book would not have been written without the support of my mother and father and my wife, Ann. In large part this is a product of my parents' many years of instruction, encouragement, and sacrifice. Ann contributed editorial assistance, moral support, and necessary diversions, and she carried more than her share of family responsibilities for many months while wondering if it would ever be finished.

A number of errors of interpretation, fact, and style have been prevented by the many unselfish people who have assisted me. I assume responsibility for those that remain.

M. Kenneth Bowler

The Nixon
Guaranteed
Income
Proposal

Chapter One

Introduction: Background and Method

Several million Americans who are aged, blind, or disabled and also poor are a bit better protected against the ravages of inflation as a result of the introduction this week of the first broad Federal guarantee of a floor under income for the needy.... On a national basis, ... the new program (Supplemental Security Income program—SSI) is expected to put a billion extra dollars this year in the pockets of elderly and handicapped persons now on the fringes of destitution.

New York Times editorial, January 3, 1974

Reform of welfare programs has been a high priority item for several years in both the legislative and executive branches of government. ... The implementation of SSI ... will begin this reform process for the programs affecting the aged, blind, and disabled.... Because it does not affect the family welfare program, SSI represents only a small step toward general welfare reform. Prior to the legislation's enactment, welfare reform on a much broader scale was contemplated. However, the House and Senate could not agree on how to deal with the major aid program for families with dependent children—AFDC.

Subcommittee on Fiscal Policy, Joint Economic Committee, U.S. Congress, *Report on The New Supplemental Security Income Program*, October 1973

A major shift in U.S. welfare policy occurred in January 1974 when the federal-state public assistance programs for the aged, blind, and disabled that had been in operation for 35 years were replaced with the Supplemental Security Income

(SSI) program. The new SSI program represents several significant and fundamental changes in cash assistance programs for the poor. It provides a federally financed and administered guaranteed minimum income for needy aged, blind, and disabled Americans with uniform national eligibility standards; it transfers primary administrative and financial responsibilities for adult cash assistance programs from the states to the Federal Government; and it increases benefits for many public assistance recipients and makes approximately 2.8 million individuals eligible for cash assistance for the first time.

The enactment and implementation of the SSI program was the outcome of a four-year review of existing welfare programs and debate within and between national executive and legislative institutions over the issue of radical welfare reform. President Nixon initiated public debate in August 1969 when he unveiled a set of welfare reforms the Administration had been developing for nearly eight months. The most innovative of the proposed changes was the Family Assistance Plan, or FAP as it came to be known. This was a new program with the underlying objective that the "Federal Government" provide "a basic income" for all needy families with children "in whichever state they live." [1]

Conceptually, FAP represented a shift from the assumptions and concerns underlying existing public assistance programs to those associated with the negative income tax—one form of a guaranteed income. In operation, FAP would replace the aid-to-families-with-dependent-children (AFDC) component of public assistance with a federally administered and financed, low-benefit-level guaranteed income for all families with children ($1,600 per year for a family of four). Under this new program approximately ten million members of "working poor" families would be eligible for federal cash benefits for the first time.

In regard to the other major public assistance programs—aid to the aged, blind, and disabled (OAA, AB, and APTD)—the Administration's welfare reform package recommended the establishment of nationwide uniform eligibility standards and a national minimum payment level of $90 a month per person. However, the existing federal-state administrative structure and matching fund arrangement would be maintained for these programs. The Administration originally estimated that FAP and the other proposed changes would increase annual federal welfare expenditures 4 to 5 billion dollars (which amounted to a 138 percent increase over the previous year's public assistance expenditures), and that they would double the number of Americans eligible for cash assistance benefits from 12 to 24 million.

Given the widespread and often intense dissatisfaction with public assistance, particularly the rapidly expanding and increasingly expensive AFDC program, a Nixon welfare reform plan was not unexpected. Recommended modifications in AFDC were quite predictable. But no one expected this Administration to propose and energetically seek congressional approval of the establishment of a guaranteed income, federal takeover of AFDC, and the largest single expansion of welfare since the implementation of the 1935 Social Security legislation. Few proposals would represent a more radical change in U.S. domestic policy or dramatic shift in the "normal" response of national political leaders to welfare problems over the past several decades: a response Gilbert Steiner has characterized as "tireless tinkering with the status quo."[2]

With only minor changes, Nixon's welfare proposal was approved by the House Ways and Means Committee and passed in the House of Representatives by a vote of 243 to 155, just eight months after it was publicly announced. John Osborne referred to House passage of a guaranteed income for families with children as "the miracle of the 1970 congressional session."[3] However, the House-approved welfare reforms did not pass the Senate in the 91st Congress.

When the 92nd Congress convened in January 1971, Nixon announced that the enactment of his welfare reform bill would be "White House priority number one" and his "major legislative goal in 1971."[4] The House Ways and Means Committee met in executive session for five months engaged in what Chairman Wilbur Mills described as "the most thorough-going, extensive and intensive review and analysis" his committee had ever made of public assistance and U.S. social welfare policy.[5] On May 17, 1971, Ways and Means approved legislation containing a modified version of Nixon's Family Assistance Plan and the new Supplemental Security Income program.

The Committee's bill, which passed the House of Representatives in June, would replace AFDC, OAA, AB, and APTD with federal guaranteed income programs for families with children (FAP) and aged, blind, and disabled adults (SSI), and double both federal public assistance costs and the number of individuals eligible for cash assistance. In October 1972, fifteen months after receiving the House bill, the Senate approved the new SSI program but rejected the most innovative component of the House-approved welfare legislation—replacing AFDC with the Family Assistance Plan.

This book is an account and analysis of the development of FAP and the Nixon Administration's decision to sponsor a guaranteed income for families with children in 1969; the modification and approval of Nixon's welfare proposal by the House of Representatives in 1971; the approval of the SSI program and defeat of FAP in the Senate in 1971; and the substantive changes in federal cash assistance programs that were developed and debated, rejected or adopted between 1969 and 1973.

THEORY AND METHOD

A Decision Making Framework

In the following chapters the executive and legislative actions pertaining to FAP and SSI have been organized within a decision making framework derived from a number of authors including Simon, Snyder, Rosenau, and

Lindblom.[6] As stated by Rosenau, underlying the decision making approach to politics is

> ... the simple notion that political action is undertaken by concrete human beings and that comprehension of the dynamics of this action requires viewing the world from the perspective of these identifiable actors.[7]

The basic principle of the approach is that the perspectives and actions of political actors or policy makers are reconstructed in terms of, and for the purpose of explaining,

> one main form of behavior, the decision to pursue one course of action rather than many others that might be pursued.[8]

The essential elements of policy change suggested by a decision making focus include the processes and conditions associated with shifts in the attention of policy makers to particular policy issues and courses of action, the development or design of new policies, and the mobilization of support for and final selection of particular innovative policy actions.[9]

This study examines the *decision making processes,* the *decision conditions,* and the *substance of welfare policy decisions* reached in the White House, House of Representatives, and the Senate in the case of FAP and SSI, and attempts to link process and conditions to substantive policy changes proposed and approved.

Decision making processes, as defined here, are the intellectual and interactive, formal and informal activities by which policy makers respond to public problems and arrive at policy decisions, including attention directing, agenda setting, and policy review, choice, design, and support mobilizing processes.

Decision conditions include circumstances or factors within and outside the political institutions that affect both the nature and outcome of these decision activities or processes. The implicit distinction between decision processes and decision conditions is that the former focuses on *how* a policy decision was reached and the latter focuses on *why* a particular course of action was approved or disapproved.

Policy substance refers to the following components of public policy:[10]

1. The *Conceptual* Component: the explicit and implicit goals, values, identified problems and conditions, social images, and assumptions of causal relationships which constitute the general symbolic context, rationale, and justification for prescribed governmental courses of action.

2. The *Technical* Component: the prescribed course of action (administrative structures and arrangements, operating principles, programs) for achieving the goals and promoting the values. Or, the explicit rules and procedures which, in varying degrees of specificity, inform those who implement and administer the policy what to do, how, and when.
3. The *Consequential* Component: the costs and achieved results of a particular course of action as well as other intended and unintended social, economic and political consequences.

Identifiable alterations or shifts in conceptual, technical, or consequential dimensions of a particular policy or program constitute policy change.

This conceptualization of public policy, combined with the decision making framework outlined above, suggests that policy change occurs when in the process of reassessing an existing policy or program the attention and preferences of enough decision makers shift to new problem interpretations, policy objectives, or administrative arrangements with significantly different results or consequences. One way, then, of explaining policy change (and a focus that suggests an analytical link between substance and process in political decision making) is to try to describe the process and conditions associated with the shift in attention and preferences of policy makers to innovative policy alternatives.[11]

The following analysis describes the changes in conceptual, technical, and consequential components of U.S. welfare policy contained in the welfare decisions made in the White House and Congress. It then attempts to explain these decisions by identifying the processes and conditions associated with the shift in attention and preferences of national policy makers to the policy innovations FAP and SSI represented.

DATA

The most important source of data was off-the-record, semistructured interviews with some of the Administration and Congressional officials who participated in the decision making activities associated with FAP and SSI.[12] Other sources of information, which in some cases provided a check on the accuracy or validity of the interview data, included newspaper accounts and the public record (committee hearings, committee votes, the Congressional Record, White House and Department of Health, Education, and Welfare statements and reports); limited access to verbatim transcripts of the 1971 Ways and Means executive sessions on welfare reform; and personal observations of the welfare debate I made while working from January through September 1971 as an American Political Science Association Congressional Fellow in the offices of Senator Abraham Ribicoff and House Ways and Means member James C. Corman.

ORGANIZATION

Chapter Two contains an analysis of U.S. welfare policy and programs as of 1972. Chapter Three examines the changes in existing policy proposed by Nixon, or the substance of the welfare decisions made by the White House in 1969. The processes and conditions associated with the development of FAP and President Nixon's decision to sponsor a guaranteed income for families with children are described in Chapter Four. The welfare policy decisions made by Ways and Means and the House of Representatives in 1971 are examined in Chapter Five. Chapter Six describes the processes by which Nixon's welfare plan was reviewed, modified, and approved by Ways and Means in 1971 and the conditions associated with House approval of a guaranteed income. Decision processes and conditions associated with the Senate response in 1972 to the House approved welfare legislation, and major changes in welfare policy enacted between 1969 and 1974, are examined in Chapter Seven. In Chapter Eight decision making processes and conditions in the White House and Congress associated with FAP and SSI are compared with the "incremental change" model of decision making, and elements of a complementary "radical change" model of decision making are suggested.

Chapter Two

The State of Welfare 1972

*We are a benevolent nation. We have always been. We have never
willynilly let our unfortunate, disabled people suffer. Some have,
I know. But we have never willynilly let it happen. Fundamentally,
we want to help all such people, the aged, the blind, the unfortunate, the uneducated. . . .*

—Congressman Phil Landrum
1970

*There are more people in poverty today than there were last year
and yet we have some $31 billion budgeted to help end poverty in
1972.
. . . We may find that much of the money that is being spent to
alleviate poverty does not bring a single person out of poverty.*

—Senator Abraham Ribicoff
1971

At the time it was enacted, and for many years later, the Social Security Act of
1935 was considered revolutionary because it "changed both the concept of
personal economic security in the United States and the nature of federal-state
relationships in the welfare field."[1] Until this time, income security had been
for the most part the responsibility of the individual and aiding the poor the
responsibility of charitable organizations and local governments. The Social
Security Act, which established federal social insurance and public assistance
programs, identified income security and aiding the poor as federal responsibilities and thereby marked the establishment of a new governmental function
at the national level.

    Between 1935 and 1972 a wide variety of federal programs were
enacted with the purpose of combating poverty and providing individuals and

families with some measure of income security. In August 1971 the Nixon Administration, at the request of Senator Abraham Ribicoff, submitted a report to the Senate Finance Committee which listed 170 different federal programs in existence at that time which "provide benefits to the poor."[2] What follows is a description of the primary conceptual, technical, and consequential elements of U.S. social welfare programs in 1972—before changes resulting from the welfare policy review initiated by the Nixon reform proposal had been implemented.

This description groups the programs into four major categories—social insurance, public assistance, income in-kind, and rehabilitation and opportunities programs—and provides the basis for discussion in following chapters of the extent and nature of change in U.S. welfare policy represented in the reforms proposed and enacted between 1969 and 1972.

U.S. WELFARE PROGRAMS IN 1972: OBJECTIVES, PRINCIPLES, AND PROCEDURES

Underlying U.S. social welfare policy is the conviction that income derived from employment is the basic source of economic security for all Americans. The wide variety of federal programs that attempt to encourage employment opportunities, the imposition of minimum wage requirements to insure adequate income from employment, federally supported training, education, and other "manpower" programs aimed at increasing the employability and income-earning skills of individuals, and the federal-state employment services that attempt to bring individuals and jobs together should be considered key elements in U.S. social welfare policy. In other words, the fundamental strategy of the policy is to encourage employment opportunities that provide adequate income.

Social Insurance

Other programs, which should be considered as supplemental to this basic strategy, can be grouped into four supplementary levels of protection against poverty. The first is *social insurance* and the major programs in this category are indicated in Table 2–1.

The purpose of these programs—Old Age Survivors Insurance, Disability Insurance, Unemployment Insurance, and Workman's Compensation—is to provide

> a permanent, systematic national mechanism to protect the majority of workers against some of the major economic hazards of life by assuring them of continued income, from government sources, when normal income ceased because of loss of job, old age, and similar factors.[3]

Table 2-1.   Major Social Insurance Programs, Benefit Outlays, and
Recipients in Fiscal 1972

Programs	Benefit Outlays (billions)	Recipients (millions)
Old age survivors insurance	$34.5	24.3
Disability insurance	4.0	2.8
Unemployment insurance	6.4	15.4
Workman's compensation	3.0	Not available

Source: U.S., Congress, Joint Economic Committee, *Public Income Transfer Programs,*
James R. Storey, December 1973; U.S., Congress, Senate, Committee on Finance, *Information on Federal Programs to Aid the Poor,* 92nd Congress, 2nd sess., February 1972.

To be eligible for the cash benefits provided by these programs, a person, or
a member of a family, must have been employed for a specified length of
time in a covered occupation and made contributions toward the financing
of benefits during this employment period. Old age survivors insurance, or
Social Security, is the basic means of providing a level of income security for
the worker and his family; at present about nine out of every ten persons
who are working for a living are covered by this program.[4]
        Since enactment in 1935, certain principles have been important
in directing the operations of social insurance programs. First and foremost
is the notion that the benefits they provide for the worker and his family
"grow out of his own work," or that they are a sort of an extension of the
individual's own earnings. Within statutory established minimum and maximum payment levels, the monthly benefits reflect the amount of prior contributions in that the more a person earns and contributes the higher his benefits.
Related to this is the notion, reinforced by the contributory nature of the
financing, that the benefits are "earned" and that eligibility is a matter of
"right." In other words, the benefits do not carry the stigma of "charity," no
means test is required to receive them, and if an individual can fit himself in
the legal definition of a beneficiary, the officials in charge have no discretion
to withhold his benefits.[5]
        The administration of these programs and delivery of benefits is
highly formalized, simplified, and automated, requiring a limited amount of
contact between recipients and administrators.

Public Assistance
        The second set of programs is *categorical public assistance.* The
major public assistance programs operating in 1972 are shown in Table 2-2.
These programs—Aid to Families with Dependent Children, Old Age Assistance,
Aid to the Blind, Aid to the Disabled, and Veterans' Pensions—were designed
to supplement social insurance and employment as the primary source of in-

Table 2-2.   Major Public Assistance Programs, Benefit Outlays, and Recipients in Fiscal 1972

Programs	Benefit Outlays (billions)	Recipients (millions)
Aid to families with dependent children (AFDC)	$6.7	10.8
Old age assistance (OAA)	2.5	2.3
Aid to the blind (AB)	.1	.1
Aid to the disabled (APTD)	1.5	1.1
Veterans' pensions	2.5	2.3

Source: U.S., Congress, Joint Economic Committee, *Public Income Transfer Programs,* James R. Storey, December 1973; U.S., Congress, Senate, Committee on Finance, *Information on Federal Programs to Aid the Poor,* 92nd Congress, 2nd sess., February 1972.

come security by providing cash assistance to needy individuals *unable to work* and to certain groups with special needs or status such as veterans.[6]

The central objective was to provide at least a minimum subsistence level of aid for the poor who for some obvious reason cannot be expected to support themselves by working. To be eligible for these benefits an individual must be poor; that is, he must prove his present income and resources are below a specified level, and he must also fit into one of the following categories: aged, blind, permanently and totally disabled, families with dependent children where one parent is deceased or otherwise absent from the home (or, in 25 states, where the father is unemployed), and veterans.

There are several underlying principles and concerns that have had a major effect on the development and operation of public assistance. Most important is the notion that cash assistance should not be made available to everyone who is poor, only those who are poor "through no fault of their own." Therefore, federally aided, means-tested, cash assistance programs were designed only for the selected categories of "unemployables" or "deserving" poor identified above.[7]

Another "fundamental doctrine" of the original Social Security Act that contained both the social insurance programs and public assistance was that the two types of programs were to be carefully distinguished in terms of administration, funding, program purpose, the nature of the benefits, and the recipients. For example, as contrasted with Social Security or unemployment insurance, public assistance benefits are considered unearned, and not to be received by anyone as a matter of right but as public charity. Any stigma associated with the notion of charity or the "public dole" is justified as a means of preventing idleness and discouraging individuals from applying for public assistance.

Furthermore, social insurance is viewed as a necessary and permanent component of U.S. social welfare policy and the total economic enterprise, whereas public assistance programs have been considered temporary—emergency or interim programs that would gradually "wither away" when everyone had earned protection under the social insurance programs.[8]

Another central assumption in the design of public assistance was that the programs should be managed by governments closest to home, "where judgment of what is 'really needed' and what the taxpayers can 'afford to pay' is alleged to be most reliable."[9] As a result, with the exception of veterans' pensions, the decision to operate the programs listed in Table 2-2 (AFDC, OAA, AB, and APTD), until the implementation of the SSI program in January 1974, was with the states, as to a large degree was the determination of who was eligible for benefits, how much assistance was granted, and under what conditions.[10]

The extent of federal financing varied from state to state in accordance with formulas established for each program. The Federal Government provided financial encouragement for participation, but it could not compel states to offer these programs. On the other hand, if a state chose to implement one or more of the programs and provided its share of the funds, it could set whatever benefit level it chose and the Federal Government was obligated to meet whatever its share of the total cost turned out to be according to the statutory matching formula. Consequently, there was (and still is in AFDC) a significant amount of disparity from state to state in terms of eligibility requirements, program coverage, administrative practices, payment levels, and cost to local taxpayers for public assistance.

In July 1972, maximum yearly benefits paid to a family of four under AFDC varied from $720 in Mississippi to $4,332 in Michigan and $4,500 in Alaska; maximum yearly payments to an aged couple under OAA ranged from $1,380 in Maine to $3,960 in California and $4,100 in Alaska;[11] the percent of the states' public assistance expenditures paid by the Federal Government ranged from 34 percent in Alaska to 82 percent in Mississippi during fiscal 1972;[12] and the amount expended per inhabitant for public assistance in fiscal 1971 ranged from $13.02 in Indiana to $85.55 in California.[13] By 1972, state control over standards and requirements had declined as federal regulations increased. However, the states still had more control over public assistance than did the Department of Health, Education, and Welfare.[14]

In 1972 three-fourths of those receiving cash benefits under the four major programs (AFDC, OAA, AB and APTD) were AFDC recipients, and this one program accounted for over 60 percent of the total cost for public assistance. AFDC recipients are viewed by many as undeserving in the sense that they are to blame for their destitution because of idleness, laziness, immorality, or alcoholism.[15] This attitude on the part of the public, some legislators, and some of those who administer the program has resulted in the establishment of time consuming, complicated, and highly discretionary investigations to verify eligibility, as well as requirements that attempt to regulate the morality, mobility, and life style of the recipients.[16]

Income In-Kind

Federal programs that supplement low incomes through direct provision of goods and services make up a third component of U.S. welfare policy. The major "income in-kind" programs are listed in Table 2-3. These programs—Medicare, Medicaid, food stamps, food distribution programs, public housing—were enacted in response to the "discovery" in the 1960s of poverty, malnutrition, disease, inadequate housing, and health care among much of the low income population,[17] and the realization that the private market cannot supply sufficient quantities of these goods and services with necessary speed or at a price many low income Americans can afford.

Along with the desire to alleviate hunger, sickness, etc., several ideas have guided and influenced the development and course of these programs. A central theme is that providing the needy with assistance in the form of in-kind benefits assures that the family will use a portion of its resources on food and health care.[18] In other words, it is another means of regulating behavior by constraining what the poor can buy with their resources. From this perspective the programs constitute a form of compulsory budgeting. Also, there is the notion that adequate health care, nutrition, and housing might enable some of the recipients to become more self-sufficient.

Medicare should be distinguished from the other programs in Table 2-3. It is a national hospital and medical insurance program for the aged administered by the Social Security Administration. The underlying principles and administrative procedures are the same as those discussed in relation to the social insurance programs. Medicaid, on the other hand, is an optional

Table 2-3.   Major Income In-Kind Programs, Benefit Outlays, and Recipients in Fiscal 1972

Programs	Benefit Outlays (billions)	Recipients (millions)
Medicare (health care for the aged)	$8.5	9.8
Medicaid (health care for the poor)	7.0	19.0
Food stamps	2.0	10.0
Public housing	.8	1.0
Food distribution programs	.9	32.0

Source: U.S., Congress, Joint Economic Committee, *Public Income Transfer Programs,* James R. Storey, December 1973; U.S., Congress, Senate, Committee on Finance, *Information on Federal Programs to Aid the Poor,* 92nd Congress, 2nd sess., February 1972.

program of health care for the poor, managed by state and local authorities with shared federal and state financing. It is a means-tested program with eligibility standards and benefit levels determined by state and local authorities under certain federal guidelines.

As of 1972 the food stamp and food commodities programs had never been in operation in some parts of the country. In other income in-kind programs—public housing for example—the demand far surpasses the supply. In sum, there was no guarantee that a poor person would receive Medicaid, food stamps, or public housing benefits, and when he did the application process was, as with public assistance, time consuming, inconvenient, and complicated.

Rehabilitation and Opportunities

The fourth category of programs comprises what has been labeled the "rehabilitation and opportunities strategy" for combating poverty in the U.S. Several are listed in Table 2–4.

These programs provide the poor with counseling, training, job placement services, financial incentives for working, and penalties for not working—all with the objective of raising their income earning capacities. Although most legislators, administrators, and welfare experts agree that the purpose of these programs is to help the poor become self-supporting, there is disagreement, at least in terms of problem focus and emphasis, as to why this is a legitimate or justifiable use of public resources.

To some, helping the poor become self-sufficient means "transforming welfare recipients into breadwinners,"[19] which they hope will

Table 2–4. Major Rehabilitation and Opportunities Programs, Benefit Outlays, and Recipients in Fiscal 1972

Programs	Benefit Outlays (billions)	Recipients (millions)
Childhood development (Head Start)	$ .4	.6
Educational programs for the disadvantaged	1.8	Not available
Employment services	.2	"
Manpower programs	1.2	"
Vocational Education and rehabilitation programs	.6	"
Work incentive program	.2	.2
Community action operations	.6	8.0
Social services	.7	10.7

Source: U.S., Congress, Joint Economic Committee, *Public Income Transfer Programs,* James R. Storey, December 1973; U.S., Congress, Senate, Committee on Finance, *Information on Federal Programs to Aid the Poor,* 92nd Congress, 2nd sess., February 1972.

eventually reduce the number of persons receiving welfare and thereby reduce welfare costs. From this perspective, social services and rehabilitation is an attempt to rescue the principle that public assistance would wither away with the growth of social insurance programs.[20] Others support these programs primarily because they might increase the earnings of the poor and thereby reduce poverty and the emotional and physical suffering it produces.

The concept of social services and rehabilitation was enacted into law with the 1962 amendments to the public assistance programs, which authorized 75 percent federal matching funds to states for certain prescribed services and rehabilitation programs. At the time of their enactment there were 3.1 million AFDC recipients, which represented a 40 percent increase since 1955 despite relatively high employment and continued expansion of social insurance coverage. The objective, or hope, of these amendments is stated with some clarity in the report of the House Ways and Means Committee:

> The new approach . . . places emphasis on the provision of services to help families become self-supporting rather than dependent on Welfare checks. The bill would . . . provide incentives to recipients . . . to improve their condition so as to render continual public assistance . . . unnecessary. . . . Experience has shown that adequately trained personnel can be one of the largest factors in reducing, ultimately, the cost of public assistance programs.[21]

The strategy of "preparing the welfare population emotionally and vocationally to become labor market participants"[22] (or, "getting poverty out of the people"[23]) was restated in the War on Poverty legislation. The antipoverty programs that were enacted in 1964 focused on changing people and the educational and training systems, "without altering economic policies or public assistance policies which would actually redistribute income or expand the number of jobs and wages available to the poor."[24]

By 1967 the number of AFDC recipients had increased to 5.3 million and faith in social services and social workers as poverty reducing mechanisms was rapidly decreasing. That year Congress approved and President Johnson signed into law what Daniel Moynihan called "the first purposively punitive welfare legislation in the history of the American national government."[25] According to Gilbert Steiner, as the 1967 Social Security Amendments made their way through Congress,

> the old slogans—services instead of support, rehabilitation instead of relief—were abandoned and work incentives became the new thing in the continuing search for relief from relief cases.[26]

With the intention of halting the increase in welfare costs which was occurring mainly in the AFDC program, these amendments ordered the so-called "AFDC freeze," which limited further federal financial matching funds after June 1968 for the Aid to Families of Dependent Children program. They established the Work Incentive Program (WIN), which expanded work training programs, made *mandatory* the referral for training or work of "appropriate" AFDC adults (including the mothers of preschool children not needed at home), authorized a training incentive payment of $30 a month, and authorized more funds for day care facilities. As a work incentive, recipients would be allowed to keep the first $30 of monthly earnings plus one-third of any additional earnings.

The "rehabilitation and opportunities" programs are based on the assumption that poverty is the result of individual handicaps or deficiencies such as the lack of work skills, education, motivation, or knowledge about jobs. The remedies are therefore directed at changing individuals and, as summarized by Martin Rein, together they comprise a strategy with the following main characteristics:

> *education and manpower* retraining to teach literary and occupational skills, *social services* to provide counseling and concrete services such as day care to facilitate the transition from welfare to work, combined with an incentive to improve the level of living for those who work. . . . Finally to these inducements has been added a *compulsory* feature, which requires welfare mothers to accept training and/or work.[27]

COSTS AND EFFECTS OF WELFARE PROGRAMS IN 1972

Expenditures and Distribution of Benefits

The twenty-two major programs and the estimated federal, state, and local expenditures for fiscal 1972 are shown in Table 2-5. As indicated, they cost $99.6 billion. It was estimated that from 50 to 60 million individuals derived benefits from one or more of the programs in 1972.[28] One-quarter of the $100 billion went for the Poverty Entitlement Programs, which provided benefits specifically for the poor, or low income persons. These were means-tested programs and the amount of benefits received were generally based on the current cash income of the recipients. An estimated 25 to 30 million persons received benefits from one or more of these programs, which is considered to be a good approximation of the true size of the nation's 1972 "welfare rolls."[29]

Three-quarters of the $100 billion was spent on the Normal Entitlement Programs, which provided benefits for individuals and families— some of them poor—for reasons other than poverty such as prior work experience or veteran status. Most of the benefits distributed under these programs

Table 2-5.   Major Social Welfare Programs and Benefit Outlays for Fiscal Year 1972
(billions of dollars)

Program	Benefit Outlays		
	Total	Federal	State & Local
Poverty Entitlement Programs			
AFDC	$ 6.7	$ 3.7	$ 3.0
OAA	2.5	1.7	.8
AB	.1	.06	.1
APTD	1.5	.8	.7
General assistance[a]	.7	–	.7
Veterans' pensions	2.5	2.5	–
School lunch program	.5	.5	–
Food stamps	2.0	2.0	–
Food Distribution programs	.3	.3	–
Public housing	.8	.8	–
Medicaid	7.0	3.9	3.1
Total poverty programs	$24.6	$16.3	$ 8.3
Normal Entitlement Programs			
Social Security	$34.5	$34.5	–
Disability insurance	4.0	4.0	–
Railroad retirement	2.1	2.1	–
Civil service retirement	3.4	3.4	–
Other retirement programs: federal	4.0	4.0	–
state, and local retirement[a]	3.3	–	3.3
Unemployment insurance	6.4	6.4	–
Workmen's compensation[a]	3.0	.2	2.8
Veterans' medical care[b]	2.2	2.2	–
Veterans' compensation[b]	3.6	3.6	–
Medicare	8.5	8.5	–
Total normal programs	$75.0	$68.9	$ 6.1
Total all programs	$99.6	$85.2	$14.4

Source: U.S., Congress, Joint Economic Committee, *Public Income Transfer Programs,* James R. Storey, December 1973.
[a]Expenditures are for calendar year 1970.
[b]This program is in part an income-tested or poverty entitlement program.

went to the nonpoor; however, they did prevent millions of persons from requiring benefits under one or more of the Poverty Entitlement Programs. It was estimated by the Nixon Administration that in 1972, twenty-two percent of the $32 billion in benefits paid out under the Old Age and Survivors Insurance programs, 23 percent of the $4 billion disability insurance benefits, and 22 percent of the $9.5 billion spent under Medicare went to the poor, or to persons with incomes below the Census Bureau defined poverty level.[30] Another study indicated that in 1965, forty-six percent of the poor house-

The administrative styles and procedures associated with the
ograms differed significantly. In general, the eligibility determination and
her administrative procedures associated with programs that distributed
nefits primarily to nonpoor recipients, the Normal Entitlement Programs,
re simplified, automated, nondiscretionary and no means test was required.
ministrative processes associated with programs that provided benefits
marily for the poor were just the reverse.

Antipoverty Effect

Existing programs and expenditures in 1972 provided a level of
nomic security for many Americans and benefits which improved the living
ditions of many low income individuals and families. However, they did not
viate poverty in the United States. According to a Census Bureau report
lished in November 1971, there were about 25.5 million persons with
mes below the poverty level of $3,968 for a nonfarm family of four in
0: about 13 percent of the total population. This represented an increase
.2 million, or 5.1 percent, since 1969 and marked the first significant annual
ease in the poverty population since 1959, the earliest year for which
parable data are available.[32]

A Census Bureau report published in June 1973 showed that in
1 there were 25.6 million persons with incomes below the poverty line and
this decreased to 24.5 million in 1972, which was still slightly above the
9 figure of 24.3.[33] The decrease of 1.1 million from 1971 to 1972
ably reflected a 10 percent increase in Social Security benefits which took
ct January 1, 1972 inasmuch as many of the people whose income rose
e the poverty level in 1972 were elderly, white individuals.

One reason existing programs had not eradicated poverty is that
were not intended to. Social insurance was supposed to prevent destitu-
among workers, not cure it. Public assistance was supposed to help the
s provide whatever level of aid they deemed appropriate to certain
ified groups of people who could not be expected to provide for themselves—
o all poor people. The objectives of the income in-kind and rehabilitation
ams were to prevent starvation and disease in the short run, and to cure
ty, not immediately by direct assistance, but through the long term
ss of helping the poor develop the knowledge, values, and skills that would
e them, eventually, to get a job that provides an adequate income.

There were many poor people in the United States who did not
y for any of the direct assistance programs, not all of the programs were
ting in every part of the country, and in many areas where they did
the benefits were not adequate. The Census Bureau report indicated
bout 30 percent of the families with incomes below the poverty line
70 were receiving social security benefits and 30 percent received some
e from public assistance. As some of these were the same families, less

Table 2-6.   Distribution of Fiscal 1972 Welfare Ex
Income of Recipients and Nature of Benefits
(billions of dollars)

	Benefits			
Recipients	In-Kind & Services		Cash	
Poor	$14.0	(66%)	$18.9	(24%)
Nonpoor	7.3	(34%)	59.4	(76%)
		(100%)		(100%)
Total	$21.3		$78.3	
	(21%)		(79%)	

Source: U.S., Congress, Joint Economic Committee, *Public Income Tr*
James R. Storey, December 1973; U.S., Congress, Senate, Committee
tion on Federal Programs to Aid the Poor, 92nd Congress, 2nd sess., F

holds receiving social security checks had their yearly incom
poverty level by these benefits.[31]

Table 2-6 shows the distribution of cash and in-
benefits to poor and nonpoor recipients. The Census Bureau
poverty was used to distinguish the poor from the nonpoor,
latter group with incomes just above the poverty level of $3
technically "nonpoor." The dollar figures and percentages a
from the several sources listed. Although they represent onl
mations of actual expenditures, they do indicate the genera
social welfare benefits in 1972.

As shown, most of the benefits (approximately)
the nonpoor. This is because, as indicated in Table 2-5, 75
benefit outlays were for Normal Entitlement Programs, wh
reasons other than poverty. About four-fifths of the tota
lays were in the form of direct cash assistance and 20 perc
of income in-kind or services.

However, the two general types of benefits we
equally among the poor and nonpoor recipients. About 7(
fourths of the $78.3 billion in cash benefits went to the n
by the Census Bureau, and the remaining one-quarter wer
On the other hand, the poor received about two-thirds of
service benefits. In sum, by 1972 we had forged a social v
provided primarily cash assistance, most of which went to
not necessarily undeserving or "unneedy" persons. Appro
in benefits went to the poor as a result of existing progra
50 percent of this was in the form of goods and services
health care, counseling, training, and rehabilitation progr

than 60 percent of the poor were receiving any cash assistance. And, the 50 to 60 percent of the 25.5 million poor people who were receiving some cash still had a yearly income of less than $3,968.[34] (Many of those defined as poor were receiving benefits from the income in-kind and service programs not included in the Census Bureau calculation of yearly income.) Those who were not receiving any cash assistance were, in large part, the "working poor": the individuals and their families who worked full or part time so they were not eligible for public assistance, but whose yearly earnings were less than $3,968.

Political Reactions and Policy Issues

A good many people, including some of those involved in the formulation and funding of U.S. welfare programs, were disturbed in 1972 because they thought there were too many programs costing too much money. They worried that existing programs were undermining the fundamental value of employment in a free enterprise system as the basis of income security in the United States. Others were dismayed at the relatively small percentage of the public resources spent in combating hunger, poverty, and disease. And, there was a growing number of people who were disturbed by the fact that in spite of 170 different programs, four intervention strategies, and yearly expenditures amounting to $100 billion dollars, poverty, hunger, malnutrition, and inadequate health care would still not be eliminated in the United States.

The Senate Finance Committee was holding hearings on the Nixon welfare reform proposal when the 1971 Census report showing a significant increase in poverty between 1969 and 1970 was released. Senator Abraham Ribicoff of Connecticut, a member of the Committee and former Secretary of Health, Education and Welfare, found the increase in poverty most perplexing. In reaction to the report he offered the following observations and suggestions to the then Secretary of HEW, Elliott L. Richardson.

> As I look at the figures that I have, 25.5 million Americans live in poverty. If these Americans had no income whatsoever it would take $29.9 billion to bring them up to the poverty level. But these 25.5 million do have income amounting to $18.5 billion. Therefore, an additional amount of some $11 billion could move everybody above the poverty level.
>
> Now if we are making expenditures of $31 billion on poverty programs, and if there is a great question as to what portion of the 25.5 million poor people are being taken out of poverty because of these programs, and if you consider that by the elimination of $11 billion worth of these programs we might be able to take everybody out of poverty, I think we should start examining the need for all of these programs. . . . I think that the executive branch, . . . and we as Senators and Congressmen who keep voting

these huge sums of money to end poverty, ought to know what we are getting for our money. There are more people in poverty today than there were last year and yet we have some $31 billion budgeted to help end poverty in 1972.

. . . We may find that much of the money that is being spent to alleviate poverty does not bring a single person out of poverty. Therefore, we can take that money and increase what we want to spend to really take people out of poverty by providing them direct financial assistance.[35]

Ribicoff was aware that many of those with incomes below the poverty level were receiving assistance in the form of health care through Medicaid and Medicare, food stamps, and food commodities which were not included in the Census Bureau Report. He was also aware that this statement to Secretary Richardson reflected some ideas which were *not* reflected in existing welfare policy and programs.

In the first place he was assuming an income definition of poverty and an income identification of those deserving public assistance; he implied that what the poor need most is money and not rehabilitation or income in-kind; and he was suggesting that an objective of U.S. welfare policy was, or should be, the elimination of income poverty by raising everyone's income above a certain minimum level. The enactment of legislation establishing programs that incorporated and were consistent with the logic of these concepts would represent a radical change in U.S. social welfare policy: the most significant change since the Social Security Act of 1935.

Ribicoff understood this because it represented a shift in his own thinking. He was the Secretary of HEW who promoted and defended in Congress the 1962 welfare amendments which put an emphasis on "services instead of support, rehabilitation instead of relief, and training for useful work instead of prolonged dependency."[36] In a memorandum to the Ways and Means Committee in support of the social service amendments he said, in 1962:

. . . too much emphasis has been placed on just getting an assistance check into the hands of an individual. If we are ever going to move constructively in this field, we must come to recognize that our efforts must involve a variety of helpful services, of which giving a money payment is only one. . . .[37]

The apparent inconsistencies in Senator Ribicoff's 1962 memo and his remarks to Secretary Richardson in 1971 reflect two basic controversies in U.S. social welfare policy in 1972 and at the present time.

First, should the policy and programs focus primarily on the economic needs of the poor and concentrate on providing an adequate level of assistance for all those in need, or should the preoccupation be with reducing the welfare rolls and welfare costs with an emphasis on training, rehabilitation, social services, work incentives, and compulsory work and training requirements? Second, when assistance is provided, should it be in the form of direct cash transfers, income in-kind, or, as at present, some of both?

And the shift in the Senator's thinking about the appropriate objectives and techniques of U.S. social welfare policy reflected in the two quotes suggests some of the important changes contained in Nixon's welfare reform proposal announced in August 1969.

Chapter Three

Welfare Policy: The Nixon Reforms

Income by right is not politically feasible in the near future. The President will not support it and Congress would not pass it if he did.

　　　　　　　　　　　—Bill Cavala and Aaron Wildavsky,
　　　　　　　　　　　　Spring 1969

Family Assistance is a system of graduated income maintenance provided as a matter of right to all persons with dependent children.

　　　　　　　　　　　—Daniel Moynihan, July, 1970

FAP: "A NEW DEPARTURE IN SOCIAL POLICY"

Public statements by Nixon Administration officials described the welfare reform plan revealed by President Nixon on August 8, 1969 as a "revolutionary effort to reform a welfare system in crisis"[1] and a "new departure in social policy," not simply "an incremental change—a marginal improvement in an old program."[2] It represented "total reform," according to official statements, because it would replace the Aid to Families with Dependent Children program with "a new family assistance system"; and because family assistance was the "cornerstone" of a new overall approach or strategy which would produce changes in all major social welfare programs.[3]

According to President Nixon, the fundamental proposition of this new approach, labeled an "income strategy," was

That the best judge of each family's priorities is that family itself, that the best way to ameliorate the hardships of poverty is to provide the family with additional income—to be spent as that family sees fit.[4]

23

In other words, the basic thrust of this new strategy was to increase the buying power of the poor by providing them with cash to purchase food and other essentials as opposed to developing "elaborate secondary markets wherein the poor are required to obtain the goods and services—housing, clothing, food, and whatever—that other persons obtain in a general market."[5]

Officially, the present "crisis" in welfare that necessitated radical reform was the result of four problems with the present welfare system:

1.   The wide disparities in benefit levels and eligibility requirements through-out the country and the resulting inequities and undesirable incentives.
2.   The inadequacy of benefits and persistence of poverty in many parts of the country.
3.   The ineffective and inefficient administrative structure and demeaning eligibility determination procedures.
4.   The dramatic and seemingly uncontrollable increase in welfare costs and caseloads in recent years, which was adding to the financial problems of states and large cities.

The essential elements of Nixon's welfare proposal can be described in relation to these problems.

Reducing the Inequities and Improper Incentives

The official public documents and statements emphasized that the first priority of the reform plan was to "correct, insofar as possible," three inequities produced by the present system: (1) the state-to-state inequities resulting from the wide differences in benefit levels and eligibility require-ments among the states; (2) the inequitable treatment of low income, male-headed families relative to female-headed families in the 25 states that had *not* adopted the AFDC-UP program, which provided benefits for families where the father was living at home but was unemployed; and (3) the inequities between those who work (the "working poor") and those who do not (the "welfare poor") in areas where welfare benefits were higher than wages from low paying jobs.[6]

The Administration charged that these inequities were wrong in principle and intolerable in operation because in the 25 states without the AFDC-UP program they provided an economic incentive for unemployed fathers to leave their families so the wife and children would be eligible for benefits. In those states where the AFDC-UP program was operating and the benefits were higher than earnings from low paying jobs, there was an economic incen-tive for low wage earners to quit work and go on welfare. And, the state-to-state inequities *might* be enticing poor people from rural areas where welfare benefits were low to move into already overcrowded urban areas with higher benefits thereby adding to the financial pressures of many large cities.

With the objective of reducing these inequities and improper incentives, the Administration proposed that the present AFDC program be scrapped and a new, federally funded and administered program called the Family Assistance Plan (FAP) be instituted in its place. This program would provide direct federal payments to *all needy families with children,* which included present AFDC, AFDC-UP recipients, and, for the first time, poor families headed by full time male workers—or the 2 to 3 million "working poor" families. The presence of a child in the household would be the key to eligibility, which meant that poor childless couples and single individuals would be ineligible for benefits.

The basic yearly federal payment for an eligible family would be at the rate of $500 a person for the first two family members and $300 for each additional member, which would establish a federally guaranteed minimum payment of $1,600 for a family of four with no other income. States in which existing AFDC benefits were higher than the proposed federal payment would be required to continue to pay the difference between the FAP guaranteed minimum and what they were paying to *present recipients.* They would not be required to supplement the federal payment to the "working poor."

Administration officials argued that this new program, with a federal income floor of $1,600, would reduce the disparity in state payments at least at the minimum payment level. And, by making all families with children eligible for benefits, FAP would reduce the incentives for family breakup and the work disincentives that existed in the current system. Also, as a financial incentive for members of families to work, the first $60 a month or $720 a year earned by the family plus 50 percent of further earnings up to a cutoff point of $3,960 would be completely excluded or disregarded in computing the family's monthly benefits.

In order to reduce state variations and inequities in the existing programs for the aged, blind, and disabled, the Administration proposed to combine these categories into one "Adult program." The basic federal/state administrative and funding arrangements that existed under OAA, AB and APTD would not be changed; however, there would be federally defined, nationally uniform eligibility requirements and a nationwide minimum payment of $90 a month for all adult recipients.

Adequate Payment Levels and the Persistence of Poverty

Under FAP, a family of four who was eligible for the $1,600 federal cash minimum would also be eligible for approximately $750 worth of food stamps for a total value of about $2,350, or slightly more than two-thirds of the poverty level as of 1969. The Administration recognized that a program with a basic benefit below the poverty level would *not* eliminate poverty. Nevertheless, it was labeled a "substantial improvement" and "a major attack on poverty" on the grounds that it represented an increase in payment levels in ten states and for about 20 percent of the present recipients, and because it would raise the incomes of almost two million persons above the poverty level.

While the present AFDC program provided benefits for only 17 percent of the poor and 35 percent of all poor children in the country, according to the Administration, FAP would cover 65 percent of all the poor and virtually 100 percent of all poor families with children.[7] The proposed $90 per month minimum payment for the aged, blind, and disabled would provide a yearly income for the adult recipients that was above the 1969 Census Bureau poverty level of $2,100.

According to public statements by Administration spokesmen, limited financial resources and the decision that providing benefits for the "working poor" was the first priority, necessitated the exclusion of needy, non-aged, and childless individuals and couples from benefits, as well as the below-poverty-level benefit levels for poor families with children.[8]

Ineffective, Inefficient, and Demeaning Administrative Procedures

Three administrative problems of the present system were identified in public discussions of the welfare proposal. First, under the present public assistance programs the Federal Government did not have adequate control over the "allocation of its own resources." It was simply obligated to pay its share of whatever the different states' cost happened to be.[9] Second, the double or triple layers of administrative agencies (federal, state, and local) were inefficient and costly. The present administrative structure did not take advantage of all "the economies of scale which . . . an automated and nationally administered system can have."[10] Finally, the present administrative procedures were often too complicated, discretionary, arbitrary, and demeaning.[11]

On grounds of administrative efficiency and control, the reforms were proposed as a major, first step in the federalization of public assistance. Along with the establishment of a new federal program for families and setting national eligibility and payment standards for the adult programs, states were given the option of contracting with the Social Security Administration for federal administration of the adult programs and the required state supplementation of federal payments to families.

To reduce some of the indignities associated with welfare, to "lessen welfare redtape" and "to cut out the costly investigations so bitterly resented as 'welfare snooping,'" the Administration proposed that the program be "administered on an automated basis" and that the federal payment "be based upon a certification of income, with spot checks sufficient to prevent abuses."[12]

Increasing Welfare Costs and Caseloads
and Hard-Pressed States and Cities

It was initially estimated that the proposed reforms would add
12 million persons to the welfare rolls and increase federal welfare costs by $4.4
billion dollars. President Nixon described this increase in costs and caseloads as
the "initial investment" or "startup costs" of a new business enterprise that
would "yield future returns to the nation."[13]

An implicit, if not explicit, official justification for making the
"working poor" eligible for benefits was the notion that recent increases under
the present system were largely the result of low wage earners quitting their
jobs and going on welfare. Supplementing their wages, it was argued, would
encourage the "working poor" to continue working and thereby curtail the
"dramatic" increases that have occurred under the present system.

Along with the already mentioned financial incentive for ablebodied recipients to maintain or find some form of employment, the proposal
contained a requirement that recipients register for employment or training
and accept training or a suitable job opportunity when offered. This requirement applied to ablebodied mothers unless they had children under the age of
six or if the father was living at home and either working or duly registered.

To increase the effectiveness of the work requirement and financial incentive in reducing the number of welfare recipients by enhancing their
ability to support themselves, the bill authorized $600 million for a major ex-
pansion of training and day care facilities. It also provided for an additional $30
a month training allowance for recipients who participated in any training
program. Together, these provisions, according to public statements, would
eventually produce a reduction in welfare costs and the number of welfare
recipients.

The proposal guaranteed all states an immediate reduction in present
welfare expenditures. This was done with the "50-90" rule which specified
that, for the first five years after the changes were enacted, every state would
have to spend at least 50 percent of the amount it would have spent under the
present public assistance programs; but no state would have to spend more
than 90 percent of the expenditures it would have incurred under existing law.

In other words, every state was guaranteed a 10 to 50 percent
savings on welfare costs for at least five years. The amount of savings for each
state would depend upon how much it cost to supplement the federal payments
up to current benefit levels. Any cost for supplementation that went above 90
percent of what the state would have spent for public assistance would be
absorbed by the Federal Government.

Some of these measures—a new federal cash assistance program
for families with children including the "working poor," a $4.4 billion dollar

increase in federal welfare expenditures, and the addition of 12 million to the welfare rolls—represented unexpected and major reforms in current policy. The problem now is to identify the extent and nature of policy change they would entail if implemented.

THE NIXON PROPOSAL: CONCEPTUAL, TECHNICAL, AND CONSEQUENTIAL POLICY CHANGES

By definition a social welfare program does four things: it (1) defines eligibility and thereby identifies the recipients of certain benefits, (2) specifies the nature or type of benefits, (3) establishes the values or amount of benefits that are to be distributed, and (4) prescribes the procedures and techniques to be used in their delivery.[14] These are the basic policy questions which must be resolved in the process of designing any welfare program.

Reflecting the perceptions, assumptions, and values of the policy makers, the decisions reached regarding these four components determine the nature and operations of the program. The following analysis identifies conceptual and technical changes President Nixon's reform plan would have made in these components of welfare programs in effect at the time it was introduced, and suggests some important potential consequences of these policy changes.

Conceptual and Technical Change

The Recipients of Benefits.   The Nixon proposal contained three important changes in eligibility requirements for federal cash assistance programs:

1. All families with children whose family income was less than a certain specified level would be eligible for benefits, regardless of whether or not the father was employable or unemployable, employed or unemployed, living at home or elsewhere.
2. Eligibility requirements for the federal payment to families and the state supplemental payment would be standardized nationwide.
3. For the aged, blind, and disabled, federal standards would be established with respect to resource limitations, the definitions of blindness and disability, and other nonfinancial eligibility requirements which varied from state to state under current law.

The first of these changes represented an important shift in fundamental concepts and assumptions associated with the existing public assistance programs. For example, a basic concept of public assistance is that "poor people can and should be separated into classes of those who either 'can' or 'will' work and those who 'can't' or 'won't.'" [15] Public assistance is for those who can't work—*not* for those who can but won't or for those who do but don't earn enough to adequately provide for themselves and their families.

FAP, by making all families with children and with incomes below a specified level eligible for cash benefits, would eliminate the categorical distinction between those who can and can't work. Most important, it would shift the focus of federal cash assistance programs from the problem of "economic dependence," i.e., those unable to work, to the problem of income poverty—people with incomes below a specified level. Under FAP the target group would not be the "unemployables," but the "children in poverty." In the identification of those eligible and deserving of cash assistance, it would shift the focus from the *characteristics of individual applicants* to the *income of families.* [16]

Another key concept underlying the selected categories of recipients in public assistance is that of "fault" or "blame." [17] The aged, blind, disabled, and dependent children are seen as deserving of cash assistance because it is not their fault they are poor. Conversely, public assistance at least implies, by not granting benefits, that any ablebodied adult who is poor is personally at fault—because he is lazy, undisciplined, unwilling to work, etc. The income definition of eligibility in FAP would modify, by implication, this notion of fault by extending some of the blame to the economic system for not supplying adequate job opportunities and for maintaining jobs that pay insufficient wages.

The Nature of the Benefits. The proposed reforms would not make a significant change in the types of benefits that were distributed under current law. Cash recipients, under the Nixon plan, as with present public assistance recipients, would be eligible for food stamps, surplus food commodities, Medicaid, public housing, social services in effect under current law, and a variety of employment and training programs and services including a $30 a month training allowance.

Conceptually, however, FAP would entail an important shift in federal cash benefits. The minimum payment would constitute an "income floor," a specified minimum level of yearly income which every American family with children would be guaranteed by federal law. The requirement that ablebodied adults must register for work or training, as it was stated in the provisions of the bill sent to Congress in 1969, did not in concept or effect make FAP any less of a low level, federal guaranteed minimum income for families. If a father of four refused to register for work or to take a job when offered, his family would be penalized $300. The effect of the work requirement, in other words, would be to reduce the yearly income guarantee for a family of four from $1,600 to $1,300. The family would still have a legal right to a federal cash grant at a specified level.

The cash benefits paid to the "working poor," families with a full time worker but with a yearly income of less than the established maximum payment under FAP, would constitute a governmental system of wage or earnings supplementation necessitated by the prevalence of jobs that do not pay adequate salaries. The establishment of a federal guaranteed minimum income and a system of wage supplements would represent a radical departure from the assumptions and purposes of public assistance.

The Value of Benefits.   Because the states were required to supplement the federal payment up to current public assistance benefit levels, the proposal would only affect the level or value of cash benefits in those states that were providing AFDC recipients less than $1,600 for a family of four and OAA, AB, and APTD recipients less than $90 per month. It would increase the amount of cash payments received by public assistance recipients in these states up to the $1,600 minimum for families and $90 monthly minimum for adults. Using the July 1969 figures, under FAP the maximum yearly benefits paid to a family of four would range from $1,600 (the federal minimum) in Mississippi to $3,984 (the $1,600 federal minimum plus state supplementation up to the existing AFDC payment level) in New Jersey.

The states were not required by FAP to supplement federal payments to the "working poor." Consequently, in the highest paying states like New Jersey, New York, and Connecticut the "working poor" would probably still be worse off than those AFDC recipients eligible for the FAP payment plus state supplementation. The amount of benefits a low wage earner would receive under FAP would depend on the size of the family and the amount of family income from earnings. A family of four with no outside earnings would be eligible for $1,600: $500 for the mother and father and $300 for each child. A seven-member family with no earnings would receive $2,500 per year.

Table 3-1 shows how the level of family earnings would affect the amount of the FAP payment and the total yearly income of a low income family of four. For example, a family with earnings of $1,000 would be eligible for $1,460 in FAP benefits (i.e., $1,600 minus $140: $140 equals the family's earnings of $1,000 minus the first $720 and 50 percent of the remaining $280). The total yearly income of this family would be $2,460 ($1,000 in earnings plus the $1,460 FAP payment).

If the family earned $2,000, they would be eligible for $960 in benefits (i.e., $1,600 minus $640: $640 equals the family's earnings of $2,000 minus the first $720 and 50 percent of the remaining $1,280). Their total yearly income would be $2,960 ($2,000 in earnings plus the $960 in FAP benefits), which is $500 higher than the family with a yearly income of $1,000. A family with a yearly income amounting to $3,000 would be eligible for a FAP supplement of $460. When the yearly income of a family of four reached $3,920 they would no longer be eligible for cash benefits.[18]

Under the proposal, an elderly couple would be guaranteed $2,160

Table 3-1. Yearly Benefits and Total Income for a Family of Four Under FAP

Family Earnings	Amount of Earnings Disregarded[a]	FAP Payments[b]	Total Family Income[c]
$ 0	$ 0	$1,600	$1,600
500	500	1,600	2,100
1,000	860	1,460	2,460
1,500	1,110	1,210	2,710
2,000	1,360	960	2,960
2,500	1,610	710	3,210
3,000	1,860	460	3,460
3,500	2,110	210	3,710
4,000	2,360	0	4,000

[a]In computing the federal cash payment, a family would be allowed to "disregard" $60 per month ($720 per year) as work related expenses, plus one-half of additional earnings up to $3,920.

[b]Federal cash benefits payable to a family would be computed by subtracting the family's earnings, minus the amount disregarded, from the basic FAP benefit of $1,600 for a family of four.

[c]Total family income would be the amount of family earnings plus the federal cash (FAP) payment.

a year in cash benefits ($90 per recipient per month aggregated on a yearly basis), while a family of four would be guaranteed only $1,600. In other words, the Nixon reforms would perpetuate the disparity in benefit levels between adult categories and the families that existed under the current system.

The proposal of a nationwide minimum payment level for the aged, blind, and disabled slightly above the current Census Bureau defined poverty line reflected a shift in thinking about welfare benefits to the concept of a nationally defined minimum amount of income necessary to purchase the minimum requirements of food, clothing, and shelter.[19]

The Delivery of Benefits: Government Jurisdiction. The proposed reforms would maintain the existing federal-state structure of administration and funding for aged, blind and disabled recipients of cash assistance. For the families, the states were given three administrative alternatives: (1) federal administration of the federal payment and the state supplement; (2) federal administration of the federal payment and state administration of the state supplement; and (3) state administration of both the federal and state payments.

In those few states where the FAP minimum benefit levels were higher than existing maximum AFDC payments (in August 1969 this included Alabama, Arkansas, Georgia, Louisiana, Mississippi, South Carolina, and Tennessee), these options were quite meaningless because no state supplementation would be required (or expected!). In these states the AFDC program would be abolished and replaced with a completely federal guaranteed income for families with children.

For the other states there were incentives in the form of savings on administrative costs and strong encouragement from HEW officials for them to opt for federal administration of both the federal payment *and* the state supplement to families. These measures reflected a primary objective of the welfare reform proposal: reducing state influence and increasing federal control over U.S. welfare policy and programs.

The Social Security Act of 1935 represented a large change in public policy because it marked the beginning of the Federal Government's involvement in the business of public relief. The Nixon proposal represented another major change because its enactment would initiate proceedings leading to the dissolution of the federal-state partnership in public assistance. In intent and effect this would violate a fundamental tenet of existing policy: welfare should be managed by governments closest to home where judgment of what is really needed and what the taxpayers can afford to pay is most reliable.[20]

The Delivery of Benefits: Administrative Procedures.   It was not clear in the legislation sent to Congress the extent to which, or in what way, the reforms would simplify the procedures and remove the "indignities" involved in applying for cash assistance as Administration officials promised. Application procedures were left up to the Secretary of HEW to determine, and it was not specified whether or not a simplified application form would be used or if the process would involve time consuming home visits by social workers to check up on applicants' information.

The mandatory work registration and work and training requirements were not new. The 1967 amendments required all ablebodied AFDC recipients, including mothers with school-age children, to register for manpower services, training and employment under the Work Incentive Program (WIN). Essentially, FAP would federalize the work related programs in WIN. It would give the federal Department of Labor greater control over the operations of the various component activities and in the determination of those who were capable of participating.

The extent to which FAP would increase administrative efficiency was unpredictable because of the different administrative options available to the states. In fact, federal administrative responsibilities and processes could be quite complicated and inefficient under FAP if a substantial number of states chose different options. However, by equalizing benefits for families up to the $1,600 minimum in the low benefit states and putting a ceiling on payments in the high benefit states, FAP probably would increase the predictability of federal welfare costs and provide the Federal Government greater control over welfare expenditures.

Potential Consequences

Full consequences of the changes proposed by Nixon were un-predictable. The *actual* cost of the new Family Assistance Plan, and number of FAP recipients; its effect on the family stability, work effort, and movement of recipients; its general antipoverty impact; and the political support or opposition it would generate would be known only after several years of operation. However, the Administration provided information that indicated potential consequences of the proposed changes along the following dimensions.

Cost of the Nixon Reforms and Public Assistance. Total federal costs of the proposed changes were initially estimated at $7.6 billion. This was $4.4 billion more than the Federal Government spent on public assistance in 1968, the most recent figures available when the changes were first presented. Based on these figures, the Nixon reforms would mean a 138 percent increase in federal expenditures for cash assistance programs. The major components of the $4.4 billion increase included: [21]

Family assistance payments	$3.0
Adult public assistance changes	0.4
Federal payment to states under the "90-50" rule	0.1
Training and day care	0.6
Administration and other	0.3
Total	$4.4

Another set of figures was presented to the Ways and Means Committee in March 1971 which can be used to compare the estimated full year cost of the proposed reforms with the estimated full year cost of public assistance under current programs for fiscal year 1972. These figures are shown in Table 3-2. By this time the estimated cost of the Nixon plan had increased from $7.6 to $9.7 billion, as indicated. However, according to these figures, the cost of existing programs was increasing so rapidly that in 1972 the proposed changes would increase federal expenditures by only 50 percent as compared to the 130 percent increase indicated earlier.

This estimated 50 to 130 percent increase (depending upon which year is used for comparison) is much larger than any recent yearly increase in federal costs for public assistance, as is indicated in column 5 of Table 3-3. In fact, it is larger than all of the previous five-year increases in federal costs from 1951 to 1966, and it is comparable to the 96 percent increase that took place from 1966 to 1971.

Table 3-2. Estimated Cost of the Nixon Reforms and Public Assistance Under Existing Programs in Fiscal 1972 (billions of dollars)

Program	Nixon Reforms	Existing System	Net Cost of Nixon Reforms	Percent Increase Under Nixon Reforms
Payments to families (AFDC)	$5.0	$3.7	$1.3	35
Payments to adults (OAA, AB, APTD)	2.5	2.1	.4	16
States savings clause	.6	–	.6	100
Total	$8.1	$5.8	$2.3	37
Administration	$ .7	$ .4	$ .3	
Training	.4	.2	.2	
Day care	.5	.1	.4	
Total	$1.6	$ .7	$ .9	129
Grand Total	$9.7	$6.5	$3.2	49·

Source: U.S., Congress, House, Committee on Ways and Means, "Statistical Information Related to Family Assistance Provisions," 92nd Congress, 1st sess., 1971, Tables II–1, II–3, II–4.

Table 3-3. Expenditures of Federal, State, and Local Governments for Cash Payments and Administration of Federally Funded Public Assistance Programs, Fiscal Years 1951-1971 (millions of dollars)

Year	Total Cost	Percent Change	Federal Share	Percent Change	Percent Federal Share
1951	$ 2,205		$1,188		54
1956	2,707	+23	1,463	+23	54
1961	3,714	+37	2,169	+48	58
1966	5,094	+37	3,053	+41	60
1967	5,247	+ 3	3,206	+ 5	61
1968	5,869	+12	3,524	+10	60
1969	6,804	+16	4,006	+14	59
1970	8,223	+21	4,748	+19	58
1971[a]	10,329	+26	5,979	+26	58
1966–69		+34		+31	
1966–70		+61		+56	
1966–71		+103		+96	

Source: U.S. Department of Health, Education, and Welfare, *Trend Report: Public Assistance Data* (Washington, D.C.: Government Printing Office, 1971); U.S. Department of Health, Education, and Welfare, *Public Assistance Statistics,* July 6, 1971.

[a]Administrative costs have been estimated on basis of previous years' costs.

Welfare Rolls Under the Nixon Reforms and Public Assistance. In December 1969, or shortly after Nixon introduced his welfare proposal, there were 10,271,000 persons receiving assistance under the federally supported public assistance programs. It was initially estimated that under the Nixon reforms 22.4 million Americans would be eligible for cash assistance. In other words, it was estimated they would have at least doubled the 1969 welfare rolls.

Table 3–4 compares the projected number of recipients under FAP with the number under the existing system for the years 1972 through 1975. According to these figures, the proposed changes would add 10 million recipients in 1972, an increase of 72 percent over the current system. As indicated, the addition of "working poor" families to the welfare rolls would account for almost all of the increase (approximately 9.7 million of the 10 million new recipients).

Table 3–5 shows the yearly increase in the number of public assistance recipients since 1965 and the five-year increases since 1950. The estimated 80 to over 100 percent increase in recipients that would occur under FAP is three times as large as any yearly growth under existing cash programs since 1965. It is larger than any five-year increase since 1950, including 1965 to 1970, which was the period of such rapid expansion.

Table 3–4. Projected Eligible Recipients Under the Nixon Reforms and Under Current Law, 1972–1975
(millions of persons)

	1972	*1973*	*1974*	*1975*
Nixon Reforms				
Persons in families eligible for FAP only[a]	9.7	8.9	8.2	7.5
Persons in families eligible for FAP and state supplement[b]	10.9	12.3	13.8	15.5
Adult category[c] recipients	3.5	3.6	3.8	4.0
Total	24.1	24.8	25.8	27.0
Existing Programs				
AFDC recipients	10.8	12.1	13.6	15.3
OAA, AB, APTD (adult category) recipients	3.3	3.4	3.6	3.8
Total	14.1	15.5	17.2	19.1

Source: U.S., Congress, House, Committee on Ways and Means, "Statistical Information Related to Family Assistance Provisions," 92nd Congress, 1st sess., 1971.

[a]"Working poor" families.

[b]AFDC recipients.

[c]Aged, blind, and disabled recipients.

Table 3-5.   Number of Public Assistance Recipients in December of
Each Year Indicated
(thousands)

Year	Total	Percent Change	AFDC	Percent Change	AFDC Percent of Total
1950	5,184		2,233		43
1955	5,075	- 2	2,192	- 2	43
1960	5,854	+15	3,073	+40	53
1965	7,125	+22	4,396	+43	62
1966	7,411	+ 4	4,666	+ 6	63
1967	8,111	+ 9	5,309	+14	66
1968	8,896	+10	6,086	+15	68
1969	10,271	+16	7,313	+20	71
1970	12,758	+24	9,660	+32	76
1971	13,825	+ 8	10,653	+10	77
1965-70		+79		+120	

Source: U.S., Department of Health, Education, and Welfare, *Trend Report: Public Assis-
tance Data* (Washington, D.C.: Government Printing Office, 1971); U.S. Department of
Health, Education, and Welfare, *Public Assistance Statistics* (Washington, D.C.: Government
Printing Office, July, 1971).

Besides increasing the number of cash recipients, FAP would
drastically alter the composition of the AFDC population in the United States.
As indicated in Table 3-6, the AFDC population in 1969 was primarily female-
headed families, 50 percent were black, only 27 percent lived in the South
and 82 percent of the family heads were unlikely to have engaged in any work
experience. In contrast, the FAP population would be half male, predominately
white; the largest concentration would be in the South where wages were low
and two-thirds of the recipients would be engaged in full or part time work.[22]

Benefit Levels Under the Nixon Reforms and Public Assistance.
The Administration promised that with mandatory state supplementation no
one presently receiving cash benefits under public assistance would be worse
off if the reforms were enacted. Figures released in December 1970, which
estimated that 14.4 million poor Americans "would be better off" under the
Nixon proposal than under the current programs, are shown in Table 3-7. About
17 percent of the 14.4 million included present public assistance recipients
who would receive higher payments under the Nixon plan.

Over one-third of those receiving OAA, AB, and APTD would receive higher benefits because of the proposed $90 per month minimum pay-
ment for "adult" recipients. And 800,000, or about 10 percent of the present
AFDC recipients, would be better off under FAP. Most of these were families
living in the South where AFDC payments were lower than the $1,600 FAP

Table 3-6.   Distribution of Families Under Aid to Families with
Dependent Children Program in 1969, and of Families Eligible
for the Family Assistance Plan in 1972

	Percentage Distribution	
Characteristic	AFDC 2,400,000 Families	FAP 3,617,000 Families
Sex of Family Head		
Male	18.7	50.1
Female	81.3	49.9
Race of Family Head		
White	48.3	61.4
Nonwhite	51.7	38.6
Region of Residence		
Northeast	30.9	21.1
North Central	19.8	20.3
South	26.8	42.7
West	22.5	15.9
Work Experience of Family Head		
Worked full time all year	7.8	30.9
Some work during year	10.1	37.0
No work during year	82.1	31.3
Military	0	.9

Source: U.S., Congress, House, Committee on Ways and Means, "Statistical Information Related to Family Assistance Provisions," 92nd Congress, 1st sess., 1971; Charles L. Schultze *et al., Setting National Priorities: The 1972 Budget* (Washington, D.C.: Brookings Institution, 1971), p. 177.

minimum. As is indicated, 12.5 of the 14.4 million that would be better off were persons who received no benefits under public assistance—primarily the "working poor"—who would be eligible for cash benefits if FAP became law.

In sum, the Nixon welfare reform proposal represented major policy innovation because it would entail significant shifts in important conceptual, technical, and consequential elements of the existing public assistance programs, especially Aid to Families with Dependent Children. In theory, the Family Assistance Plan represented a shift to the concerns, concepts, and objectives of the Negative Income Tax—one type of guaranteed income.

This included recognition of the need for a national cash assistance program that supplements the income of low wage earners as well as aiding those unable to work; a shift from "economic dependency" to a national "income" definition of poverty and eligibility for federal cash assistance; and a shift in problem definition and policy objective from that of fighting poverty by assisting those unable to work, to reducing poverty by raising the income of all families above a specified level.

Table 3-7. Administration Estimates of the Number of "Poor Persons" Who Would Be "Better Off" Under the Nixon Reforms Than Under Existing Public Assistance Programs

Client Group	Millions	Percent of Cases Under Existing Programs, 1971
Families		
(1) Persons not covered under existing programs	10.8	–
(2) Present AFDC recipients in states paying less than the FAP minimum including Food Stamp bonuses	.8	9.9
(3) Others[a]	1.5	–
Total	13.1	9.9
Adults		
(1) Persons not covered under existing programs	.1	–
(2) Present adult cases in states paying less than the $90 monthly minimum	1.1	36.3
(3) Others[b]	.07	–
Total	1.3	36.3
Grand Total	14.4	16.9

Source: U.S., *Congressional Record,* December 7, 1970, p. S19521.

[a]Includes state supplemental cases not eligible for AFDC because the state does not have the AFDC-UP program or because of changes in eligibility standards under FAP.

[b]Includes new APTD cases made eligible by the national definition of disability.

In operation, FAP would amount to a federally controlled, low-benefit-level guaranteed income for families with children quite similar to negative tax programs proposed by Robert Lampman and the President's Commission on Income Maintenance Programs.[23] The federal cash benefits would be supplemented in most states by food stamps, surplus food commodities, Medicaid, and, for the nonworking poor families, by a modified AFDC program under tighter federal regulations.

The Nixon proposal would not have completely eradicated income poverty. However, it would have raised the incomes of all of the aged, blind, and disabled and many of the "working poor" families above the 1969 poverty line;[24] and produced the largest single expansion of welfare, in terms of costs and caseloads associated with federal cash assistance programs, since the implementation of the original Social Security legislation.

The next chapter describes the policy making procedures and conditions associated with the unexpected decision within the Nixon Administration to design and sponsor these fundamental and extensive changes in U.S. welfare policy.

Chapter Four

Welfare Policy Process: The White House

But for those who are able to help themselves, what we need are not more millions on welfare rolls but more millions on pay-rolls. . . .

—Richard M. Nixon, 1968

Our studies have demonstrated that tinkering with the present welfare system is not enough. We need a complete reappraisal and redirection of programs. . . .

—Richard M. Nixon, 1969

. . . we are going to have welfare reform, and . . . every family in America will have a minimum income.

—Richard M. Nixon, 1971

When President Nixon took office in January 1969 it was not apparent what he would do in regard to welfare. In May 1968, in an address to the Association of American Editorial Cartoonists, he stated: "at the present time I do not see a reasonable prospect that I will recommend . . . a guaranteed annual income or a negative income tax. . . ."[1]

In accepting his party's nomination for the Presidency in August 1968, he said that the present welfare programs had failed and promised to make some changes. His references to cutting the cost of federal welfare programs and moving people from welfare rolls to payrolls suggested that any changes he might propose as President would be in the "conservative" direction of the 1967 welfare amendments, which put a freeze on federal welfare expenditures and attempted to reduce the number of AFDC recipients by requiring them to accept work training or employment.[2]

In contrast, at one point during the campaign he said "it was unfair and nonsensical for states such as Mississippi to pay its welfare recipients $20 a month while northern industrial states provided payments of $100 a month." To the surprise of many, he promised to recommend the imposition of a "national standard" that would reduce these disparities in welfare payments.[3] The establishment of national eligibility and payment standards, without changing the federal-state or categorical structure, had been recommended by several advisory commissions and was expected to be the next "liberal" modification of public assistance.[4]

Radical reform proposals that would replace public assistance with some type of guaranteed income (e.g., a negative income tax or family allowance) had been around since the late 1950s.[5] However, the advocates of radical change had generated little interest on the part of policy makers or the general public and, for several reasons, to them the election of Richard Nixon meant at least another four years before any action in this direction would be taken.

In the first place, nothing had happened to make the welfare situation any worse than it had been for the past five to ten years: "There was no sudden new crisis in welfare."[6] The poor and those receiving welfare, the people who would benefit from a more generous and less onerous welfare system, had voted for Humphrey—if they voted at all. And a Gallup Poll taken in January 1969 indicated that 62 percent of the public was opposed to a "guaranteed income" of $3,200 a year (less than 50 percent of those making under $3,000 favored such a program); however, 79 percent were in favor of the government's guaranteeing enough "work" so that a family would be assured of at least $3,200 a year.[7]

On August 8, 1969, after eight months of information gathering and analysis, disagreement and debate, maneuvering, bargaining, and decision making within the Administration, President Nixon announced his unexpected decision to propose and seek congressional approval of a guaranteed income for families with children to replace the present AFDC program. The first part of this chapter describes the development of President Nixon's welfare proposal in terms of what appeared to be the major stages in the decision making processes that yielded FAP and the other proposed reforms: setting the domestic agenda; policy choice; and policy and program design.

DECISION MAKING PROCESS

Welfare Reform and the Nixon
Domestic Agenda

Upon taking office, President Nixon was primarily interested in matters of foreign policy and generally more concerned about international than domestic problems. He told an interviewer in November 1967, "I've

always thought this country could run itself domestically without a President.
. . . All you need is a competent Cabinet to run the country at home. You need
a president for foreign policy. . . ."[8] There was no indication of a shift in
his thinking about the primary responsibility of the President when he entered
the White House in January 1969. However, Administration officials interviewed agreed that, at least as compared to other domestic issues, from the
beginning of his Administration Nixon was "very concerned about welfare."
According to Daniel Moynihan, Nixon's Urban Affairs adviser,

> Five days before the inauguration he had sent a memorandum to
> me, Finch, Attorney General John Mitchell, and his legislative
> assistant Bryce Harlow asking for a 'thorough investigation' of the
> 'New York welfare mess,' which he suspected was typical of that
> all over the country.[9]

Because of his concern and request for information, Moynihan says that within a few months of taking office Nixon was receiving "more and better information about the problem of welfare than any of his predecessors. . . ."[10]

John Osborn, who, according to a former Nixon staff member,
"probably has the best access to the White House staff of any reporter in
Washington,"[11] claims Nixon came to the presidency with a "genuine conviction" that the welfare system was "an 'utter disaster' and required fundamental change."[12] It was this conviction, according to Osborn, which led
Nixon to appoint Moynihan—a proponent of radical welfare reform—his Urban
Affairs adviser, and to establish a preinaugural task force to study welfare.
The conflicting reactions among Nixon's top domestic advisers to the report
and recommendations of this task force marked the beginning of the debate
over welfare reform as an item for the Nixon Administration's national domestic program.

The welfare task force report, which was leaked to the press in mid
January 1969, recommended the establishment of national eligibility standards
for the four public assistance programs, a national minimum payment level
of $40 per month per AFDC recipient, and a national minimum payment of
$70 per month for all other categories, or alternatively, $65 per month for
OAA recipients and $90 for AB and APTD recipients.

It also proposed increasing the federal share of public assistance
costs, requiring all states to participate in the AFDC-UP program, mandating
the use of a declaratory (or simplified form) application for eligibility determination, and repealing the freeze on federal expenditures for AFDC contained
in the 1967 welfare amendments. It was estimated that these changes would
increase federal public assistance costs by $1 to $1.5 billion, depending on
the minimum payment established for the adult categories.[13]

In other words, the task force recommended important "liberal" modifications without challenging the basic principles or structure of public assistance. More radical or extensive change was pretty well ruled out at the beginning by the focus and constraints established by the task force director, Richard Nathan. At the outset, Nathan instructed the task force members that they should try to see what could be done "to improve the present system within the constraint of a $2 billion limit." He explained in an interview,

> This was my constraint. I wanted to see what could be done to make it a better, more equitable system within this limit. We focused primarily on the problems and inequities of the present system, and the need for national eligibility requirements and payment standards. . . . Our recommendations represented important changes, but—and let me emphasize—not as significant as the changes eventually proposed in the Family Assistance Plan. Some of our recommendations were kept and more significant changes were added as the process unfolded.

Nathan's reading of the economic and political constraints indicated that the incremental, low cost improvements recommended by his group were the most they could reasonably hope for. However, several members were pessimistic about how much of an improvement these modifications would actually make, as indicated in the following paragraph from the task force report.

> It is the conviction of some members of the Task Force that incremental improvements in the public assistance program will fail in the long run to provide a basic income maintenance system that encourages family stability, stresses work incentives, and enables the development of efficient service delivery and modern program management. It was argued, however, that incremental gains must first be sought, before drastic overhaul can be justified. . . . If the implementation of the Task Force's recommendations and similar measures does not provide satisfactory progress, we believe the new Administration should turn its attention to longer-run alternatives, such as . . . the negative income tax, children's allowances, etc.[14]

At the first meeting of the Administration's Urban Council, President Nixon told Nathan he had read the report of the task force and commented, "I liked it, but Everett Dirksen didn't." The implication was that he was willing to go along with the proposed "liberal" welfare reforms, but he knew they would not set well with some of the more conservative members of the party and his staff. He was right. Arthur Burns, long time associate and Nixon's chief adviser on domestic affairs, soon made it known he was opposed to the task force recommendations. According to Nathan, Burns

> wrote a memo to the President summarizing the work of all of the task forces—he had been asked by Nixon to do this—in which he was stridently critical of our report and said it should be discarded and a new task force set up to take a more responsible and rigorous look at this subject.

Burns opposed the Nathan proposals because they would *expand* welfare. While he agreed the welfare system was in serious trouble, he was convinced that the way to improve the situation was through measures that would *reduce* welfare costs and caseloads. This would constitute true, "effective" welfare reform. Furthermore, he argued that the major domestic issue was inflation and that the central thrust of the Nixon domestic program should be curbing inflation by keeping to a minimum the costs of both new and existing programs. Unless they could come up with changes which would cut federal welfare expenditures, he did not think welfare reform was an appropriate item for the Nixon agenda.

However, Robert Finch, another old friend of the President's and the new Secretary of Health, Education, and Welfare, liked the task force recommendations. And Moynihan believed they were at least a constructive step in the right direction. Moynihan's formal assignment was to head a special cabinet level committee concerned with urban problems. It was not clear what this would entail or how much influence he would have as the sole "liberal Democrat" in the new Republican Administration. What was predictable was that on certain issues he and Burns would not see eye to eye. (This was as predictable as it was unpredictable that Richard Nixon would be the first president to advocate a guaranteed income.) Welfare was one of those issues.

For several years Moynihan had been associated with liberal anti-poverty policies and advocated radical change in public assistance. In 1968, in an article entitled "The Crisis in Welfare," he charged "major national political leaders" with consistently avoiding serious involvement with the problems of welfare, and he called for "a thorough reassessment of public welfare." On the basis of his assessment he concluded that "the problem of the poor is that they are excluded from the larger society because they do not have the income needed to sustain an 'average' life." The solution he proposed was to replace public assistance with a guaranteed annual income for everyone in the form of a universal family allowance system.[15]

In 1969, as the President's adviser for urban problems, Moynihan not only believed welfare reform should be a part of the Nixon agenda, but that it should be the first and major item. Consistent with this opinion, he

designated a subcommittee of the new Urban Affairs Council he was heading
to study welfare reform. Initially, he viewed the imposition of national eligibility and payment standards, as recommended by the task force, as a pretty
big step for the Nixon Administration and Congress. Believing that the more
radical reforms which he preferred were unfeasible, through his welfare subcommittee reports, memos and personal conversations he proceeded to convince
Nixon that he should recommend to Congress the Nathan task force proposals.

The conflicting positions of Moynihan and Finch on one side and
Burns on the other regarding the status of welfare reform on the domestic
agenda provided the first issue, the first round of debate, and the first of
several difficult decisions for Nixon in the formation of his welfare proposal.
Sometime late in February or early March, the President went against the advice of Burns and concluded that welfare reform would be a major component
of his domestic program. Several reasons were repeated in the interviews as to
why Nixon arrived at this position. First was Nixon's personal commitment
to making some "constructive changes" in the present system and the fact
that the Nathan recommendations were available and had substantial support
both from within and outside the Administration. Also, most agreed that
Finch and Moynihan were very influential. Nathan put it this way:

> . . . credit has to go to Finch, who planted the seed by interesting
> him [the President] in the task force report and supporting the
> recommendations. The President listens to Finch on these matters.
> Credit must also go to Pat Moynihan. He fertilized the seed planted
> by Finch.

Policy Choice: What Kind of
Welfare Reform?

When the Administration let it be known in early March that
welfare reform would be included in the forthcoming domestic program, they
did not have a formal proposal ready to submit to Congress. Apparently,
Nixon believed that with some facility the Nathan recommendations could be
transformed into a legislative proposal which he and at least some of his key
advisers could support. He soon discovered that however difficult the decision
to do *something* about a particular problem might be, it is often less difficult
and less debatable than the choice of just exactly what it is you are going to
do—or, selecting an appropriate solution.[16]

The Administration had made a commitment to do something
about welfare and now they needed to formulate a course of action. As the
process of policy choice and development unfolded in the coming months,
new participants entered the debate, the range of issues and possible solutions
expanded, the nature of the controversy changed, and the intensity of disagreement increased.

Several of the participants interviewed indicated that Nathan might have underestimated what at least some of Nixon's men were interested in and willing to do regarding welfare; or, that from the beginning there were some who felt the task force recommendations did not "go far enough." When they were presented to the welfare subcommittee of the Urban Affairs Council in early February, Secretary Schultz pointed out that they would not do anything to help the "working poor," and another voiced a concern that they would not provide enough "new benefits to present recipients."

Steiner reports that Finch's response to the recommendations was, in effect, "is that all?" [17] Whatever his specific reservations, shortly after receiving the task force report Finch turned it over to his undersecretary, John Veneman, for review and comments. Veneman assigned this task to Worth Bateman, who was the deputy assistant secretary for planning and valuation at HEW.

Bateman was one of several Democratic holdovers from the Johnson Administration who for several years had openly advocated replacing public assistance with a negative income tax. He convinced Veneman that the task force recommendations were insufficient; and, with the knowledge of Finch, a group was formed under the direction of Veneman and Bateman for the purpose of developing an alternative to the Nathan task force proposals. Bateman selected James Lyday, then at OEO, Mike Mahoney and Charles Hawkins of HEW, and Tom Joe, Veneman's assistant, to work with him on the committee. Bateman's and Lyday's commitment to a negative income tax was well known; both had designed and advocated low-benefit-level NIT proposals at various times during the Johnson Administration. One HEW official explained:

> You have to understand that there has been a conspiracy among lower level bureaucrats in favor of a negative income tax since 1965. They are Democratic appointed officials—most of them economists—who have been pushing for a negative tax program since 1965. They organized the hearings on NIT proposals before the Joint Economic Committee in 1968. Every time there was a review of welfare during the Johnson Administration these guys would propose some form of a negative income tax program, but they could never get Johnson or Wilbur Cohen (Secretary of HEW) to go for it. What happened was that some of these guys, Bateman, Lyday, and Mahoney, stayed on for a while under Nixon and got involved in the welfare debate through Veneman.

Within a matter of days the Bateman group presented Veneman a memo, "no more than a few pages long," which outlined their alternative to the task force proposals, In essence, they recommended that the AFDC pro-

gram be replaced with a federally funded and administered negative tax program
for all families with children—including the "working poor." They proposed
a $1,500 minimum payment level with a 50 percent earnings disregard and a
$3,000 cutoff point. This new program for families would be administered by
either the Social Security Administration or the Internal Revenue Service.
To qualify for benefits, applicants would be required to file a simple statement
of earned income every three months. Spot checks would guard against cheating. They recommended that the task force provisions dealing with the aged,
blind, and disabled programs be maintained. It was estimated that their plan
would cost about $1.98 billion.

A member of the Bateman group explained the development of
their proposal in the following way:

> We felt the exclusion of the "working poor" was the major inequity
> in the present program and that, in fact, this inequity would be
> made worse if you improved the present system—along the lines
> suggested in the Nathan proposal—and didn't include low income,
> male-headed families. . . . We concentrated on familes with children
> because we felt they were the ones in the worst shape. The adult
> programs (AB, OAA, APTD) were pretty good as compared to
> AFDC. . . . We were sorta backed into the $1,500 benefit level by
> the $2 billion fiscal limit set up by Nathan and the need to set a
> level that, with supplementation up to the present payment levels,
> would provide some financial savings for the states over the present
> program.
>   We felt we had a pretty modest proposal and that we didn't want
> to have to reduce the benefit levels below the $1,500 minimum,
> which we would have had to do if we included individuals and
> couples without children and stayed within the fiscal limit of $2
> billion.

It was apparent that they viewed their proposal as a politically and economically
feasible first step toward the complete replacement of public assistance with
a negative tax program. They hoped it was politically feasible because it would
eliminate AFDC, which few supported, and economically feasible because they
estimated it would cost no more than the task force proposal. They defended
their recommendations to Veneman on these grounds and on the basis that
their plan would have the same effect as Nathan's proposal in reducing inter-
state disparities in eligibility and payment standards. In addition, they argued
that, because it provided benefits for *all* families with children, their plan would
reduce the inequitable treatment of male-headed and "working poor" families
and thereby reduce the work disincentives and incentives for families to break
up that existed under the present AFDC program.

The Bateman group had no difficulty convincing Veneman their plan was superior to Nathan's recommendations. Finch was receptive as well and told them he would support their proposal if Nathan would. Several well planned and prepared meetings between Nathan and the Bateman group followed. A member of the Bateman committee described what happened.

> First we convinced Veneman and Finch. Then the job was to sell it to Nathan—and that wasn't very difficult. We saw our job as accepting his adult provisions and getting him to accept our family program. . . . Essentially, we convinced him that he had the same objections to his proposal that we and others had, and that our suggestions were what he considered proper solutions. In fact, I am surprised that Nathan still distinguishes between us and himself.

Other administration officials, those not associated with the Bateman group, in describing what happened emphasized that Nathan "did not know that Bateman and others had been working on an alternative proposal," and he was "not aware" of the preparation for the meetings with him.

Nathan's position remained somewhat ambiguous, probably because his boss, Robert Mayo, director of the budget, opposed FAP at least until it was made public. However, apparently Finch sensed enough support from Nathan for him to go ahead and present the Bateman plan to a March 24 meeting of the Urban Affairs Council Welfare Subcommittee. Prior to this meeting, John Price, Moynihan's assistant and a staff assistant to the welfare subcommittee, showed the plan to Moynihan. Price said in an interview,

> I was in favor of a negative income tax program for various reasons and, in fact, had tried to convince Moynihan at one time that it was better than family allowances which he advocated in his 1967 article on welfare. I had him read a *Yale Law Review* article on the subject.
>
> I remember showing him the Bateman plan—at the time it proposed a $1,500 minimum with a 50 percent tax rate. After looking at it he decided "it was the solution to their problem."

Veneman, Bateman, and the other members of the committee realized the radical nature of the plan Finch would be presenting to the Cabinet members. They carefully developed a "low key" and guarded presentation which, for obvious reasons, made no reference to a negative tax program or a guaranteed income. They recommended to Finch that the plan be presented as the "Honest Christian Anti-Communist Working Man's Family Allowance National Defense Human Resources Rivers and Harbors Act of 1969." This was shortened to the Family Security System.[18]

Finch and Moynihan, Attorney General Mitchell, Secretaries Stans, Schultz, and Hardin, and Martin Anderson, an assistant to Arthur Burns,

attended the subcommittee meeting. According to interviews and other reports
of this meeting, the Cabinet members did not appear to grasp the radical
nature of the Family Security System—which was the intention of the Bateman
group. However, Martin Anderson, an economist from Columbia who was
filling in for Burns, did. Evans and Novak report that "as Finch read the paper
Anderson's eyes almost popped out of his head." Moynihan, who was in charge
of the meeting, "routinely" directed the Urban Affairs Council to provide some
cost estimates of the Finch proposal—just as though nothing had been said
that ought to shock anybody. At this Anderson demanded, "Now, wait a
minute, . . . let's call a spade a spade." "Anybody who wants to call a spade
a spade," replied Moynihan, "should be made to use one."[19]

   Finch was unable to persuade a majority of those present to support sending a favorable report on the Family Security System to the President.
Nevertheless, it was clear that Finch and Moynihan preferred this negative tax
plan developed by holdover bureaucrats from the Johnson Administration
to the Nathan task force proposal. In other words, Veneman, Bateman, and the
others had been successful in shifting the *attention* and *preferences* of two
key presidential advisers to radical welfare reform in the form of a negative
tax for families with children.

   Despite the fact that the proposal was not approved by the subcommittee, Finch and Moynihan immediately proceeded to convince Nixon
that this was the course of action he should pursue. Two days after the Urban
Affairs subcommittee meeting Moynihan sent a memo to the President stating,

> *The essential fact about the Family Security System is that it will
> abolish poverty for dependent children and the working poor.*
> The cost is not very great. *Because it is a direct payment system.*
> The tremendous costs of the poverty program come from *services.* . . .
> The Family Security System would enable you to begin cutting
> back sharply on these costly and questionable services, and yet to
> assert with full validity that it was under your presidency that
> poverty was abolished in America.[20]

   It was inevitable that Arthur Burns would oppose the Family
Security System advocated by Finch and Moynihan. In general, he remained
convinced that the Administration should focus on fighting inflation and cutting
federal expenditures. On the subject of welfare policy in particular, Burns and
Moynihan were poles apart. In the 1968 article, Moynihan had advocated a
system of family allowances that would provide *every* American family, not
only the poor, with a guaranteed minimum level of federal cash benefits in
order to reduce the stigma attached to welfare. In contrast, Burns, according
to a report by Spivak of the *Wall Street Journal,* was convinced that cash

hrust was to develop programs that would reduce the welfare rolls, at least
n the long run, by turning welfare recipients "into taxpaying, self-sufficient
workers."[24] It was somewhat ironical, and possibly even embarrassing, that
Burns would advocate expanding the measures and continuing in the spirit of
the 1967 welfare amendments that Moynihan had described as "so intolerably
inhumane, placing enormous pressure on weak and abandoned women, help-
less and surely innocent children," that "Dickens would have been hard put
to invent a credible sponsor."[25]

Nixon now had two alternative courses of action to choose from:
one focused on *reducing poverty* and the other on *reducing welfare.* In retro-
spect, Finch described the situation as

> "a classic confrontation" between innovators and incrementalists,
> between . . . "those who recognize that the present system is just
> a disaster and that we had to break out of the mold, and those
> who wanted to rewrite the old system."[26]

With two proposals which differed substantially in terms of the extent of
change proposed, problem focus, policy objectives, preferred means, and
desired and predicted consequences, what had been low level skirmishes turned
into a full-fledged "battle of memorandums."[27] Moynihan and Finch were
the principal advocates on one side and Burns, with the support of Robert
Mayo and David Kennedy, Secretary of the Treasury, on the other. It became
public knowledge that two competing proposals were being debated within
the Administration and that at times the debate was quite intense. The issues
were so complex and the disagreements between the major contenders so
fundamental that sometime in May Nixon began soliciting comments from a
number of additional people both within and outside the Administration. One
of the participants explained,

> The President sent letters to people all over the country asking
> them to comment on one or both of the proposals. These were
> friends of his, people he knows and whose advice he trusts—several
> of them were people in academics. He also solicited comments
> from several members of the Cabinet who weren't seen as experts
> in this field, or who publicly would be thought to have very little
> interest in the issue—Melvin Laird, for example. To my knowledge
> the President had not done this on any prior issue and he hasn't
> done it since—I mean soliciting memos from all over. He was very
> involved in the decision. As a result there were stacks of memos,
> most of which were circulated.

The contending parties within the Administration did not focus
solely on the substantive aspects of the two proposals. Economic and political

benefits should be limited not only to the poor, but to the poor '
unable to support themselves."

> Mr. Burns believes that the work incentives that underl
> enterprise system will be eroded if welfare becomes a "ı
> all the poor. Mr. Burns reasons, "It seems inescapable th
> and more people would make the purely rational decisio
> main idle rather than work." . . . There's a great risk, he ı
> corrosive effect on moral values and attitudes, not only iı
> of recipient adults but on their children as well." . . .[21]

Shortly after assuming his White House post, Moynihan stated in a tele
interview:

> I feel the problem of the poor people is they don't have eno
> money and I would sort of put my faith in any effort that pı
> more resources into the hands of those that don't now have t
> . . . cold cash. It's a surprisingly good cure for a lot of social
> ills.[22]

In other words, Moynihan favored a welfare system that would provide cas
and allow recipients maximum discretion in the use of available resources.
Burns, on the other hand, opposed a $1 billion increase in the food stamp
program on grounds that federal expenditures on programs for the poor wer
already too high and that food stamps were not an effective means of combating malnutrition and poverty, because "you can use them to buy Coke or
potato chips." He argued that the government should "teach people about
proper diet and provide the very poor well-balanced food parcels."[23]

In late April Burns concluded that Nixon could not be dissuaded
from proposing some kind of welfare reform, so he devised an alternative to
the Finch-Moynihan plan. Instead of the Family Security System, he recommended mandating state participation in AFDC-UP and establishing national
eligibility and payment standards ($40 per month for AFDC and $65 for OAA,
AB, and APTD)—recommendations of the Nathan task force he had so vigorously opposed a few months earlier. To these task force recommendations
he added the expansion of federal work training, job placement and day care
programs, and the establishment of a stronger, more enforceable requirement
that all AFDC recipients, including mothers with school-age children, accept
available jobs or participate in job training programs. (AFDC mothers would
not have to comply if day care services were not available.)

The emphasis of the proposal was on the work requirement, training, job placement, day care and other work related elements. The central

considerations were an important part of the discussion and debate. According to one participant:

> A meeting in late April degenerated into an argument over cost
> and a quibbling over figures, with Burns and Moynihan disputing
> each other's cost estimates of their respective proposals. Burns
> said his plan would cost $1.0 billion and the Finch/Moynihan
> $3.0. Moynihan argued that the Burns plan would cost $1.8 billion.

As a result of this meeting a "technical committee" was set up under the direction of Paul McCracken to determine independently the probable costs
of the two plans. The McCracken group concluded that the Burns plan would
cost $1.9 billion, the Finch-Moynihan plan as proposed $2.3 billion; and, if
single individuals and childless couples were included in the Finch-Moynihan
proposal, it would cost $3.1 billion.

Political arguments in support of the Burns plan included the contention that it would be easier to gain Congressional approval of a plan containing incremental changes in existing programs than it would be to get support
for a proposal which represented a sharp break with current policy. Burns
said Congress would be more receptive to his proposal because it cost less and
because it included stringent work requirements similar to the ones the House
and Senate approved in the 1967 welfare amendments. Also, it was argued that
neither Congress nor the general public wanted a guaranteed income or a welfare change which would increase the welfare rolls.

The Finch-Moynihan group, on the other hand, believed they had
a proposal which, in the words of Veneman, "had a good change of being
accepted by Congress." He said,

> There are two ways, as I see it, to change public policies. One is
> to propose something really far out one year that you know will
> never pass, but will at least open discussion in an area. Or, you can
> attempt to come up with something that is feasible the first try.
> This is what we tried to do—we wanted something that provided
> the necessary changes, but which had a good chance of being
> accepted as introduced. We wanted a proposal that would be
> supported by state and local leaders, legislators and the public.

Finch, Moynihan, Veneman, and others maintained that the Family Security
System would draw support in Congress and elsewhere because it would abolish
AFDC, or *because* it represented a break with current policy. They argued that
the Burns plan was nothing more than another attempt to rehabilitate a failing program that no one supported. They also stressed the need for a new,
first term president "to become identified with new proposals in areas of public concern."

Moynihan, through memos and word-of-mouth, pointed out that although small policy changes are easier to get enacted, presidents are *not* remembered for their incremental changes. On June 6, Moynihan sent a memo which, according to several people interviewed, was "supposed to have persuaded Nixon to go with the Finch-Moynihan proposal." He defended the Family Security System as a more effective antipoverty program than the Burns proposal, and added:

> I am really discouraged about the budget situation in the coming three to five years. I fear you will have nothing like the options I am sure you hoped for. Even more, I fear that the pressure from Congress will be nigh irresistible to use up what extra resources you have on a sort of 10 percent across-the-board increase in all the Great Society programs each year. This is the natural instinct of the Congress, and it is hard for the President to resist.
>
> If your extra money goes down that drain, I fear in four years' time you really won't have a single distinctive Nixon program to show for it all. Therefore I am doubly interested in seeing you go up now with a genuinely new, unmistakably needed program. . . .
>
> We can afford the Family Security System. Once you have asked for it, you can resist the pressures endlessly to add marginal funds to already doubtful programs. This way, in 1972, we will have a record of solid, unprecedented accomplishment in a vital area of social policy, and not just an explanation as to how complicated it all was.[28]

Unofficially the Administration promised in early March that a welfare reform plan would soon be submitted to Congress, and in his April 14 message on domestic legislation Nixon made it official:

> Our studies have demonstrated that tinkering with the present welfare system is not enough. We need a complete reappraisal and redirection of programs which have aggravated the troubles they were meant to cure, perpetuating a dismal cycle of dependency from one generation to the next. Therefore, I will be submitting to Congress a program providing for the reform of the welfare system.[29]

By the end of May the Administration still did not have a proposal drafted, and the sheer amount of information and commentary that had been generated was adding confusion to a complicated and difficult decision. At this point, the President asked George Schultz, the Secretary of Labor, to review the two plans that had been put forward and the several large binders of memos that had been collected. Schultz turned the assignment over to his assistant, Jerome Rosow.

In June, when Schultz and Rosow completed their review and submitted a report on the two welfare plans, Nixon's White House staff was still debating the history, substance, economics, and politics of welfare and no reconciliation or decision as to a particular course of action seemed imminent. By this time, the Administration was feeling pressure from Congress to produce some of the domestic legislation that had been promised.

The report prepared by Schultz, Rosow, and Paul Barton, subsequently labeled the "Schultz Plan," recommended that the Administration's welfare proposal include: national eligibility standards and a $65 monthly minimum payment for the adult categories as recommended by the Nathan task force; the federally funded and controlled negative income tax for families as proposed and supported by Finch and Moynihan; and the day care, work training, job placement components—minus the work requirement—advocated by Burns.

Instead of a work registration requirement in the families program, they proposed an "earnings disregard" of $20 per week, or $1,042 a year, as a "financial incentive" for recipients to increase their work efforts. In other words, in calculating on the basis of family income the amount of cash benefits the family is eligible for, the first $20 of weekly earnings plus 50 percent of earnings above this would be "disregarded," or, it would not be deducted in determining the federal benefit. They argued that this would provide an effective means of encouraging work because a family would always have more income if someone was working. Emphasizing the financial incentive of the earnings disregard, the day care, work training, and job placement components, the report characterized the new federal program for families as "a welfare reform that encouraged work and self-sufficiency."

Essentially, they argued, it was a work supplement program that would provide an effective incentive for the "working poor" to keep working and encourage and assist the nonworking ablebodied recipients to find some kind of employment. The basic objective of the new program would be to *ease* people out of welfare and into work. In other words, the report argued that the "Schultz Plan" was consistent with the concerns articulated by Burns even though it included a negative tax program for all families with children.

The recommendations contained in the Schultz report were defined by Moynihan as representing a third alternative welfare proposal. He described it in a news conference as a "compromise," and a "comprehensive" plan which contained features of the other two proposals.[30] In other words, according to Moynihan, the situation had changed. The President now had three proposals to choose from and one of them was a kind of "synthesis." However, to Burns and Mayo, the Schultz recommendations represented an endorsement of the Finch-Moynihan plan, and not an acceptable compromise or synthesis.

Nixon left for Rumania shortly after receiving the Schultz memo. While abroad he made "daily phone calls" back to the White House and HEW asking questions related to the different welfare plans. When he returned to Washington he informed his staff that he had decided to go with the Schultz plan, to which he would add the work requirement contained in the Burns proposal.

Several of those interviewed believed that Nixon had decided what he wanted to do before receiving the Schultz report and recommendations and that it had very little influence in the policy choices he made. However, they all agreed that the Schultz memo was a crucial part of the process because it provided an opportunity and vehicle for the President to inform his advisers of the decisions he had reached and to initiate the next stage, that of designing a program, preparing a legislative proposal, and writing speeches. One participant explained,

> I don't know how important the Schultz memo—and its support for the Moynihan-Finch plan—was in persuading the President which way to go in this decision. I mean, some say he had made up his mind before he went to Rumania and before the Schultz report, but that he was concerned about Burns. However, the Schultz plan was very important as a means of announcing his decision to support the liberal position.

Program Design

With the basic policy decisions made, a White House working group was set up under the direction of John Ehrlichman to design a program and prepare the legislative proposal. In a news conference on July 15, Moynihan described the situation.

> We've put together what we think is a very nice creature. We got all the parts and we wound it up and marched it down to the White House, and we've had people down there working on it, playing with the parts, and I can't guarantee you what's going to come marching back onto Capitol Hill.[31]

Different explanations were offered as to why the special White House group was established instead of having the experts in HEW design the program. One reason was the White House hoped this would minimize leaks to the press regarding the nature of the program, and another was that it increased Nixon's influence in the process of developing specific components of the program. Others said the President was concerned about the opposition of Burns, Mayo, and others to his decision and that the White House group was created as an attempt to increase support for the new proposal. Its members included Martin Anderson, who represented Burns; Richard Nathan, representing Mayo and the OMB; Robert Patricelli from HEW, representing Finch;

Jerome Rosow, representing Schultz at Labor; and Edward Morgan, an assistant to Ehrlichman, who was the group chairman.

The group started working around the 4th of July and continued for about three weeks. Their task, as described by Patricelli

> . . . was to work out the technical details and put the proposals into legislative detail. By this time the major decisions had been made by the President: to go with the liberal position of a completely federal program, which included the working poor, and to include the work requirements wanted by the conservatives.

However, they soon became bogged down with the same policy conflicts which had impeded the process during the preceding six months, and the equally troublesome problem of coordinating the proposed changes with existing welfare programs. As two of the participants explained,

> We all pretty much agreed that national standards and eligibility requirements were needed. The directive from the President was to include the working poor; however, not everyone in the group agreed on this and at times arguments would flare up over the issue. . . .

> Martin Anderson, Burns's representative, came in one day with charts pointing out the problems of including the working poor, of coordinating state supplementation with other programs and with the tax rate under the Schultz-Moynihan-Finch plan. He was the Senator Williams of the White House working group. However, the decisions to include the working poor and to replace AFDC with a federal program had already been made by the President.

Insufficient information and disagreement among the members complicated and delayed the design of major components of the new program. The most troublesome decisions included devising an effective and fair work requirement and penalty for noncompliance, specifying payment levels and the earnings disregard, and coordinating the earnings disregard and tax rate in the new federal program with the state supplemental payment and the food stamp program. A member of the group recalled,

> After we had included the working poor we looked at the total cost of the proposal and saw that most of the cost was due to the working poor and that we weren't doing much for the present recipients with a $1,500 minimum payment. There were several suggestions. At one time we tried a minimum of $1,750 with a $450 disregard which came out to about the same total cost.

We finally just sort of settled on $1,600. Labor was very concerned about maintaining a high disregard as a work incentive—however, that got cut in the last few days from $1,040 to $720 per year. When we cut it we didn't know that this amounted to $60 a month. . . . We thought we had settled the food stamp problem by deciding not to cash them out. . . . The problem of coordinating the federal program with a 50 percent tax rate and the state supplementation stopped us for over a week.

When they could not work out an acceptable compromise on a particular issue they would first take it up with the Cabinet members they were representing. If they still could not reach an agreement, they would take the problem to Ehrlichman. One member explained,

On matters of lesser importance he would make the decisions; on important matters it would go to the President. The President would know how each of us felt in these cases. Each of us had a vote, but we didn't know how much weight it had relative to the votes of other members of the group. The final decisions were made by the President. We felt communication with him was good. . . . He would ask Ehrlichman how we were doing. Ehrlichman would try a few of our decisions out on him and then let us know his reaction.

The participants interviewed identified the existence of conflicting points of view, the role of fiscal and political constraints, and both the availability and absence of information as important in determining the general features and specific details of the new program they produced. For example, because of the different policy positions and recommendations put forward by Burns and Finch and represented in the White House group by Anderson and Patricelli, the proposal included both a negative tax plan for families with children and work requirements with provisions for expanding day care, training, and job placement programs. And, at the insistence of Secretary Schultz, an earnings disregard was included that increased the total cost by $1 billion.

If for no other reason, political considerations dictated a federal minimum payment high enough to provide all states with some reduction in welfare costs—this meant they could not drop below $1,500. At $1,500 very few AFDC recipients would receive higher payments. However, the cost of raising the minimum to $1,700 was prohibitive. In other words, budgetary and political constraints pretty much determined that the minimum payment for a family of four be somewhere between $1,500 and $1,700. It was set at $1,600.

The existence of data and a computer model which provided estimates of the number of eligible recipients and total program costs at different payment levels, earnings disregard levels, and tax rates, was important in determining and defending the benefit provisions that were finally agreed upon. Several members believed the cost and caseload projections which extended over a five to ten year period were crucial in Nixon's decision to support the program they had designed. One said,

> The President was very impressed with the computer output which estimated the costs and caseloads. I think the fact that the technology and information necessary to do this was available to us was very important in obtaining the President's final approval. It seemed to be accurate and quite precise as to probable consequences of a program using different minimum payments, tax rates, . . .

The computer cost and caseload estimates helped establish minimum and maximum limits, but members of the working group had to select the precise benefit schedules, earnings disregard, tax rate, and financial penalty for not complying with the work requirement that would be written into the legislative proposal. And, as one said, they "just didn't know what would happen if certain measures were put into effect." The alternatives were limited by political and fiscal considerations, but choices as to exact numbers were made on the basis of intuition and "conspicuous solutions" or "natural meeting points."[32]

The final Cabinet level debate on welfare before Nixon announced the Family Assistance Plan over national television on August 8 was unplanned and unappreciated. What had been scheduled was an August 6 meeting of the full Cabinet at Camp David for the purpose of a final briefing on the welfare proposal the Administration was going to send to Congress. Nixon was supposed to have "made it quite clear at the outset" they were not there to debate the bill, that he thought the debate had gone on long enough. "He felt he had heard from everyone and had made his decision." Now he wanted their support for what he had decided was the Administration's welfare reform proposal. However, Arthur Burns, Vice President Agnew, Paul McCracken, Robert Mayo, and Secretaries Kennedy and Romney interrupted the briefing to indicate opposition to the proposal. The opposing comments by Burns, Mayo, and the Vice President were described as "lengthy and vociferous." Secretaries Finch and Schultz, Antipoverty Director Donald Rumsfeld and Moynihan defended the plan. The only concession Nixon made as a result of this meeting was to change the name of the program from the Family Security System to the Family Assistance Program.

Nixon said after the meeting that if a vote of the Cabinet members had been taken there would have been 11 votes against the proposal and 4 in favor—Finch, Schultz, Rumsfeld, and Secretary of Defense Melvin Laird. At a small informal gathering immediately following the unscheduled debate, Moynihan commented: "For a bunch of Republicans who are used to sitting around at board of director meetings and letting the chairman make the final decisions, they weren't very hierarchical today."

DECISION MAKING CONDITIONS

Administration officials interviewed agreed that Nixon's decision to sponsor the Family Assistance Plan was unexpected; and that if enacted it would represent major innovation in U.S. welfare policy. They identified three conditions as reasons *why* the Nixon Administration ended up proposing radical change in AFDC: the failure of AFDC; the availability of an innovative course of action; and the commitment of the President and some of his advisers to reforming welfare.

The "Welfare Crisis"
In almost every interview, the first reason given for Nixon's decision to support FAP referred to the "problems" and "dissatisfaction" with AFDC—or the "crisis in welfare." For example, three responded:

> Because of the crisis situation in welfare, everyone felt something had to be done—everybody wanted change.

> . . . the overwhelming dissatisfaction with the present system.

> The intensity of the problem is an important element left out of the incrementalist model—as well as the ability of *new* policy makers to see new problems or to see old problems and offer new solutions. The welfare system is a disaster and has been for a long time—it amazes me that changes hadn't been offered a long time ago.

The specific "problems" with the present system that were mentioned included the inadequacy of payment levels, inequitable treatment of male-headed and "working poor" families, and inefficient and oppressive administrative procedures. But there was agreement that the "real pressure" for change was the increasing costs and caseloads in the AFDC program, and not the problems just mentioned. One said, "The costs of welfare, mainly AFDC, were skyrocketing—increasing three times as fast as state revenues. That was the real pressure and reason for the change."

They indicated it was not simply the existence or perceived existence of these problems that explained FAP. It was the way in which some public officials and members of the public were reacting to these problems, especially the increase in costs and caseloads, that brought welfare to the attention of Nixon and some of his advisers and created a situation conducive to change.

First, and possibly most important, governors and mayors from the large industrial states where welfare expenditures were highest were pressuring the Administration and Congress to tighten up administrative procedures and increase the federal share of public assistance costs. They constituted an influential, politically important interest group lobbying for welfare reform in the general direction of increasing federal financial participation and control.

By 1969, many of the senators and congressmen serving on committees with jurisdiction over public assistance and HEW officials responsible for administering public assistance programs believed the present system—especially AFDC—was simply out of control. Some congressmen and senators, for example, blamed the failure of the 1969 welfare amendments to stop rising costs on the unwillingness of state and local AFDC administrators to enforce the work requirement and other provisions of the WIN program. They felt as though they could not effectively regulate welfare because under the present federal-state system they had limited control over those who administer the program at the state and local levels. Officials at HEW were concerned that they could not adequately explain the rapid expansion of AFDC, or why individual states had widely varying experiences in regard to the growth of AFDC. They were most concerned about cutbacks in public assistance programs initiated by Congress or individual states if costs continued to increase at the present rate—and they did not know if the expansion of the last ten years would continue or not.

In other words, the general reaction or position of many legislators and administrators was that the present welfare system was a failure—not so much because it was *not* fulfilling certain objectives or dealing effectively with a particular problem (the kind of condition that can possibly be dealt with through modifications and marginal adjustments)—but because the economic and political consequences of continuing with the present system were highly unpredictable, unexplainable, and appeared uncontrollable. To many of those responsible for defining, evaluating, and administering welfare, what might happen if they continued in the same direction with the same programs was as unpredictable as what might happen if drastic changes were implemented.

According to the interviews, radical change appeared desirable and possible because opposition to the present system was "almost unanimous" and included intense dissatisfaction among welfare recipients and the general public. One Nixon official explained that FAP was proposed because "*everyone* was dissatisfied with AFDC."

> The recipients in many places are unhappy because of low benefits and long waiting lines. There is a great deal of discontent among those who administer the program—I mean when you have a 40 percent turnover you know there is something wrong. Public animosity has increased toward welfare—mainly because the public

doesn't know anything about the problem. Everyone knows someone that they think is getting welfare, and shouldn't be, or they
have heard or read in the newspaper about someone illegally receiving welfare.

Others stated:

The extent of public concern over welfare was important. The increase in costs and recipients, and local politicians using this as a
political scapegoat for rising taxes, produced a public reaction
which demanded change. Local politicians have been using welfare
as a scapegoat for years. Reagan uses it. The problems of California
are much bigger than welfare but Reagan, Rockefeller, Ogilve, and
others have been using it as a scapegoat for rising taxes, so there
was a demand that something be done.

New Presidents need to become identified with new proposals
in situations like welfare. He needs to at least announce as soon as
possible new proposals containing dramatic change. The public and
Congress expect this.

The "welfare crisis" was not so severe nor public "demands" for
change so intense in 1969 that the President was compelled to respond. However, obvious problems with existing programs certainly provided an incentive
to develop a better system. And the extent of public concern and dissatisfaction
provided an opportunity to derive political and personal credit for having at
least attempted to make constructive changes. Moynihan, the prudent professor,
made certain Nixon perceived the potential political and personal opportunity
resulting from the "crisis in welfare." In a memo written in June 1969 he told
the President,

From the most conservative to the most liberal ranks, an amazing
number of members (of Congress) agree that AFDC must go. Thus,
I would argue that if you move now, you will dominate the discussion. Congress will be discussing your proposal. It hardly matters
what final form it takes, or how many times we change our position
in the process. The end result—if you wish it to be—will be your
change.[33]

In sum, the "welfare crisis" in 1969 included an influential interest
group advocating change; welfare policy makers and administrators discouraged
at either the nature or failure of the 1967 welfare amendments and uncertain
what would happen if drastic changes were not made; and relatively widespread
and intense public dissatisfaction, which provided an opportunity to propose

some changes that, hopefully, would be good for welfare and that most likely would be good for Mr. Nixon and the Republican Party.

An Accessible Innovative Alternative

Given the conditions just described, it was predictable, but not certain, that in 1969 congressmen, senators, and the President would propose changes in public assistance, or at least in the AFDC program. What was not predictable, and cannot be explained solely on the basis of widespread and intense dissatisfaction with the existing system, was that President Nixon's first major domestic proposal would be to reform welfare by replacing AFDC with a negative tax program for all families with children, instead of proposing some incremental changes like the Nathan task force recommendations.[34]

The problems and discontent with welfare were the primary reasons Nixon was interested in the issue and why welfare reform became a key feature of the Nixon domestic agenda. And, as indicated, the nature of the discontent and reaction of some legislators, administrators, and members of the public to the welfare situation was such that it would encourage Nixon and his advisers to at least consider any proposals for major change that were available and came to their attention.

According to Administration officials, an equally important set of conditions that must be considered in attempting to explain why Nixon ended up proposing radical welfare reform included the immediate accessibility of an innovative course of action, the status of this proposal among recognized welfare experts, and the availability of information by which it could be evaluated. For example, several of those interviewed gave the following "second" or "other" reasons why radical welfare change was proposed.

> . . . because of the availability and imminence of a proposal containing change in an area where change was needed. . . .

> The intellectual history and evolution of income maintenance is most important in explaining why change was possible. By this I mean that for several years economists have been working on alternative welfare programs and around 1965, under the auspices of OEO, people like Tobin and Friedman were able to come together and restate as well as publicize their schemes which used the income tax system—the negative income tax proposals. These ideas had gained credibility. Another aspect of the intellectual history of FAP is the discussion of the disintegration of the black family as a result of poverty and ghetto life. It was important that the originator of this discussion—Moynihan—was in the White House.

> . . . we were able to harness the intellectual energy and capability

necessary to make the change. A great deal of information had been collected regarding the poor and the operations of the welfare system and it was available to us. We had the negative income tax models as well as others. Knowledgeable and interested individuals were also available.

In other words, substantial research and theoretical work had been done in the income maintenance field. Innovative courses of action were available and visible. Furthermore, as a result of their research, writing and, in some cases, governmental service, some of the proponents of the different guaranteed income schemes—Moynihan, Robert Lampman, James Tobin, Milton Friedman, Harold Watts, Joseph Pechman—were now recognized by many as *the* "welfare experts."

By the late 1960s, panels and task forces set up to discuss and study welfare included these and other proponents of radical welfare reform along with or in place of people like Wilbur Cohen, Fedele Fauri, and Elizabeth Wickenden who had developed and administered, and were more more committed to, existing public assistance programs. Most important, by 1969 there was a consensus among the recognized experts, including those who created and administered the existing programs, that sooner or later, gradually or all at once, public assistance should be replaced with some form of a nationwide, federally financed and controlled income maintenance program.

When the Family Assistance Plan was announced by Nixon, conflict among those advocating different forms of a federal guaranteed income "was unexpectedly invited and promptly shut off" as many of them within the following months rallied to its support.[35] Those who indicated support for FAP, both before and after it was made public, included family allowance advocates Moynihan and Mitchell Ginsberg, negative tax advocates Lampman and Friedman, plus Wilbur Cohen and several other past Secretaries of HEW.[36]

The general agreement among welfare experts that public assistance should be replaced with some type of a federal minimum income program and the support for FAP voiced by recognized experts, according to the participants interviewed, were important in Nixon's decision to sponsor radical reform. Equally significant was the availability of information and techniques by which some of the consequences (e.g., impact on state and federal welfare costs and caseloads) of such a change could be predicted. The members of the White House working group who designed the Family Assistance Plan emphasized, as pointed out earlier, how impressed Nixon was with the cost and caseload estimates they were able to provide because of the available data and computer program. It could have been argued, and probably was, that with this information they could be at least as certain what would happen if FAP were implemented as they could be about what might happen if it were not, given the unpredictable nature of public assistance over the past five years.

Writing in the mid 1960s, Gilbert Steiner said that American public assistance policy had remained stable since 1935, despite growing dissatisfaction with it, because of the unpredictable consequences of change and the "absence of an informed, influential group with a better idea."[37] By 1969, discontent with public assistance had increased. Some new "welfare experts" had emerged. They had developed an alternative to public assistance and generated information by which they could defend it and estimate important consequences. Furthermore, a new President had just been elected who, along with some of his key advisers, was interested in welfare reform; there were people in HEW who, given the opportunity, could transmit this policy alternative and supporting information to the President, and there was someone close to the President who was uniquely qualified to defend substantively and politically the policy changes involved.

The Right People Were in the Right Place at the Right Time

During the congressional hearings on the Economic Opportunity Act of 1964, Congressman Robert Taft, Jr. asked Sargent Shriver, President Johnson's director of the poverty war, "Why, at this particular point, are we going ahead with a poverty program as such in an omnibus bill?" Shriver replied, "It is a question of timing. . . . There is a time when the timing is right to bring things together to go ahead and solve the problem."[38] In almost every case, at some point in their response to the question "why was radical welfare reform proposed?" those interviewed said something very similar to the answer Shriver gave Congressman Taft. "The time was right, that's why."

> There was a strong feeling that the timing was correct. This was very important—a sense that this was the appropriate time for a change.

> The time was right for dramatic change, especially with the change in Administration. A new Administration can always do things that an old one couldn't. Wilbur Cohen didn't have the guts to ask Johnson to make these changes. But a new Administration can make changes—it doesn't matter if it is Democratic or Republican.

> The timing was right for a change in welfare. Everyone was dissatisfied with the present system including the members of the Ways and Means Committee. Let me say, it was the right time for a Republican to suggest a change and get it accepted if he wanted to. I'm afraid if Humphrey had presented the same program it wouldn't have passed in the House. Let's face it, these changes

are not popular with Republicans. Many of the Republican congressmen who voted for it did so because some arms were twisted and
because of party loyalty. If a Democrat had presented this bill it
would have received essentially no Republican or southern Democrat support in the House—I'm convinced!

The "time was right" response encompassed several conditions
which Administration officials believed were important in Nixon's decision
to propose FAP. The "time was right," for example, because of the problems
and discontent with the present system and because an innovative alternative
was available. It also referred to two other less tangible conditions: the development of a situation in which certain individuals were in particular positions at
a particular time; and, the development, or artful creation, of a strong "sense"
and "belief" that this was a unique, sort of historic situation in which certain
individuals could do something no one else could do—only they, possibly
only at this time, could accomplish an important and worthwhile task.
         The interest in welfare that Nixon brought to the presidency, vague
and ambiguous as it might have been; the interest that Finch had or soon developed; and Moynihan's preoccupation with welfare reform during the first
nine months of the new Administration are crucial in explaining FAP. And it
was probably just as important that Nixon came to the presidency with a
secondary interest in domestic affairs in general as it was that he was interested
in doing something about the welfare situation in particular. Neither he nor
Finch, the new Secretary of HEW, had strong substantive or strategic com-
mitments to the existing welfare system. They were not as aware or as concerned,
for example, as was Wilbur Cohen, HEW secretary under Johnson, that an
attempt to make drastic changes, because of extensive investigations and
prolonged debate, might produce an antiwelfare backlash and the creation of a
sytem even less equitable, adequate and effective than the existing system.
Because of their interest in reforming welfare, but lack of information and
commitment relative to the present welfare programs, they were open and
receptive to proposals for drastic change.
         From the moment it was first announced, doubts about Nixon's
commitment to FAP and welfare reform had been expressed, often by someone who had just finished praising the proposal and Nixon for proposing it.
The participants interviewed believed that Nixon came to the presidency with
an interest in welfare, with a desire to improve the present system but without
any clear or detailed ideas about how to do it. (Of course he also wanted to
be reelected in 1972 and those interviewed indicated that the two objectives
appeared quite compatible to the President at the time he announced FAP.)
The point emphasized in the interviews was that welfare reform would not
have become a key feature of Nixon's domestic program, that FAP would not
have been developed and proposed, if Nixon had not come to the presidency
with an interest in making some changes in public assistance.

Nixon's initial interest in welfare is important in explaining FAP; and, it is equally important that some of his key advisers were committed to welfare reform and that they and the individuals they had to depend on for assistance and information had the necessary technical skills, information, and political insight to develop, in a relatively short period of time, specific proposals that appeared sound and economically and politically feasible.

For example, the fact that by Inauguration Day they had a set of relatively inexpensive recommendations *in hand,* in the form of the Nathan Task Force Report, was important in Nixon's decision in February, against the advice of Burns, to make welfare reform a part of his domestic program. The existence and nature of this report were due in large part to the energy and previous experience of Richard Nathan and the fiscal constraints he established. In 1967 he served as associate director for program research on the Kerner Commission, which recommended essentially the same changes in public assistance that were contained in the task force report Nathan prepared for the Nixon Administration.[39]

In explaining why it was, however, that Nixon ended up proposing radical change in welfare, and not the incremental changes recommended by Nathan, one has to include the interests and personality of the new Undersecretary of HEW, John Veneman, who was asked by Finch to review the report; and Veneman's reliance upon leftover Democratic economists in HEW during the early months of the Nixon Administration. Tom Joe, Veneman's assistant whom he brought from California, offered the following explanation of why Nixon proposed radical change.

> Timing was very important. I mean there were all the pressures, the fiscal problems of cities, the protests and the welfare groups complaining. And then it just happened that men like Veneman were put in the position of doing something about welfare. . . . Veneman had served on the welfare committee ever since he was first elected to the state legislature in California. When the Federal Government came up with the Medicaid program, most states just put in a one page, or less, bill and took the federal matching money with little if any thought given to the structure of the program. But in California, and Veneman was instrumental in this, they took the money but they also formulated the "California System" of medical aid for the poor. . . . Nathan came up with a "reform program," which was simply an incremental change providing fiscal relief for the states with some change in benefits. Veneman took this and, as he had done with Medicaid, he started over and he came up with FAP, which contains what I consider "programmatic change" in welfare. Someone else would probably have just accepted the Nathan proposals.

In other words, Veneman had a special interest in welfare, he was familiar with the public assistance programs, he had had experience in developing welfare proposals, and he liked to leave his mark on matters that concerned him.

A critical juncture in the process that produced FAP, a development central to explaining why Nixon ended up proposing radical change, was Veneman turning to Worth Bateman for help in reviewing the Nathan recommendations. Quite predictably, Bateman came back, almost immediately, with the same recommendation he had made many times in the past to other Undersecretaries and Secretaries of HEW: that AFDC be replaced by a low-benefit-level negative tax program. This was a last ditch attempt before Bateman left HEW and, as much to his surprise as anyone's, the new Republican hierarchy at HEW was receptive to the recommendation.

The support of Secretary Schultz for the Finch-Moynihan proposal came at a critical time, and his report demonstrating that the negative tax plan was not necessarily inconsistent with conservative rhetoric and concerns made it easier for Nixon to reject, for the second time in the welfare debate, the recommendations of Arthur Burns. However, in explaining why Nixon's attention shifted to the negative tax plan developed by Bateman and why he decided to propose radical welfare reform, the participants interviewed agreed that the presence, advocacy, and influence of Finch and Moynihan were most important.

> In understanding why Nixon went for FAP you have to include the fact that Moynihan was here and was advocating welfare reform; and, that Finch was also in favor of making some changes. Finch's support was important because the President trusts his judgment.

> A lot of credit [for FAP] has to go to Finch, who planted the seed by interesting him [the President] in the task force report and supporting the recommendations. The President listens to Finch on these matters. Credit must also go to Pat Moynihan. He fertilized the seed planted by Finch. . . . Moynihan was very important in his own great way. He sent a lot of memos telling the President that this was a historic decision—"more important than the English Corn Laws"—something that would be remembered. These were very important . . . he had the President's ear. Even though he was not involved in developing the specifics of the reform package, in his own way he played a crucial role. His memos kept the President's interest and support during the long debate. I've saved all his memos.

> Moynihan wasn't as influential in the writing of the bill as many think—including the President. However, after we came up with the bill he was one hell of an advocate—and this was important.

As suggested in the last statement, Moynihan's role and activities

in the development of FAP were somewhat controversial. Some of the participants felt Nixon and the news media gave Moynihan more credit for the
proposal than he deserved. For example, in a televised interview held a few
days after Moynihan left the Administration, Nixon referred to him as "the
author of the Family Assistance Welfare Reform" and added:

> ... I want to say I am proud that he was a member of our staff
> for two years. And his legacy, and I promised him the day that he
> left, the day before Christmas—his legacy will be that we are going
> to have welfare reform, and that every family in America with
> children will have a minimum income.[40]

Others, those who had supported Burns during the long debate, accused Moynihan of unfair tactics, such as leaking the Nathan Task Force Report, the
Bateman Plan, and the "Schultz Synthesis" to the press and thereby creating
pressure on Nixon to come up with a welfare proposal. Some felt he should
have been more straightforward about the nature of the Bateman Plan and
the Schultz proposal.

There was general agreement, however, on two points. First,
"Moynihan's role was primarily that of persuasion, not that of formulating
the policy." Second, had he not been there, the chances that Nixon would
have proposed FAP, or something like it, were slim. In regard to his role of
an advocate for FAP, one of the participants stated:

> One should not underestimate the importance of that role in
> policy decisions like this one. His memos were great. They were
> more enjoyable than Burns's and, I think, intellectually his argu-
> ments were superior.

There are several reasons why Moynihan was a particularly effective advocate of FAP. In the first place, although he was the lone "liberal
Democrat" in a Republican Administration, he and Nixon agreed on the
general point that many of the "liberal" federal programs were failing, especially in the area of social welfare; and that the loss of public confidence in the
government because of programs failing to live up to promises was a major
problem facing the Nixon Administration.[41]

Also, Moynihan was a recognized expert on poverty and public
relief. He had written quite extensively on the subject, been involved in the
development of the "war on poverty" programs; and he was deeply committed
to reforming public assistance. Because of the disorganization in domestic
policy making during the first year of the Nixon Administration and the am-
biguity of his particular role, Moynihan was able to devote a great deal more
of his time and energy to promoting FAP than Burns, who had more general responsibilities, or Finch, who had other problems and responsibilities

at HEW. Finally, Moynihan not only understood the problems of the poor and public welfare, he also understood the political problems and personality of President Nixon. He pointed out to Nixon on more than one occasion how his support of FAP could help him with the American electorate in 1972 and U.S. historians later. Nixon was interested in both.

According to interviews, the President was receptive to Moynihan's contention that this was a unique opportunity to do something that should be done and only Nixon could do because he could get business and the Republicans in Congress to support FAP: that it would be an accomplishment for which he would be remembered. One explained,

> Nixon, with the encouragement of Finch and Moynihan, believed he had a unique opportunity to make some necessary changes in our welfare system. He became convinced that *he* could make a real dent in the problem. It was a mess—it was terrible that nothing had been done but "tinkering," as Gil Steiner calls it, since the '30s. He could make the changes because he could get Republicans to support them. . . . Also, it was in line with the theme of his campaign, which was that people were discontented with the government because of the programs that weren't working. And, that we needed to reexamine existing institutions and programs and make necessary changes. This was a perfect policy area to follow through on this theme because the existing system is in such bad shape and everybody is complaining about it. . . . It was an area that fit in with what the President wanted. The President's sense that this is what *should* be done was important. He made the final decision and has to be given credit for it. His feeling of public discontent with government and distrust of existing institutions— the kind of things John Gardner talks about so eloquently, too eloquently I think—is important in the President's decisions on domestic issues.

Nixon's Commitment to FAP

Of course it is impossible to provide a complete account of Nixon's motives or reasons for proposing FAP, or to establish the strength of his commitment to radical welfare reform at the time it was proposed. The preceding analysis suggests an explanation for Nixon's decision to sponsor FAP with the following basic elements.

First, the problems and dissatisfaction with the existing welfare system had come to his attention before he was elected and he came to the presidency interested in the issue and the possibility of improvement. Several of the men he had chosen to advise and assist him in domestic matters were also interested in welfare reform. Widespread public dissatisfaction with the AFDC program, and pressure from state and local officials to make some changes, provided an incentive and the political opportunity to propose reform. An innovative policy alternative endorsed by recognized experts was presented to him. Trusted advisers argued energetically and apparently effectively that it would be to his political advantage to sponsor this proposal and, if implemented, the changes it contained would establish a more effective, equitable and desirable welfare system.

Given the division among his top advisers, it is safe to assume that Nixon's commitment to FAP wavered. At times, after talking to Moynihan or Finch, he believed it was the right thing to do politically and because it would reduce poverty. Other times he worried about the effect of a guaranteed income on the work efforts of the poor and how he would defend a proposal that doubled federal welfare costs and recipients. Most of the time, however, his attention was focused on other matters, especially those pertaining to foreign problems. When pressed in private by senators, congressmen, governors, or members of his staff, his consistent response, according to interviews, was that he was "not absolutely sure FAP would work" or "that it would take us down the right road." But he felt "something had to be done about welfare" and he was convinced the present system "was taking us down the wrong road."

Chapter Five

Welfare Policy: The Nixon, Mills, and Byrnes Reforms

We knew that soon after the first announcement the liberals would attack us for not doing enough for the poor and the conservatives would call it socialism. The day after President Nixon announced FAP over television Moynihan was talking to him on the phone. The President had had a couple of martinis and was feeling great. Moynihan asked him if he had read Reston's column today saying, "it was fabulous." After a pause he added, "enjoy it while you can!"

> —Administration Official
> 1971

The miracle of the 1970 congressional session is that the House Ways and Means Committee and then the full House approved the Nixon income measure (FAP) with few substantive changes, none of them destructive and many of them improvements.

> —John Osborne
> 1970

Legislation containing FAP and the other proposed welfare changes described in Chapter three was introduced in the House of Representatives on October 3, 1970 by John Byrnes, Ranking Republican on the House Ways and Means Committee. Ways and Means held public hearings on the Administration's proposed welfare reforms from October 15 through November 13 and then went into executive session. With only minor modifications, Nixon's welfare bill, including the Family Assistance Plan and national eligibility and payment standards for the aged, blind and disabled programs, was reported out of Ways and Means in March 1970 and approved by the House of Representatives in a 243 to 155 roll call vote April 16, 1970.

Throughout the summer and fall of 1970, FAP remained stalled in the Senate Finance Committee where, essentially, the liberal members of the committee argued that the benefits were inadequate and conservatives opposed it because it would increase welfare costs and recipients. The Administration made several modifications in response to criticism by committee members but were unable to persuade a majority to support the House passed negative tax program for families with children.

On December 11, 1970, with only three weeks remaining in the 91st Congress, the Finance Committee reported a conglomerate bill containing an import quota on shoes and textiles, a new catastrophic illness health insurance program, an increase in Social Security benefits, modifications in Veterans Pensions, Medicare and Medicaid, and provisions providing for limited pilot tests of the Family Assistance Plan. On the Senate floor, Senator Abraham Ribicoff of Connecticut and Senator Wallace Bennett of Utah, both members of the Finance Committee, offered a somewhat liberalized version of FAP as an amendment to the Social Security provisions of the Finance Committee bill. A motion to delete the Ribicoff/Bennett Amendment on December 19 was defeated 15 to 65.

From December 19 through the 28th, the Finance Committee bill was filibustered by opponents of the trade provisions, supporters of the Ribicoff/Bennett Amendment who wanted to block passage of the committee's provisions to test FAP, and opponents of the Ribicoff/Bennett Amendment who were opposed to the enactment of FAP. Finally, on December 28, when it was apparent that no decision regarding the reform of AFDC could be reached, Senator Russell Long, Chairman of the Finance Committee and a leading opponent of FAP, offered a motion to delete the Ribicoff/Bennett Amendment from the committee bill. This time the motion carried 49 to 21 and FAP was defeated.[1]

Failing to get Senate approval in 1970, Nixon announced that enactment of the welfare reforms proposed in August 1969 would be "White House priority number one" and his "major legislative goal in 1971." When the first session of the 92nd Congress convened in January 1971, the Ways and Means Committee began meeting with Administration officials in executive session to draw up legislation containing major changes in public assistance programs as well as modifications in Social Security, Medicare, and Medicaid. On May 17, 1971 the Committee, with three dissenting votes, reported a welfare reform bill which was approved by the full House several weeks later.

H.R.1, the welfare reform legislation approved by the Ways and Means Committee and passed by the House of Representatives in 1971, represented radical policy change in that it proposed fundamental and comprehensive change in all public assistance programs. In this chapter H.R.1 is compared with the original Nixon welfare reform plan with the objective of identifying the most significant differences between the two proposals. The

following chapter provides an account of the process by which Ways and
Means developed and approved H.R.1, and an analysis of conditions associated
with this process and the approval of radical welfare change by both the Committee and the House.

H.R.1: TECHNICAL CHANGES

The Recipients of Benefits

Under H.R.1, needy aged, blind, and disabled adults and families with
children and incomes below a specified level would be eligible for a minimum
federal cash payment. In other words, families eligible under the original Nixon
plan, including the "working poor," would be eligible for federal cash benefits
under H.R.1. Plus, under the House bill, adult recipients of public assistance
would also be eligible for a federal minimum cash benefit.

The Nature of the Benefits

In the Nixon proposal there was no restriction against cash recipients participating in any of the other benefits in-kind, service, or rehabilitation
programs. Under H.R.1, persons eligible for federal cash assistance, including
families, aged, blind, and disabled adults, would *not* be eligible to participate
in the food stamp program.

H.R.1 deleted provisions in the Nixon bill for special work training
projects and replaced these with a new public service employment program.
$800 million was authorized to provide 200,000 public service jobs for welfare
recipients in fiscal 1973.

The Value of the Benefits

Under the new federal program in H.R.1, eligible families would
receive $800 for each of the first two family members, $400 each for the
third, fourth, and fifth members, $300 each for the sixth and seventh mem-
bers, and $200 for the eighth member. A family of four with no other income
would receive $2,400 a year under the Committee's bill, as compared to $1,600
in the original Nixon plan. No family could receive more than $3,600, regard-
less of family size, and payments at a rate of less than $10 per month would
not be made. As in the Nixon proposal, the first $720 of a family's yearly
earnings would not be included in reducing cash benefits. However, under
H.R.1 only *one-third*, rather than one-half, of the earnings in excess of $720
per year would be excluded. Table 5-1 shows how family earnings would
affect the federal cash payment and total yearly income of a low income family
of four under H.R.1. The annual disregard of $720 plus one-third would enable
a family of four to continue receiving benefits until its income reached $4,140
(at which point the benefit rate would be $10 a month or less). In the Nixon
program the cutoff point for a family of four was $3,920.

Table 5-1.   Yearly Benefits and Total Income for a Family of Four Under H.R.1

Family Earnings	Amount of Earnings Disregarded[a]	Federal Cash Payments[b]	Total Family Income[c]
$ 0	$ 0	$2,400	$2,400
500	500	2,400	2,900
1,000	813	2,213	3,213
1,500	980	1,880	3,380
2,000	1,147	1,547	3,547
2,500	1,313	1,213	3,713
3,000	1,480	880	3,880
3,500	1,647	547	4,047
4,000	1,813	213	4,213
4,500	1,980	0	4,500

[a]In computing the federal cash payment a family would be allowed to "disregard" $60 per month ($720 per year) as work related expenses, plus one-third of additional earnings up to $4,140.

[b]Federal cash benefits payable to a family would be computed by subtracting the family's earnings, minus the amount disregarded, from the basic federal benefit of $2,400 for a family of four.

[c]Total family income would be the amount of family earnings plus the federal cash payment.

For the aged, blind, and disabled, the Nixon proposal set a minimum payment level of $90 a month per person within the existing federal-state administrative framework. H.R.1 would replace the present state programs with a new federal program, which would assure aged, blind, and disabled persons a minimum monthly income of $130 for fiscal year 1973, $140 for fiscal 1974, and $150 for fiscal 1975 and thereafter. For married couples the amounts would be $195 for fiscal 1973 and $200 for fiscal 1974 and after.

The Committee bill did not require the states to supplement these federal benefits for either family or adult recipients, as did the Nixon plan. And the Federal Government would not pay any of the cost of supplementation unless the cost to a state for supplementing up to present payment levels exceeded that state's 1971 welfare expenditures. At the request of liberal members of the Committee, Wilbur Mills introduced an amendment on the House floor which provided that states with present public assistance payments higher than the federal minimums in H.R.1 *would supplement* unless the state legislatures passed legislation to the contrary.

The Delivery of Benefits

Government Jurisdiction.   H.R.1 would replace the existing federal-state public assistance programs (AFDC, OAA, AB, APTD) with new, *federal*

negative tax programs for families (FAP) and aged, blind and disabled adults
(SSI). If a state supplemented the federal programs, it had the option of con-
tracting for federal administration of the state payments, in which case the
Federal Government would absorb all administrative costs.

Administrative Procedures. An important change from the Nixon
plan was that under H.R.1 the *families* eligible for benefits would be divided,
for administrative purposes, into two groups. Those families in which there
was an employable person would be in the Opportunities for Families program
(OFF), which would be administered by the Department of Labor. The Family Assistance program (FAP) would be for those families in which there was
not an employable person. FAP and the new federal program for the aged,
blind, and disabled would be administered by HEW. Payment levels for families in OFF and FAP would be the same. Also, H.R.1 included an emergency
aid provision, not in the Nixon proposal, authorizing those administering the
programs to provide new applicants who appear to be eligible, and who have
an emergency, an advance payment of up to $100.

Several changes were introduced in H.R.1 in an effort to "tighten
up" the administration and cost of welfare and to "prevent welfare fraud."
For example, federal appropriations for social services, with the exceptions
of child care and family planning services, were limited to $800 million for
1973. This, in effect, would put a limit on the existing open-ended appropriations for these programs. States would be allowed to impose a residency
requirement as part of the eligibility standards for state supplemental payments. Provisions were added making it a misdemeanor for a person to travel
across state boundaries for the purpose of avoiding the support of his children,
and making a deserting parent obligated to the United States for the amount
of any federal payments made to his family.

For the families in the OFF and FAP programs, payments would
be made only after a personal interview and the presentation of "convincing
evidentiary materials" such as birth certificates and tax and Social Security
records. Social Security numbers would be assigned to all members of a family
to prevent duplication in payment. A $3,000 ceiling was placed on the amount
of excluded income, such as the earnings of students and earnings used to pay
child care costs, which would require detailed accounting, listing, and verify-
ing of family income as far back as nine months prior to the date of application. In other words, there would be no simplified declaration process of
eligibility determination. Penalties for failure to present accurate information
which resulted in an overpayment were strict and severe. After a family had
received benefits for two years another application and full investigation would
be required.

H.R.1 maintained the work requirement in the Nixon proposal and
extended it to require those recipients working full time to register for programs

aimed at upgrading their work and annual income. Also, in order for mothers with children to be exempt from this requirement they would have to have children under the age of 3, instead of 6 as in the Nixon plan. Under the Nixon proposal, benefits would not be paid to an individual if he refused without good cause to participate in "suitable" manpower or training programs, or to accept "suitable" employment made available to him or her. In H.R.1 the word "suitable" was dropped. In its place the Committee listed several conditions under which work could be refused: where the wages offered were at an hourly rate of less than 3/4 of the minimum wage, and where "the individual had a demonstrated capacity, through other *available* training or employment opportunities, of securing *available* work that would better enable him to achieve self-sufficiency."[2] The penalty for failure to register or participate in work or training would be a reduction in the family benefits of $800, as compared to $300 a year under the Nixon plan.

Also, under the Committee's bill, individuals eligible for benefits because of incapacity due to alcoholism or drug addiction would be required to take rehabilitation treatment in order to receive monthly payments.

H.R.1: CONCEPTUAL CHANGE

Modifications made by the Ways and Means Committee generally extended the conceptual changes contained in the original Nixon recommendations. H.R.1 represented a dramatic shift to the assumptions and objectives of the negative income tax and other guaranteed income proposals. It would establish a national income definition of eligibility for federal cash assistance and guarantee by federal law a minimum level of yearly income for the aged, blind, disabled, and all families with children.

The level of benefits payable would be determined on the basis of family size and amount of family income from other sources. It emphasized the provision of direct cash payments as opposed to food stamps and other in-kind benefits. The authorization of 200,000 public service jobs for welfare recipients would move the Federal Government into the role of the "employer of last resort," which had been advocated by many as a necessary complement to the War on Poverty programs and income maintenance schemes like the negative income tax.[3]

In effect, H.R.1 would establish a federal guaranteed minimum income for the aged, blind, and disabled at a level above the existing poverty line. For families with children it would establish a federal guaranteed income under which the $2,400 minimum payment for a family of four was equal to about 3/4ths of the existing poverty level for a family of that size. These federal cash benefits could be supplemented by existing in-kind and service benefits (Medicaid, Social Services, etc.), with the exception of food stamps, and it was expected by Committee members and Administration officials that the states would provide a cash supplement for all present public assistance recipients at least up to current payment levels.

H.R.1: POTENTIAL CONSEQUENCES

It was estimated that federal costs of the programs for families and adults under H.R.1 would have been $14 billion in 1973, and total costs to all levels of government $17.5 billion. As shown in Table 5-2, this would have meant a 100 percent increase in federal public assistance expenditures in 1973 and a 31 percent decrease in state expenditures, amounting to a 45 percent increase in the costs of existing cash assistance programs for all levels of government. The federal share of total costs in 1973 would have been 80 percent under H.R.1 as compared to 58 percent under existing public assistance programs.

Table 5-2. Estimated Cost of H.R.1 and Public Assistance Under
Existing Programs, Fiscal 1973
(billions of dollars)

Level of Government and Program	*H.R.1*	*Existing Programs*	*Net Cost of H.R.1*	*Percent Increase Under H.R.1*
Federal Government				
Payments to families (AFDC)	$ 5.5	$ 3.9	$1.6	41
Payments to adults (OAA, AB, APTD)	4.1	2.2	1.9	87
State savings clause	1.1	–	1.1	100
Total	$10.7	$ 6.1	$4.6	75
Administration	1.1	.4	.7	
Training	.5	.2	.3	
Public service jobs	.8	–	.8	
Child care	.8	.3	.5	
Support services	.1	–	.1	
Total Federal Cost	$14.0	$ 7.0	$7.0	100
State Government				
Payments to families (AFDC)	3.1	3.3	–.2	
Payments to adults (OAA, AB, APTD)	1.5	1.4	.1	
State savings clause	–1.1	–	–1.1	
Administration	–	.4	–.4	
Total State Cost	$ 3.5	$ 5.1	–$1.6	–31
Total All Governments	$17.5	$12.1	$5.4	45

Source: U.S., Congress, *Social Security Amendments of 1971,* Ways and Means Committee Report on H.R.1, 92nd Congress, 1st sess., 1971, pp. 208-209.

The Administration produced figures indicating that under H.R.1 every state could have supplemented the federal benefits up to existing payment levels, including the value of food stamps received by current public assistance recipients, and still derived a savings on estimated welfare expenditures in 1973 under existing programs. This savings would have been increased significantly if the states turned over the administation of the state supplement to the Federal Government.

Table 5-3 shows the estimated *percent decrease* in each state's expenditures for cash assistance programs if H.R.1 had replaced existing public assistance programs in 1973. These percentages were based on Administration estimates that assumed all states would maintain current benefit levels, including food stamp benefits, and would turn over the administration of state supplemental payments to the Federal Government. Savings in 1973 welfare costs would have ranged from 13 percent in Maine and 14 percent in Vermont and Washington to 100 percent in Arkansas, Mississippi, and South Carolina, where public assistance benefits were lower than the minimum payments in H.R.1.

Table 5-4 compares the projected number of cash recipients under H.R.1 with existing public assistance programs for 1973 through 1976. It shows that in 1973 under H.R.1 there would have been 25.6 million recipients as compared to 15.0 million under the current system. This amounts to an increase of 10.6 million cash recipients, or a 71 percent increase if H.R.1 had been enacted. As indicated in Table 5-5, there would have been a potential increase in welfare recipients in every state under H.R.1. In eighteen states it would have increased the number of cash recipients by 100 percent or more and there would have been an increase of at least 50 percent in 38 of the states.

Table 5–3.   Estimated States' Savings in 1973 Welfare Expenditures Under H.R.1

Percent Decrease in State Costs Under H.R.1	Number of States	States
0–20	12	Maine, Wash., Vt., N.H., Pa., N.Dak., Idaho, Mass., Mo., Calif., Minn., Nebr.
21–40	20	Alaska, Del., Mich., Ill., N.J., N.Y., R.I., Va., Ind., Nev., Colo., Conn., Utah, Hawaii, S.Dak., Wyo., Ky., Kans., Mont., Oreg.
41–60	5	N.Mex., Ohio, Iowa, Tex., Wis.
61–80	6	Md., Okla., Ariz., N.C., Ala., Tenn.
81–100	7	Ga., W.Va., La., Fla., Ark., Miss., S.C.

Source: Percentages were derived from information presented in U.S., Congress, House, *Social Security Amendments of 1971,* House Ways and Means Committee Report on H.R.1, 92nd Congress, 1st sess., 1971, p. 216.

Table 5-4. Projected Eligible Recipients Under H.R.1 and Existing Programs, 1973-1976
(millions of persons)

	1973	*1974*	*1975*	*1976*
H.R.1				
Persons in families:				
Not covered under existing programs	9.1	8.1	7.2	6.4
Covered under existing programs	10.3	10.6	10.9	11.2
Aged, blind & disabled	6.2	6.6	7.1	7.2
Total	25.6	25.3	25.2	24.8
Existing Programs				
AFDC recipients	11.6	12.6	13.6	14.7
Aged, blind & disabled (OAA, AB, APTD)	3.4	3.4	3.5	3.5
Total	15.0	16.0	17.1	18.2

Source: U.S., Congress, House, *Social Security Amendments of 1971,* House Ways and Means Committee Report on H.R.1, 92nd Congress, 1st sess., 1971, p. 227.

Table 5-5. Projected Increase in Number of Persons Eligible for Cash Assistance Under H.R.1 in 1973

Percent Increase Under H.R.1	*Number of States*	*States*
0–49	13	Calif., Colo., Conn., D.C., Hawaii, Maine, Mass., N.J., N.Mex., N.Y., Oreg., Penn., Wash.
50–99	20	Ala., Alaska, Ariz., Del., Ga., Idaho, Ill., La., Md., Mich., Minn., Mo., Nev., N.H., Ohio, Okla., R.I., Utah, Vt., Wyo.
100–149	12	Fla., Ind., Iowa, Kans., Ky., Miss., Mont., Neb., S.Dak., Tenn., Tex., Wisc.
150–200	3	Ark., N.Dak., W.Va.
200+	3	N.C., S.C., Va.

Source: Percentages were derived from information presented in U.S., Congress, House, *Social Security Amendments of 1971,* House Ways and Means Committee Report on H.R.1, 92nd Congress, 1st sess., 1971, pp. 217–218.

The Administration predicted a 44 percent increase in the number of recipients between 1971 and 1973 under existing public assistance programs. Consequently, the extent of change in welfare costs and caseloads that would have resulted from the implementation of H.R.1 in 1973, at least according to official projections, would not have been quite as dramatic as if the original Nixon proposal or H.R.1 had been implemented in 1970 or 1971.[4]

Without mandatory state supplementation of federal benefits, the Administration could not promise, as they had done with the original Nixon proposal, that no public assistance recipient would be worse off if H.R.1 were enacted. And no official figures were made public suggesting how many poor Americans would be better off under H.R.1 than under the existing programs. [5].

Some estimates have been derived from available data which indicate how many Americans would have been better off in terms of receiving more *cash benefits* under H.R.1 in 1973. These figures are shown in Table 5-6. Because cash recipients would no longer be eligible for food stamps, for many the increase in cash benefits would not have meant an increase in the total value of welfare benefits they received under the existing programs. According to these calculations, about 17 million people would have received more cash if H.R.1 had replaced public assistance programs in 1973. Of this 17 million, 9.2 million included the "working poor" families and families with dependent children who were not eligible for cash benefits under existing law, and 2.8 million included aged, blind or disabled individuals who would have become eligible for cash benefits because of the higher minimum payment standards under H.R.1.

Table 5-6. Estimated Number of Persons Who Would Have a Higher *Cash Income* Under H.R.1 Than Under Existing Public Assistance Programs in 1973

Client Group	Number (in millions)	Percent of Cases Under Existing Programs
Families		
Persons not covered under existing programs (mainly "working poor")	9.2	–
Present AFDC recipients in states paying less than the H.R.1 minimum as of March 1971	3.1	31
Total	12.3	31
Adults		
Persons not covered under existing programs (new cases made eligible by H.R.1 eligibility standards)	2.8	–
Present adult cases in states paying less than the H.R.1 minimum as of March 1971	1.74	56
Total	4.54	56
Grand Total	16.84	36

Source: Estimates were derived from information presented in Table 5-4 and U.S., Congress, Senate, Committee on Finance, "Maximum Payment Levels for Public Assistance Programs, March 1971" (prepared by the Department of Health, Education, and Welfare, 1971).

Most of these families and adults lived in the southern states where wages and current welfare benefits were the lowest. Some of these individuals were eligible for food stamps under existing law, so it is not possible to identify exactly how many of them would have been better off in terms of the total value of benefits they received. Some 3.1 million AFDC recipients, or 31 percent of 1973 AFDC recipients, and 1.74 million aged, blind, and disabled, 56 percent of the 1973 OAA, AB, and APTD recipients, would have received more cash under H.R.1 because they lived in states where the current maximum payments were less than the minimum payments under H.R.1.

When the value of food stamps is taken into account, however, the number of AFDC recipients who would have been better off under H.R.1, in terms of the total value of welfare benefits received, is reduced to approximately 600,000, or 7 percent of the 1973 AFDC population. This would have included recipients who lived in Alabama, Arkansas, Louisiana, Mississippi, and South Carolina.

In Table 5–7 the $2,400 payment for a family of four under H.R.1 is compared with the maximum payment to an AFDC family of four in each state as of March 1971. The $2,400 minimum payment under H.R.1 ranged from 58 percent of the maximum AFDC payment in New Jersey to 247 percent in Alabama and 333 percent in Mississippi. H.R.1 would have increased cash payments to AFDC recipients in the 22 states where $2,400 amounted to more than 100 percent of the current maximum payment.

Table 5–7. Relationship of H.R.1 Payment Levels to AFDC Payment Levels as of March 1971

$2,400 (H.R.1 Minimum Payment for a Family of Four) as a Percent of AFDC Maximum for a Family of Four	*Number of States*	*States*
60–75	14	N.J., Conn., N.Y., Ill., Vt., N.H., Minn., Mass., Penn., S.Dak., Mich., Alaska, N.Dak., Wash.
76–100	14	Va., Hawaii, R.I., Kans., Iowa, Idaho, Colo., Neb., Wyo., Oreg., Calif., Wisc., Mont., Ohio
101–125	9	Md., Utah, Ky., Okla., N.Mex., Ind., Ariz., N.C., Maine
126–150	6	Del., Tex., Nev., W.Va., Fla., Ga.
150+	7	Mo., Tenn., La., S.C., Ark., Ala., Miss.

Source: Percentages were derived from information presented in Table 5–4, and U.S., Congress, Senate, Committee on Finance, "Maximum Payment Levels for Public Assistance Programs, March 1971" (prepared by the Department of Health, Education, and Welfare, 1971).

H.R.1 would not have eliminated income poverty in the United States. However, it would have increased the cash income of millions of Americans, and for many of these it would have raised their yearly income above the established poverty level. As with the original Nixon plan, it would have produced the largest single expansion of welfare since the implementation of the 1935 Social Security legislation.

Chapter Six

Welfare Policy Process:
The House of Representatives

The Committee on Ways and Means is just completing the most thoroughgoing, extensive, and intensive review and analysis which has ever been made of this program. . . . The Bill which the Committee is about to recommend to the House of Representatives will contain provision after provision designed to meet the myriad of problems which we have identified during our consideration of the subject.

> —Chairman Wilbur Mills
> May 1971

When Nixon first announced his proposal on television I was skeptical. . . . But, when we got working on the bill itself, with Byrnes supporting it and then when Mills changed his position and supported it, I decided it was the right thing to do. . . . Mills said this is a good bill because it has the middle-of-the-roaders voting for it and the extremists opposing it.

> —Republican Member of Ways and
> Means Committee
> 1971

For the first five months of the 92nd Congress beginning January 1971, the daily calendar of Congressional activities included the same listing for the House Ways and Means Committee:

> House Committee on Ways and Means, executive, to continue consideration of H.R.1, Social Security Amendments of 1971, 10 A.M., committee room, Longworth Building.

The Committee did not hold public hearings on President Nixon's welfare proposal in 1971 as they had done in 1969. Shortly after Congress got under way they immediately began executive session deliberations on welfare reform. Administration officials who were in attendance at most of the closed-door meetings during January through May included: John Veneman, John Montgomery, Charles Hawkins, Mike Mahoney, and James Edwards of HEW; Robert Ball, Commissioner of the Social Security Administration; and Jerome Rosow and Paul Barton of the Department of Labor.

Dozens of issues pertaining to Social Security, Medicaid, Medicare, and cash assistance for adults and families were reviewed, debated, and resolved by those who attended the executive meetings in February, March, and the first week of April. Over the Easter vacation, April 7 through 19, the Committee staff prepared a 30-page confidential report entitled "Description of Provisions in Confidential Committee Print of Draft Bill." When Congress reconvened April 20, they entered into the final "markup" stage and began resolving the most controversial issues by committee vote. On May 17, the Committee approved 22 to 3 a bill containing the welfare changes outlined in Chapter Five. This legislation, H.R.1—Social Security Amendments of 1971, was officially released to noncommittee congressmen, the press, and the public on May 26; it was approved by the full House June 22, 1971.

This chapter describes the membership and characteristic "style" of the Ways and Means Committee, the decision making process and procedures by which the Committee shaped H.R.1, and the conditions associated with Committee and House approval of this proposal for radical welfare change.

HOUSE WAYS AND MEANS COMMITTEE

The Congressional Committee which developed H.R.1 was composed of relatively secure and senior congressmen. Twenty of the 25 members had served in the House for at least nine years. Only four faced any opposition in the 1970 primary elections and they all received at least 55 percent of the votes cast in the 1970 general elections. As shown in Table 6-1, rural southern states were well represented on the Committee; however, a majority of the members were from urban states with large welfare populations and expenditures, including New York, California, Michigan, Illinois, Pennsylvania, Ohio, and Massachusetts.

The low party opposition scores shown in Table 6-1 suggest most of the members were "good" party men: that on issues which divided the House along party lines, Ways and Means members generally voted with the majority of their respective parties. The prevalence of low conservative coalition opposition scores shown in the table indicates a large conservative majority composed of southern Democrats and Republicans.[1] The existence of a conservative majority within the Committee, the party loyalty, relative elec-

Table 6-1. Members of the House Ways and Means Committee, 92nd Congress, 1st Session: State and Type of District, Conservative Coalition Opposition, and Party Opposition Scores for 1971

Member	State	Type of District[a]	Conservative Coalition Opposition Score[b] (percent)	Party Opposition Score[c] (percent)
Democrats				
Wilbur Mills	Ark.	suburb	21	24
John Watts	Ky.	rural	18	46
Al Ullman	Oreg.	rural	57	17
James Burke	Mass.	suburb	81	9
Martha Griffiths	Mich.	urban	41	9
Dan Rostenkowski	Ill.	urban	55	12
Phil Landrum	Ga.	rural	16	30
Charles Vanik	Ohio	suburb	93	11
Richard Fulton	Tenn.	urban	66	14
Omar Burleson	Tex.	rural	5	68
James Corman	Calif.	urban	71	12
William Green	Pa.	urban	81	6
Sam Gibbons	Fla.	urban	70	16
Hugh Carey	N.Y.	urban	83	9
Joe Waggonner	La.	suburb	1	63
Republicans				
John Byrnes	Wisc.	suburb	13	17
Jackson Betts	Ohio	rural	5	10
Herman Schneebeli	Pa.	rural	14	11
Harold Collier	Ill.	suburb	11	17
Joel Broyhill	Va.	suburb	12	21
Barber Conable	N.Y.	suburb	18	16
Charles Chamberlain	Mich.	suburb	6	12
Jerry Pettis	Calif.	suburb	10	20
John Duncan	Tenn.	suburb	13	20
Donald Brotzman	Colo.	suburb	14	17

Source: U.S., Department of Commerce, Bureau of the Census, *Congressional District Data, Districts of the 92nd Congress* (Washington, D.C.: Government Printing Office, 1971); *Congressional Quarterly Weekly Report* (Washington, D.C.: Congressional Quarterly Service, January 15, 1972), pp. 74–80, 86–91.

[a]A congressional district was defined as *urban* if 50 percent or more of the district population lived within the boundaries of one of the standard metropolitan statistical areas (SMSA) and 50 percent or more lived inside the central cities of the SMSA as defined by the U.S. Office of Management and Budget and the Census Bureau. If 50 percent of the population lived inside an SMSA but fewer than 50 percent lived inside the central city the district was defined as *suburban*. If fewer than 50 percent of the population lived inside a SMSA the district was defined as *rural*.

[b]Conservative Coalition Opposition Score: The percentage of 99 conservative coalition recorded votes in 1971 (as defined by *Congressional Quarterly*) on which the member voted in *disagreement* with the position of the conservative coalition.

[c]Party Opposition Score: The percentage of 121 House Party Unity recorded votes in 1971 (as defined by *Congressional Quarterly*) on which the member voted in *disagreement* with a majority of his party.

toral security, and suburban or urban constituencies of most of the members are important factors, which influenced both the decision process and outcome of Ways and Means welfare deliberations in 1971.

As Manley's study of Ways and Means suggests,[2] the legislative orientation and style of the members and the decision making norms and procedures of the Committee during this period are also important in understanding how H.R.1 was developed and why radical reform was approved. Manley explains, because of the recruitment criteria used, congressmen assigned to Ways and Means,

> are, in general, pragmatic in their outlook on politics, patient in their pursuit of objectives, unbending on few things, and inclined to compromise on all but the most basic issues.[3]

"Burning policy interests do not characterize" those representatives assigned to the Committee in the 1960s and 1970s.[4] The pragmatic orientation of the members is consistent with the decision making style of the Committee. Three features of Ways and Means policy making are described by Manley. The first is identified as the norm of "restrained partisanship," which means

> members should not allow partisanship to interfere with a thorough study and complete understanding of the technical complexities of the bills they consider. Members have a bipartisan responsibility to the House and to the nation to write sound legislation.[5]

Second, granting due respect for seniority and technical expertise, every member who wants to can participate in the deliberations and is given ample opportunity to present and defend his views. Third, final Committee decisions are supposed to be consensus decisions. That is, they should reflect substantive, fiscal, and political balance and compromise, and have the support not only of the Democrats, Republicans, liberals, or conservatives but of all Committee members—or at least 20 of the 25.[6]

The objective of the Committee is to design legislation that is technically sound, that at least all but a very few members of the Committee can support, and, most important, that will be approved by the full House. The general procedure in designing a bill is to incorporate as many of the members' suggestions and specific provisions as possible, to find a compromise position for most conflicts, and to settle the remaining irreconcilable disagreements by a committee vote.

A final characteristic of Ways and Means policy making at the present time is the influence of its chairman, Wilbur Mills. Mills, according to Manley, "stands out as one of the most influential committee chairmen in recent years, if not in history."[7] The source of his influence includes his formal position as Committee chairman, his years of experience in the House, the knowledge he has of the issues and legislation handled by the Committee, his willingness to do special favors for Committee members when and in whatever way he can, and his mastery of the art of what Lindblom calls "partisan analysis"—a technique of persuasion by which one policy maker finds "a way in which a policy he desires can serve the values of another policy maker to whom the persuasion is directed."[8] As is the case with most major bills, Committee members supported H.R.1 for different, and in some cases, inconsistent reasons. Mills's special ability is that of discovering the provisions, wording, and reasons—political, personal, or substantive—that persuade congressmen with different political and policy orientations to support a particular legislative proposal.

The nature of Mills's influence and leadership is that of effective attention directing and consensus building—in both the Committee and the House. In other words, what distinguishes Mills from most other members, and defines his power in the House, is his leverage in shifting the attention of House members to particular public problems and courses of action and obtaining Committee and House approval of the legislation he sponsors. He is responsive to Presidents and House colleagues, but he also exercises significant discretion in setting the Ways and Means agenda, and thereby determining the trade, tax, and welfare legislation the Committee, and House, will and will not consider. In regard to his ability to obtain Committee and House passage of legislation he supports, the members view him as a "consensus seeker" and an effective "consensus builder." According to Committee member Barber Conable, although

> the newspapers like to build up all this mystique and mystery about Mills, saying he has a secret bill or scheme for this and that, he does not come up with solutions like Minerva came out of the forehead of Zeus. This is a consensus Committee and he is a master at operating the process—but he is not a superman. More often than not the process dictates the final substance of the bill— the process of finding a consensus solution.

Manley describes him as a "democratic chairman," who

> ... is perhaps as responsive to the Committe as the Committee is to him. He no doubt has great influence with the members, but it is earned by the way he approaches his job and develops its potential. Ways and Means is highly centralized under Mills but the Committee's policy decisions emerge from an exhaustive— and collegial—process. The decisions of the Committee are shaped

and articulated by Mills, but his word comes close to being law in the Committee because he has listened to others, particularly to the ranking Republican, John Byrnes.[9]

Major bills reported by Ways and Means, at least since Mills has been chairman, are debated on the House floor under a closed rule, which means they can be amended or modified *only* by the Committee. The House membership must either accept or reject the legislation as designed by the Committee members. "In a few cases, a modified closed rule permits some kind of amendment but normally the rule is closed completely."[10] Despite, or possibly because of, the closed rule and the limitations it imposes on House members, Ways and Means bills, with very few exceptions, are approved by the House. From 1961 to 1974, the Committee lost on only three roll call votes.[11]

H.R.1: DECISION MAKING PROCESS

The decision making activities and procedures involved in the development of H.R.1 within the Ways and Means Committee have been summarized in the following account in terms of what appeared to be the three primary stages in the process: agenda setting; policy analysis and program design—consensus issues; policy analysis and program design—conflict issues.

Setting the Committee's
Welfare Agenda

The procedure used by Mills to identify welfare problems and possible solutions for Committee consideration in 1971 was somewhat extraordinary. According to the Undersecretary of HEW, John Veneman, "Mills requested" that his staff prepare a "detailed list of *all* the complaints and concerns that had been stated since Nixon first introduced FAP in August 1969." A Ways and Means staff member explained this request in the following way:

> The HEW staff, and you can tell them I told you, made . . . poor preparations for this year (1971). They came over here and we asked them if they had attempted to answer the objections made in the Senate and elsewhere, and they hadn't. And, it was damn tough to get them to do it! The first thing we asked them to do was to read through all the debates and discussions in committees and on the floor—in the House and Senate—dealing with FAP; and then to list the objections: who made them, where and when, and to suggest an answer or response. It was damn hard to get them to do it—especially to provide adequate answers. I told them this in front of the Chairman. I told them I wasn't against

them—if I had been it would have been easy, like shooting fish in
a barrel. They better be ready for the Senate this time.

Veneman's reluctance was not surprising. In the first place, the
Administration had spent nine months in 1969 debating and designing the
program where essentially the same objections had been raised by persons
who wanted more adequate payment levels and others who were opposed to
the expansion of costs and caseloads that would occur under FAP. And modifications had been made in 1970 in response to criticism in the Senate and
elsewhere. At this point, Veneman and other Administration officials believed
FAP was a sound proposal reflecting the concerns of "responsible" liberals
and conservatives. They had given up ever convincing Senator Long and
other "extreme" conservatives and liberals, as suggested in the following comments by an HEW official.

> You can talk to Senator Long and others like him and give him
> the hypothetical example of a mother with nine children. You
> point out that it will cost $4,000 to train her for a job that pays
> $2,000 and costs $1,500 a year, per child, for day care. So, you
> end up paying almost $20,000 a year in order to prevent a federal
> minimum payment of $5,000 or less for this family. And he will
> reply,"That's okay, you can't put a value on those children seeing
> a mother get up at 5:30 to go to work." Doing what? Picking
> armadillos off the highway?
>   . . . I have an amendment that, I think, if it was added we would
> get 100 percent support in the Senate. It would guarantee every
> senator and congressman a maid and housekeeper for life. I think
> that is what Long and others are really concerned about—that if
> the bill goes through they won't be able to get a maid down in
> Louisiana. . . . You know, however, there are as many dumb people
> on the liberal side of this issue as on the other side. For example,
> some congressmen and senators sit over there and think that no
> one should be required to take a job that isn't as exciting as theirs.
> Well hell! Ninety percent of the people in this country work at
> very uninteresting jobs.

Another reason Veneman and his staff balked at the request was
that the Ways and Means and Senate Finance Committee hearings added up
to almost 5,000 pages. The minutes of both Committees' executive sessions,
the two-week debate on the Senate floor in December 1970, and the House
floor debate in 1969—plus the suggestion that they also review newspaper and
magazine editorials—would add another several thousand pages. In other words,
it looked like a time consuming and potentially unfruitful job.

This agenda setting procedure represented the problem solving
and policy making logic and technique of the "professional legislator:" a process

"professional reformers" tend to view as the bane of their methods and efforts to design the best solutions to public problems. To Chairman Mills, the best things in politics are negotiable and negotiated. However, some are more negotiable than others. Certain procedural requirements and his perception of what must be done to get House approval of a bill are less debatable and negotiable than most. Veneman complied.

Eighteen people in HEW worked full time for most of January reviewing the recorded debates and discussions of FAP. Veneman explained,

> If someone said something that wasn't true then we discounted his complaint. But where someone had a legitimate objection we attempted to meet it with a justification, or to make a change and then explain it.

Charles Hawkins, who was working with Veneman in HEW during this time, recalled,

> What they came up with was about 2,000 pages with one complaint per page. Of course some of the complaints were the same. They would read: Senator so-and-so on such-and-such a day said this. I think they reduced this to 167 different individuals and about 100 different objections. They were compiled and then HEW suggested an answer to each.

The Ways and Means staff man quoted earlier complained that the Committee staff

> had to do HEW's job of reducing the number of objections and proposed changes to a workable number, as well as coming up with answers to the objections and possible changes.

On most major bills the Committee staff summarizes the objections registered during Ways and Means hearings and executive meetings for the use of the Chairman and the Committee in the final markup sessions. However, staff members acknowledge that, in the case of FAP, this procedure was more elaborate, comprehensive and time consuming than normal, reflecting the extraordinary or radical nature of the bill.

Early in February, Committee members received a confidential committee print entitled, "Changes in Family Assistance Provisions of H.R.1 Recommended by the Department of Health, Education, and Welfare." An introductory note described the contents:

> Staff Note:
> The Department submitted to the committee staff between Janu-

ary 27 and February 4 nearly 80 proposals for changes in the family assistance provisions of H.R.1. Based on discussions between the staff of the committee and the staff of the Department, the Department reduced the number of its proposals for changes to the 32 printed in this pamphlet, many of which were modified during discussions with the committee staff. Several major policy issues in family assistance are not included in this print; the Department wishes to present those issues directly to the committee.

The staff has limited its comments in this print to the specific changes recommended by the Department.

During February and March the members received five additional Committee prints recommending major changes in existing public assistance programs and numerous modifications in Social Security, Medicare, and Medicaid. The problems identified and solutions recommended in these documents constituted the Committee's agenda during the 1971 welfare deliberations, or the issues discussed at daily Committee meetings, which normally went from 10:00 to 12:00 in the mornings and from 1:45 to 4:00 or 5:00 in the afternoons.

Most important, over a period of several weeks they received what finally amounted to an 80-page document labeled, "Mr. Mills's Questions." Altogether there were 32 separate "questions" raised by the Chairman. For each question the report briefly discussed the issue involved, specified the relevant provision in the original Nixon proposal, and provided a justification by HEW for maintaining the existing provision or a recommended change and justification. The Chairman's questions dealt with a wide variety of issues including, for example, the following:

> *Mills's Question:* Should mothers with children at least three years old be required to register for work or training?
> *HEW Response:* No; mothers should not be required to work until all children reach the age of six.
>
> *Mills's Question:* Should not the amount of money to be deducted for refusing to work be increased and the person who refuses be obligated to the Federal Government for the amount of money his family received?
> *HEW Response:* Yes to the first and no to the second.
>
> *Mills's Questions:* Should not a maximum level of benefits be established, regardless of family size?
> *HEW Response:* No—it would hurt the working poor more than it would prevent illegitimacy.
>
> *Mills's Question:* Won't the states, the recipients, and other interest groups apply pressure on the Federal Government to raise the federal benefits under FAP?
> *HEW Response:* The bill contains no provisions for increasing the federal payments and no changes are recommended.

Mills's Question: Should we build a provision into H.R.1 which allows for direct payment of rent to landlords?
HEW Response: No—it is inconsistent with the assumptions of the "income strategy."
Mills's Question: Did we consider a proposal for the working poor similar to the recent proposal by the Heath Government in Britain?
HEW Response: "The British proposal for the working poor is startlingly similar to ours, with a 50% tax rate on an earned income difference between a certain standard and actual earnings." In other words, it is a negative income tax program. "In conclusion, we found nothing wrong with such an approach and in fact adopted it."

This list of Mills's questions and HEW responses formally informed the Administration and Committee members of the Chairman's primary concerns and presented some changes in the Nixon proposal eventually incorporated in H.R.1. The questions indicated that Mills was interested in a "complete federalization" of programs for aged, blind, and disabled adults, and concerned about "tightening up" the proposed FAP program for families. In general he wanted reforms that, to the extent possible, would decrease administrative costs of welfare, stabilize federal welfare expenditures, reduce fraud and overpayments, and encourage ablebodied recipients to find employment.

The Administration's formal response to Mills's list of questions was an additional 40-page document that discussed and made recommendations relative to fifteen "major policy issues." The recommendations included:

1. Increasing federal cash benefits for a family of four under FAP to $2,200 and making recipients ineligible for food stamps.
2. Maintaining the requirement in the original Nixon proposal that states supplement federal FAP benefits up to current AFDC payment levels.
3. Tightening up the administration of FAP by placing a $2,000 limit on the amount of earned income a family may have excluded from benefit computation, using Social Security numbers to identify FAP recipients, requiring the presentation of evidentiary materials such as birth certificates and tax records by applicants and a detailed interview before granting benefits, creating a nationwide system for obtaining and verifying eligibility information, and enacting a federal welfare fraud statute.
4. Strengthening the work requirement by increasing the financial penalty from $300 to $500, expanding the work training programs, and creating 200,000 public employment jobs.

Discussion in Committee meetings would drift at times from the specific welfare problems and recommended solutions identified in documents prepared by HEW and the Ways and Means staff under the direction of Mills.

And at one point during the 1971 deliberations, Committee member Al Ullman was allowed to present a proposal which the Chamber of Commerce sponsored as an alternative to FAP. This proposal would divide welfare recipients into the employables and the unemployables. Those who were poor and unemployable would continue to receive benefits through the existing public assistance programs. For the poor employables, a federal nonwelfare program would be developed with the objective of promoting "self-sufficiency" through "work expense allowances," "free child care," and "a large scale program of public service jobs." It was "a guaranteed job" program.

However, the Committee did *not* formally consider any of the other alternative proposals to FAP which had been introduced by members of the House. For example, Committee member Omar Burleson had introduced a bill that would turn welfare completely over to the states with the Federal Government returning to each state the equivalent amount of federal taxes it would take to pay for FAP or the current public assistance programs. Members of the Black Caucus in the House were sponsoring the National Welfare Rights Organization's proposal, which would replace existing social welfare programs with a federal guaranteed annual income of $6,500 for a family of four. Committee member William Green had a bill supported by the National Council of Churches, the League of Women Voters, and several other public interest groups that would federalize public assistance and provide a minimum federal payment of $3,600 for a family of four.

In other words, the attention of most of the attentive and influential members and the focus of Committee deliberations never shifted from the basic features of the original Nixon program for poor families (FAP) and a plan to federalize cash assistance for aged, blind, and disabled adults proposed during the 1971 Committee deliberations by Mills.

Policy Analysis and Program Design—
Consensus Issues

The process that produced H.R.1 was, essentially, a circumscribed search for a technically defensible response or solution to the "welfare crisis," synchronized with the engineering of a consensus within the Committee and a supporting majority on the House floor. Under the direction of Mills, this combined process of policy analysis, program design, and consensus building can be very demanding. Members acknowledge that the Committee workload, the complexity of legislation they deal with, and the procedures used and pace set by Mills enhance his influence in Committee decisions. A Democratic member told an interviewer,

> Mills's ability to put together a consensus on the Committee is often a product of the grinding pace he sets. . . . The executive sessions just go on and on. People get tired, worn out, willing to let

> Mills have his way. . . . There is so much stuff to be covered that some members are smothered by it. There is no question that this gives Mills and Byrnes an advantage.[12]

The processing of H.R.1 was more exhaustive, time consuming, difficult and demanding than usual. In public and private, Mills said it was "the most thoroughgoing, extensive, and intensive review and analysis which has ever been made" of public assistance. When the Committee finally reported the welfare bill in 1971, Mills told the members he "did not want to see welfare again for at least five years."

With respect to his own policy preferences and the way in which he arrives at specific decisions, Mills has said,

> Sometimes I know what I want to do ahead of time and sometimes I don't decide until during the hearings or even the executive sessions where we consider legislation line by line. I don't take a position in advance. because it freezes me. I may discover the position is not right. I don't like to come up the hill and down so quick. If I say something confidentially in the committee about my position on a bill, I always read about it the next day in the papers. The other members can't keep anything confidential. So I've become very cagey about discussing things ahead of time.[13]

Early in 1971 he made clear his preference for a federal takeover of existing public assistance programs for the aged, blind and disabled. "These programs," he told U.S. News and World Report, "are more or less unabused and limited in scope." And, "ultimately" he wanted "to take the elderly and the blind and the disabled out of what is called poverty."[14] In Committee he proposed that OAA, AB, and APTD be replaced with a completely federal negative tax program that would assure single aged, blind, or disabled recipients $1,560 a year and couples $2,340. With the attention of the members focused on proposed changes in programs for AFDC and "working poor" families, the Chairman's poverty level guaranteed income program for adults (later titled the Supplemental Security Income program—SSI) was accepted with little debate or disagreement.

Mills was less sure about what exactly should or could be done about the AFDC program and "working poor" families. What was certain was that in designing a new program for families Committee members would disagree. Consensus building would be difficult, and, in the end, they would have to settle for a partial consensus—a program containing consensus solutions on some elements and the preferences of the majority on the most controversial issues. In public statements Mills indicated that eventual federalization of all public assistance programs, including AFDC, was inevitable and probably desirable; but he said he was not in favor of taking over AFDC "until the deplorable mess can be corrected."

> AFDC is sadly and badly administered. . . . If AFDC can be improved so it does not become a haven for people for life, with the costs doubling every three years, then that would be another thing.[15]

Despite reservations about making the "working poor" eligible for benefits, he supported Nixon's Family Assistance Plan because he believed that with some modifications it would provide a more efficient and manageable program than AFDC.

Accepting the basic features of FAP, Mills faced the task of designing a negative tax program for families with children that he judged to be administratively superior to AFDC and that was acceptable to 90 percent of the Committee members and a majority of the House. He began by identifying and cataloguing his and all other "legitimate" objections to FAP and presenting them to the Committee as a list of problems they had to solve. His agenda did *not* include a philosophical discussion of welfare, the economic and social consequences of a guaranteed annual income, or the appropriate role of the federal and state governments in cash assistance for the poor, as had taken place within the Nixon Administration during the development of FAP and in the Senate in 1970.

Comments and debate on these abstract and unresolvable issues were interjected, but Mills kept the Committee deliberations and the attention of most members focused on the specific objections presented as separate, essentially technical problems. The Committee discussed such questions as: how can we increase benefits in those states where they are "deplorably inadequate," and "stop the bleeding-heart social workers" in other states "from giving a welfare check to anyone who asks?" How many persons will be eligible and what are the estimated state and federal costs of FAP at different federal payment levels? What kind of a work requirement can be implemented and effectively enforced? How can we "tighten up" the administration of FAP, prevent welfare cheating, and get some "control over welfare costs?"

During February and March, according to Mills, the Committee "examined and proposed answers to every significant question that had been raised in the two-year period the President's welfare reform proposals had been under discussion."[16] When conflicts arose, the procedure was to search for the compromise which was acceptable to the Administration and Byrnes, had the support of the most Committee members, and, in Mills's judgment, was technically and politically sound. Discussion of problems and possible solutions was not limited to the scheduled Committee meetings. The Chairman met privately with Administration officials, Committee and non-Committee members of the House, and with recognized experts such as former Secretary of HEW Wilbur Cohen.

Mills also released a series of "trial balloons" to test reaction to possible changes, put pressure on the Administration or Committee members to go along with tentative changes, and prepare House members, the press, and the public for the Committee product. For example, in February he told reporters he had informed the Administration that FAP had to be "rewritten extensively—and rapidly—before the Committee would consider it," especially in regard to "tightening up" administrative procedures, eligibility requirements, and work incentives.[17] He also indicated he was considering the possibility of "federalizing welfare costs" as a "substitute" for Nixon's revenue sharing proposal. Governor McCall of Oregon, Governor Rockefeller of New York, and the President let him know they wanted no substitute.[18]

Mills hoped the Committee would be finished with welfare by March. On March 16, the Committee was given a document prepared by HEW entitled: "Summary of Changes That Have Been Proposed in the Family Assistance Plan." The proposed changes included requiring mothers to take work or training unless they had children under three instead of six, changing the name of FAP to "Opportunities for Families" (noting that HEW opposed both of these changes), increasing the penalty for failure to register for or participate in work or training from $300 to $500, raising the minimum payment for a family of four from $1,600 to $2,200, and making FAP recipients ineligible for food stamps.

On March 24, a week later, reporters were told the Committee had "reached tentative agreement on a comprehensive revision of the welfare system."[19] Reflecting efforts to placate the major concerns of both liberal and conservative Committee members, by this time the minimum benefit for a family of four had been increased from $2,200 to $2,400 and the penalty for refusing to accept work or training from $500 to $800. Also, consistent with the conservative position, there was no requirement or federal financial support for state supplementation, and, for administrative purposes, FAP had been divided into two programs: OFF for families with an employable member and FAP for other eligible families.

Over the Easter recess, April 7 to 19, working from notes given to them by the Chairman, the Committee staff prepared a "draft" of H.R.1 containing a modified version of Nixon's original Family Assistance Plan and a new poverty level guaranteed income for aged, blind, and disabled adults. After Easter the Committee met in executive meetings for another six weeks but made few modifications in this draft bill, which served as the agenda for the final markup sessions.

Policy Analysis and Program Design— Conflict Issues

By April, Mills, like Nixon at the Camp David meeting of the Cabinet August 8, 1969, was weary of welfare and impatient with intransigence. Welfare reform had been before the Committee for two years, they were behind schedule this year and under pressure to begin work on revenue sharing, about which Mills had some strong reservations. He believed that to the extent possible the draft bill reflected the views of Committee members and interested, "responsible" groups. His own position was that the cash assistance programs in the draft were preferable to the present system and probably represented the best politically and economically feasible response to the present welfare situation.

However, the same day it was announced that the Committee had "reached tentative agreement," several conservative and liberal Committee members publicly voiced strong dissatisfaction with the tentative decisions and threatened opposition on the House floor if certain changes were not made. Liberals Hugh Carey of New York and James Corman of California told reporters there would be a tough fight on the floor by large urban states with high welfare costs because under the current version of the bill only the southern states would experience any financial relief. Corman added:

> The bill's ideology is clearly shown in its provision of $2,400 in federal aid to an elderly couple, but only the same amount to an ADC mother with three children. The only way you can justify that is to say that if you want a welfare mother to work, you've got to keep her children and her hungry. If you can buy that, it sure makes all the rest of this easy. . . . [T]he worst single decision we arrived at was setting the federal payment at well below the poverty line and neither mandating or encouraging the states to go above that level. If a poor family is to receive a penny more than the floor, then the state legislature must make an affirmative decision to pay all of it. I'm afraid that many state legislatures won't pay it.[20]

Conservative Joel Broyhill of Virginia still did not think the work requirements were strong enough. He told the press:

> I will insist that no one receive any assistance through the welfare program who is physically able to work but refuses to do so. I don't want any provision limiting the requirement to "suitable" employment. Any type of work should be considered suitable or reasonable to a person seeking public assistance.[21]

Three issues kept the Committee meeting on welfare right up until June 21 when the House began voting on the bill. Most troublesome, because of the persistence of the liberals and the opposition of Byrnes, was the issue of state supplementation of federal benefits. Liberals, especially Corman, Carey, and Burke, wanted a provision that would mandate state supplementation up to current payment levels in order to protect present recipients against a loss of benefits. And they wanted the Federal Government to pay part of the cost of this supplement and thereby increase the financial savings that states like California, New York, and Massachusetts with high welfare payment levels and expenditures would realize under H.R.1. The original Nixon proposal did mandate state supplementation and provided for a federal contribution of at least 10 percent under the "50-90 rule."

Veneman indicated Administration support for a similar provision early in the 1971 Committee deliberations. However, because of the increase in payments to families, the new federal program for adults, and the addition of the public service jobs, H.R.1 at this point was already several billion dollars more expensive than the original Nixon proposal, and Veneman communicated the opposition of certain Administration officials to any further cost increases.

Byrnes opposed such a provision for budgetary reasons but, most important, for reasons of administrative efficiency and control. He was "tired of governors and mayors complaining to him about the Federal Government's forcing them to spend money on federal programs," and he did not want another federal-state welfare program with dual administrative structures, responsibilities, and matching funds. He wanted the federal program to be completely federal. The states, then, could do what they wanted without any pressure or interference from the Federal Government, so long as they did nothing to undermine the principles and objectives of the federal program.

Most of the Republicans and conservative Democrats went along with Byrnes. Mills, however, thought the Federal Government should pay any cost of state supplementation up to current benefits that was in excess of a state's 1971 welfare expenditures. On May 5, responding to a somewhat heated debate between Carey, Landrum, and Veneman on this issue, he said:

> It is pretty easy for me to be for something when my state is going to be relieved 100 percent of any responsibility under the bill. And that is true of some other members of this Committee. But I am not satisfied to have the bill pass if it doesn't provide a degree of protection for other states. . . . You are not taking over the program until you take over the cost of growth. That is the whole point. . . . I think the state will continue to maintain the payments. . . . I don't think the bill will pass without the Governors of the big states supporting it.

There were three Committee votes on the supplementation issue.

On April 22 Carey sponsored a resolution which provided for the Federal Government to pay 50 percent of the cost for state supplementation of the federal benefits in all programs. It was defeated 15 to 10 with Democrats Burke, Rostenkowski, Vanik, Fulton, Corman, Green, Carey, and Gibbons, and Republicans Collier and Conable voting in support of the resolution. Burke introduced a resolution on May 5 under which the Federal Government would pay 25 percent of the costs of supplementing the federal benefits up to $3,700 (the poverty level) for the first two years, then 15 percent for the next two, 10 percent for the next two, then nothing. It was defeated 17 to 8 with Democrats Burke, Vanik, Fulton, Corman, Green, Carey, Rostenkowski, and, according to the Committee record, Ullman voting in favor of the motion.

The same day Carey moved that the states supplement the federal benefits up to the present benefit levels, including the value of food stamps, and the Federal Government pay any costs for supplementation that exceeded 75 percent of a state's public assistance expenditures for fiscal year 1971. The motion was defeated 15 to 10. Committee liberals were supported once again by Democrats Rostenkowski and Fulton and Republican Barber Conable of New York. On this motion, however, Collier voted against them and Republican Pettis of California voted with them. There were no more recorded votes on the issue. The liberals had to settle for a provision under which the Federal Government would pay only the supplementation costs in excess of a state's 1971 welfare expenditures, and an amendment introduced by Mills on the House floor, which provided that states *would* supplement unless the state legislatures passed legislation to the contrary. A liberal Committee member explained how they got this amendment:

> I tried to get the amendment accepted in the Committee but Byrnes didn't want to force the states to do anything. . . . The day before we were to vote on the rule I talked it over with Burton (Phil Burton, D-Calif.) and then I went to Byrnes and Mills and told them that the amendment would get them at least seven votes from the California delegation on the Title IV vote. They were worried about the vote—they got worried when the modified rule came out and that is why they were willing to listen. Mills told me to sound out the Committee members so I checked with about ten of them—I also contacted Veneman and told him it could mean seven votes from California and probably some more in other states. A Committee meeting was called and Mills and Byrnes presented the amendment to the members and said they supported it. Half the members didn't understand it and the other half were for it.

The second issue that had to be resolved by Committee vote involved the conflict between those who thought the work requirements in the bill were oppressive and those who did not think they were stringent enough. On April 22, Burke sponsored a motion that the draft of the bill be changed to read that mothers with children under the age of six (instead of three) would not be required to register for work. His motion was defeated 18 to 7 with Democrats Burke, Rostenkowski, Vanik, Fulton, Corman, Green, and Carey voting in favor of the change.

The same day Waggonner moved to include a provision requiring all recipient mothers with children, including those with children under 3, to register for work, and requiring any person excused from the requirement of training or work on the basis of physical illness or disability to have a certificate to this effect from a physician. This was defeated 17 to 6 with Democrats Griffiths, Burleson and Waggonner, and Republicans Collier, Broyhill, and Pettis voting in favor of the motion, Ullman voting present, and all other Committee members voting no. There were no more recorded votes on the issue.

Conservatives were successful in deleting the word "suitable" from the work requirement, which read "Every person who registered (for work) . . . would be required to participate in manpower services or training and to accept *suitable* employment," and more narrowly specifying the conditions under which someone could refuse to accept employment.

The third issue was a proposal by Mills to include in H.R.1 a 7 percent increase in Social Security benefits. This increase was opposed by the Administration, Byrnes and the other Republican members, and the southern Democrats.[22] The bill in draft form contained a provision under which "Social Security benefits would be automatically increased according to the rise in the cost of living," but no immediate increase was authorized.

The 7 percent increase was a partisan move for which the Democrats would claim full credit, and an attempt to "sweeten" H.R.1, or to make it easier for House members to support the bill or more difficult for them to go on record having opposed it. Mills's motion was defeated on April 22 by a vote of 14 to 11. The opposing majority was a conservative coalition consisting of the Committee's ten Republicans plus southern Democrats Watts, Landrum, Burleson, and Waggonner. Republicans were supporting the Administration and party leaders on this vote and the conservative Democrats had no desire to "sweeten" a bill about which they had serious practical and philosophical reservations.

On May 5 Mills proposed a 5 percent increase in Social Security benefits. His motion was defeated this time 13 to 12, with Watts switching his vote and supporting the Chairman. Several Democrats complained after the meeting that day that Waggonner, who was absent and voted against the increase by proxy, was not showing sufficient "appreciation for his elevation to the Ways and Means Committee this year."[23] Five days later, on May 17, Mills again put forward his motion for a 5 percent Social Security increase and this time it was approved 13 to 12 with Waggonner voting "yea." In explaining this switch, Waggonner said there had been "some misunderstanding" when his proxy was cast against the increase the week before.

There were two more votes taken on May 17. As a final symbolic gesture, Waggonner moved that the new FAP and OFF programs for families be separated from the rest of H.R.1 so the House could cast a separate vote on the Committee's guaranteed income for families with children. His motion was defeated 19 to 6 with Democrats Watts, Ullman, Burleson, and Waggonner and Republicans Broyhill and Duncan casting the supporting votes. Finally, the Committee voted 22 to 3 to approve H.R.1 and report it to the full House. Democrats Ullman, Burleson and Waggonner voted against a favorable report.

H.R.1: DECISION CONDITIONS

The Committee's examination of welfare in 1971, according to Mills, was more extensive and intensive than any previous consideration of the subject since the enactment of the Social Security legislation in 1935. This extraordinary examination of welfare programs yielded Committee and House approval of unpredictable, fundamental, and extensive change. The Committee members interviewed agreed that the new programs for families and adults in H.R.1 represented a major transformation in U.S. welfare policy and they identified three conditions as reasons why radical change was considered and approved: the failure of the present programs; the existence of an innovative course of action sponsored by the President; and the presence and support of congressional leaders capable of "transforming the innovative into the passable."[24]

The "Welfare Crisis": Everybody Agreed Something Had to Be Done!

Mills said it was "because the present system wasn't pleasing anybody—the recipients or those who pay for the programs" that the Committee attempted such an extensive examination of welfare and the Committee and House approved the changes in H.R.1. He added,

> I'm convinced that if these changes aren't enacted and the present system is allowed to continue we are going to see public moves to cut back on the programs and there might be a Congress willing to reduce the programs drastically.

John Byrnes said the Committee "had" to look into welfare because,

> Nobody was pleased with the present system—everyone was complaining. The taxpayers felt they were supporting too many people on welfare that didn't need to be there, and were blaming welfare

for increases in taxes. The welfare people, those on welfare, felt as though it wasn't providing them with what they needed. Then the fiscal problems of the states made it so governors and other state and local politicians were dissatisfied with the system. With everyone complaining about the system we felt we had to take a look—where there is smoke there is usually fire. I guess the Government doesn't usually look into our programs until they become so bad that everyone is complaining. When we looked at the present programs we found one hell-of-a mess.

The members, both liberal and conservative, referred to the "welfare mess" or "welfare crisis" in explaining H.R.1. One said that when Corman, a liberal, and Landrum, a conservative, can agree on changes in welfare, "you know there's a real crisis." However, while liberal and conservative members agreed there was a "crisis" in welfare, or that the present programs had failed, especially AFDC, they disagreed on the nature of the crisis or reasons for failure. Liberals emphasized the disparity in payment levels among states and between adult and family recipients, the incentives for families to break up under AFDC, and the "deplorably inadequate" payments and rigid eligibility requirements in states like Mississippi as evidence of policy failure.

Conservatives, on the other hand, said the crisis was a result of "uncontrollable" and "skyrocketing" costs and blamed states like New York where they said it was too easy to get on welfare, the benefits were too high, and the work requirement and related programs under WIN were not being enforced. In other words, there was convergence on the issue of too much leeway for states under the present system but divergence as to which states were misusing their discretion and creating the problems.

There was consensus among those interviewed that the extraordinary growth in AFDC costs and caseloads, the widespread public dissatisfaction with AFDC, and the pressure from state and local officials for financial relief were the compelling "pressures for change." A Committee staff member said,

> . . . the real pressure for change was the tremendous increase in welfare recipients and costs. If the present program hadn't grown so rapidly I don't think these changes would have been suggested or received the support that they did. Congressmen were getting letters from constituents complaining about the increasing welfare rolls and costs and complaining about someone they knew who was getting welfare instead of working. I think congressmen pay some attention to their mail and this got them interested. This is what happened in 1967 and led to the '67 amendments.

A Committee Democrat said,

> Welfare reform is an issue mainly because of public opposition
> to existing programs, much of which is based on myth and which
> has been generated by local and state elections in which candidates
> blame increasing property taxes on the growth in the welfare rolls.
> This has produced a demand for change on the part of the pub-
> lic—although much of their information about the number of
> "welfare cheaters," etc., on the welfare rolls is incorrect.

Several members indicated they were under considerable pressure from governors and mayors to support the Nixon proposal because of the financial savings
it would provide states and cities. Most of those interviewed were convinced
that lobbying efforts by state and local officials had an influence on the Committee and were especially important in obtaining House approval of H.R.1.
A Republican member explained,

> I was under a great deal of pressure from my state to push for
> state supplementation like we had last year, and I voted for sup-
> plementation, but I wasn't too disappointed when it wasn't
> mandated. I think the bill will help to relieve some of the financial
> pressure on the big industrial states that have been paying high
> benefits. . . . The Governor . . . is always a strong force when he
> is concerned about an issue. He was primarily concerned about
> fiscal relief, as he should be. When he could see that the bill was
> not going to provide a great deal of financial relief for the state,
> he was concerned about two things: that there be a federal floor,
> and that the states would be able to define the work requirements
> and other eligibility standards in regard to their supplementa-
> tion of the federal money—so long as these were not inconsistent
> with federal law.

In summing up the reasons for Committee action, Committee
member Barber Conable said that, given the intense dissatisfaction among
the recipients, the general public, and public officials, Committee members
including Mills and Byrnes

> were concerned about the drastic consequences that could result
> from the Committee's *not* taking the responsibility to do something
> in this area. The role of the Ways and Means Committee is to be
> the pressure cooker in areas like welfare, tax, and trade. We have
> to take the responsibility of doing something about problems in
> these very controversial and critical areas.

**An Accessible Innovative Alternative
Supported by the President**
Many Ways and Means members were concerned about welfare

and felt it should be on the Committee's agenda before President Nixon unveiled the Family Assistance Plan in August 1969. In part, Nixon was responding to the concerns and requests of some congressmen and senators when he
decided to include welfare reform in his domestic agenda. However, Congress
was not demanding, recommending, or expecting radical reform or a guaranteed income.

Interviews by Cavala and Wildavsky with 50 legislators in March
1969 indicated that, five months before Nixon announced FAP, the various
schemes for replacing public assistance with a guaranteed income had come
to the attention of very few congressmen or senators. And they concluded
that the reaction of all but a few "safe-seat liberals" to such a proposal would
be strong and immediate opposition on grounds of public opposition, cost,
political feasibility, and the conviction that a national guaranteed income was
inconsistent with "widely held and deeply felt American values such as achieve-
ment, work, and equality of opportunity."[25] In other words, given the
concern of some House and Committee members, and the pressure from state
officials and constituents, the Ways and Means Committee might have considered and even approved modifications in public assistance without a Presidential initiative. But a guaranteed income would *not* have been on the
Committee's agenda.

President Nixon's influence in Ways and Means and House approval
of H.R.1, his ability to "transform an unfeasible idea into one that had to
be taken seriously,"[26] reflected the general policy making roles of the
President and Congress that have become highly formalized in recent years.
That is, Congress and the public expect the President to set the national agenda,
or to identify the problems and initiate the policies that will receive formal
consideration by Congress. In reference to the Ways and Means Committee,
Manley says the President

> sets the agenda for Congress (sometimes with a nudge from senior
> legislators who assure him they can get the bill through); he de-
> termines, with important exceptions (e.g., tax reform in 1969),
> what major policy proposals Congress will look at, and when.[27]

And, in regard to social welfare policy in particular, Steiner concludes:

> White House interest and activity must be considered the sine qua
> non for change in relief policy. Not all relief policy change in
> which a president is interested will be accomplished, but none will
> be accomplished without presidential interest. Without that ex-
> pressed interest, the status quo continues; with it, the seemingly
> most hopeless of public relief causes has been transformed into
> a live issue.[28]

In general, then, while presidential interest in welfare policy might be relatively uncommon, it is even more unusual for Congress to take the initiative in this area.

The Committee members acknowledged that a guaranteed income would not have been seriously considered, let alone approved by the Committee and House, if it had not been sponsored by the President. And they agreed with Administration officials that, given the composition of the Committee and House (i.e., the existence of a conservative majority in both), sponsorship by a *Republican* President was essential in obtaining Committee and House approval of H.R.1. A Committee staff member said:

> It was possible to get approval for the changes in H.R.1 because a Republican Administration introduced them. If a Democrat had suggested them none of the Republicans would have listened or supported them and a lot of Democrats wouldn't have—especially the conservatives. Like one of the Committee members said on the House floor, I think it was Burleson, "If the Democrats had proposed this bill there would be a hole in the roof of this building."

This staff member and the Committee members who made the same observation were acknowledging the radical and "liberal" nature of the changes in H.R.1 and "a basic fact of congressional life" since the late 1930s: on policy changes like this it was possible and highly probable that a conservative coalition of Republicans and southern Democrats would form and defeat them either in Committee or on the floor.[29] The sponsorship of such a program by a conservative *Republican* President, however, drastically altered the context within which congressmen, especially Republican congressmen, perceived and responded to the issue of a guaranteed income. This was crucial in preventing the conservative coalition from defeating the proposal both in Committee and on the House floor.

At the insistence of conservatives in the White House and the Ways and Means Committee, the original Nixon proposal and H.R.1 contained elements attractive to conservative congressmen. And it was natural and credible for Nixon, his officials, Mills, and Byrnes to emphasize conservative features like the strict work requirements and to use conservative rhetoric and symbols in discussing and defending the proposal. It was also part of the strategy; a matter of conscious, careful design.

The Administration expected liberal Democrats to support the proposal even though many of them would think it "did not go far enough, the benefits were not high enough, and there was not enough savings for the big states." To get the bill approved they knew they had to get most of the Republicans to support it as well and thereby undermine the conservative coalition. They believed that with a Republican President sponsoring the bill, if they could get the support of Byrnes and Mills, and if they emphasized conservative concerns, conservative rhetoric, and the conservative features in formal and informal discussion of the legislation, they could get sufficient Republican support in the House and Senate.

They were sensitized early to the danger of even mentioning "a guaranteed income" in connection with FAP, even if the intention was to deny that FAP was such a program. At a briefing of the "Sam Devine group of conservative Republicans" before FAP had been announced publicly, the first Administration spokesman started off by saying, "This isn't a guaranteed income by virtue of the work requirements." At that point, one of the congressmen present jumped up and stormed out of the room saying he would not "even listen to a discussion about a guaranteed income." For those who asked, the standard response of the Administration was,

> No, FAP is not a guaranteed income plan. Because to be eligible for payments, applicants able to work will be required to register with their local employment offices for work or training. Anyone required to register, who refuses to do so or refuses training or a legitimate job offer, will lose his portion of the family's benefits.[30]

Another HEW official who was involved in Administration lobbying for FAP and H.R.1 said:

> The bill does provide for a greater role for the Federal Government in welfare, and it is a dressed up negative income tax form of a guaranteed income. Both of these are inconsistent with conservative philosophy, so we had to play up the work requirements. Many congressmen really believe the rhetoric on work requirements and incentives—and all of it isn't just rhetoric—others are more sophisticated and have been primarily concerned about what to tell their constituents. For them we worked up some information pointing out the work requirements and work incentives in H.R.1. They are also concerned about adding people to the welfare rolls and we have charts and information pointing out that with work requirements this bill will eventually lead to a decrease in welfare recipients.

The first and most crucial task the Administration faced was that of shifting the attention and preferences of Mills and Byrnes to radical welfare change. In 1968 Congressman William Ryan, a Democrat from New York, introduced legislation which proposed a negative tax program very similar to the Family Assistance Plan. Designed and drafted by James Lyday, who participated in the development of FAP, it provided a minimum benefit level of $2,000 for a family of four, a 50 percent tax rate on earnings, and a cutoff point of $4,000. However, it generated little interest, few congressmen knew anything about it, and it was never seriously considered by Mills, Byrnes, or the Committee as a substitute for AFDC. It took the sponsorship of the President (possibly a Republican President) as well as the incentive created by the failure of existing programs to direct the attention of Mills and Byrnes to the possibility of re-placing public assistance with a federal guaranteed income.

In addition, it took the leverage of the President and informational resources of the executive departments to persuade them to support such a proposal; or to motivate and enable them to think through, reverse, or replace some of the perceptions, assumptions, and problems they associated with welfare and a guaranteed income. Byrnes explained that, "One of the major problems we faced in trying to reform the welfare system—if not the most important problem—was a lack of understanding, both of the problem, or what was causing the increase in recipients and costs, and how to deal with the problem." He said he spent many hours with Administration officials, in his office, at the White House and HEW because

> it took me a long time to catch the point of *why* it was necessary
> to include the working poor. And I think it took the Chairman a
> while as well to see the necessity of including them in a welfare
> program. And, until you get this point, you can't understand H.R.1
> or the Administration proposal! You have to understand that
> under the present system there are some who are working but would
> be better off if they went on welfare, and that our rolls are increas-
> ing—at least in part—because these people are going on welfare.
> The father in some cases is leaving home so the family is eligible
> for welfare. Then, if you are going to include the working poor
> and try to provide an incentive for them to work, you have to set
> some kind of a minimum level of income below which a person
> is eligible for benefits—it is only by setting a minimum level (what
> some call a guaranteed income) that you can have a system that
> does include the working poor. It took a while for me to get
> this. . . . I think the system should help those who are trying to
> help themselves—and it should help those who are trying to pro-
> vide for their own welfare. Anyway, what many of the critics
> can't see is that we have a guaranteed payment level now—in every
> state. It varies from one state to another, but that's exactly what
> we have.

The long term projections of federal and state welfare costs and recipients provided by the Administration were important in both Mills and Byrnes's decision to support the new programs in H.R.1. By predicting impor-tant consequences, these projections reduced some of the risks involved in drastically changing existing policy. However, because the executive branch had a monopoly on this type of information, or because Congress did not have the computers, data, or computer experts necessary to produce these projections, effective congressional initiation of the same changes, without the assistance of the Administration or HEW, was virtually impossible.

It took the information gathering and analyzing resources of the executive branch and, given the presence of a bipartisan conservative majority, the sponsorship of a Republican President like Nixon, according to Ways and Means members, to shift the attention and support of congressional leaders and members to a proposal for radical welfare reform. In other words, there was a somewhat paradoxical situation in which a guaranteed income was most likely to be enacted when it was least likely to be initiated—when a conservative Republican occupied the White House.

Effective Congressional Leaders

Committee members agreed that the support of President Nixon was a necessary condition for Committee and House approval of H.R.1. But, it was not a sufficient condition, even when combined with the "crisis" in welfare. Those interviewed agreed and were adamant on two points: first, of the Committee members, Mills and Byrnes were the most influential in the design of H.R.1; and second, without their support the bill would not have been approved by the Committee or the House. Typical comments included: "This was a tough one; you've got to give the Chairman and Byrnes most of the credit for it." "It's Mills's bill—no matter what the Administration says." "Of course, Mills and Byrnes had the most influence in writing the bill—they were the most important." "Mills is a master craftsman, a master politician. It was his patience, skill and knowledge that got the welfare bill through—that got all of us to agree."

In other words, an explanation of why radical welfare reform was passed by the House would have to explain why Mills and Byrnes supported the proposal and then how or why they were able to get 22 Committee members and a majority of the House members to approve it.

Mills and Byrnes and a Guaranteed Annual Income

The widespread dissatisfaction with the present welfare system provided an incentive for Mills and Byrnes to design and implement reforms, possibly even drastic changes in the current law. For the past fifteen to twenty years—which included the attempts in 1962 and 1967 to improve public assistance—they had been deeply involved and exercised significant influence in the development of the welfare system. Few individuals felt a greater responsibility for the operations, or received more complaints about the problems, of public assistance. The existence and accessibility of an innovative course of action in the form of Nixon's Family Assistance Plan provided the opportunity to innovate, or made radical change possible.

However, in spite of the incentive and opportunity to innovate, interviews and other accounts indicate that, although they were willing to listen to the Administration, neither Mills nor Byrnes were initially inclined to support the President's proposal for replacing AFDC with a federal guaranteed income for families with children. Existing conditions made them receptive to the discussion and possibility of reform, but it took several months of discussion, policy review, and analysis before they arrived at the position of supporting radical change. Then it took another four to six months in 1970 and again in 1971 to move 20 more Committee members and a majority of the House to the same position.

Ways and Means and House approval of Nixon's proposal, in other words, was not inevitable, despite existing conditions highly conducive to drastic policy change. Under the same set of conditions, a different Committee chairman and ranking minority member, on the basis of their perception and analysis of problems and possible solutions, could have responded quite differently. In fact, Chairman Russell Long and ranking Republican John Williams of the Senate Finance Committee did: they rejected the President's proposal.

Mills stated many times that the fundamental problem with the welfare system was that "AFDC is sadly and badly administered."[31] In an interview he said, "Any time you have a government program that each year doubles in cost you know there is something wrong—it isn't being administered properly." More specifically, it bothered him that, although the Federal Government paid over 50 percent of the public assistance costs, under the present automated, open-ended cost sharing system the *Federal* Government was limited in what it could do to stop or slow down welfare costs or predict and control *federal* welfare expenditures. And the decentralized administrative structure made it possible for the states to ignore federal regulations like the registration for work or training requirement enacted in the 1967 Welfare Amendments.

In sum, he felt responsible for a controversial and highly discredited program over which he had limited control. Before the House Rules Committee in 1970, he said that under the present federal-state system the Federal Government was "like the fellow who has the bear by the tail going downhill."[32] He appeared convinced that the "major key" to the development of a better welfare system was a more "effective, efficient administrative mechanism."[33] The most obvious model of a more effectively and efficiently administered welfare program was the centralized and completely federal Social Security System. In his syndicated column of March 9, 1971, Joseph Kraft wrote:

> Mills wants to put welfare under responsible control. It offends his soul that the welfare system is not as efficient or honest as

Social Security, and that payments are constantly outrunning expectations in ways that compromise orderly government finance. He favors tighter standards to limit welfare fraud and the size of the welfare bureaucracy, and to raise the amount of work and job training required for benefits.[34]

The welfare situation, or "crisis," in 1970 and 1971 confirmed what Mills had suspected for several years: that welfare could not be administered effectively or efficiently under the present federal-state system. Furthermore, it was too susceptible to fluctuating political pressures at the state and local levels and, anyway, it was too expensive for the states to handle alone. So, despite sympathy for the conservative fear about the growing centralization of government or the drift of power and programs to Washington, he concluded that if they were going to establish some control over welfare costs and caseloads in states like New York, New Jersey, and California, decrease welfare cheating, and effectively enforce the work requirement enacted in 1967, they were going to have to reduce administrative discretion and centralize or federalize welfare. He explained in an interview

We have been moving toward the changes in H.R.1 since 1962. Then we left it up to the states to administer with the faith that they could do the job best—all the Federal Government did was to pay whatever cost the state legislated. In 1967 we mandated that the states institute some work programs, but didn't define how they were to do it, so we had California with a large program and New York with hardly any at all. So this time we just took it over. Under this bill the Federal Government will administer welfare. . . . As I said, we have been moving in this direction for a long time. I think the Federal Government can administer the program better. Now, this doesn't mean I don't think that there are many areas in which the local people can do the best job of running programs—in many cases they can because they are closer to the problem. But in this area it is too much of a political issue at the local level. The information we have suggests that the Federal Government can do a better job; it is easier for us to get information from the states and other Federal agencies than it is for the states to get information from federal agencies; we have the information, computers and facilities to do a better job of policing the program. . . . In the past we have not had one program but 54 different ones and the Federal Government just paid the bills. Now we will have one program under one administrator who is responsible for it.

Mills, in other words, was predisposed to go along with the federalization of AFDC as proposed in the original Nixon plan. In H.R.1, he insisted that they federalize all public assistance programs (Old Age Assistance, Aid to the Blind, Aid to the Permanently and Totally Disabled, and Aid to Families with Dependent Children), or at least take a major step in that direction.

He appeared to be less concerned about making the "working poor" eligible for welfare than he was about "tightening up," "rationalizing," or "getting some control over" the administration of welfare. However, at the insistence of the Administration and Committee liberals he accepted this major innovation in U.S. welfare policy on condition that the "cutoff point," the income level at which "working poor" families are no longer eligible for benefits, remain at about $4,000. There were two reasons he insisted on this limitation. First, the costs of the program and number of eligible recipients increased dramatically and disproportionately as the cutoff point was extended in $100 increments above $4,000 simply because there were more families in the U.S. making between $4,000 and $5,000 than there were living on less than $4,000. Second, and equally important, Administration estimates indicated that with a cutoff point of $3,920, as in the original Nixon plan, from 15 to 35 percent of the populations of most southern states would be eligible for benefits because of the low wages in that part of the country. If the cutoff point went much above $4,000, upwards of 50 percent of the families in states like Mississippi could be eligible for welfare payments.

Mills was concerned about the economic problems this might produce because, as he said, "it would create tremendous disincentives to work in some states, like mine for example, where the wages are low." Furthermore, it was going to be difficult enough for him to get many of his southern colleagues in Congress to support a federal guaranteed income, let alone one which put 50 percent of their state on welfare!

This limitation created problems in the design of H.R.1 because when they "cashed out" food stamps and increased the minimum payment from $1,600 to $2,400, with a $720 earnings disregard and 50 percent tax rate on additional earnings, the cutoff point was automatically extended to $5,520.[35] The liberals insisted that the minimum payment remain at least as high as $2,400 unless the Committee mandated a federally supported state supplementation program, which Byrnes refused to support. The dilemma was finally resolved by keeping the minimum benefit level at $2,400 but increasing the tax rate on earnings from 50 to 67 percent. This lowered the cutoff point to $4,320. Then, by providing that no payments of less than $10 per month would be made, they lowered it to $4,140. An Administration official said that, "Mills was jubilant when he discovered that with a provision eliminating payments of less than $10 a month he could drop the cutoff point $180."

John Byrnes felt that as the ranking Republican on Ways and Means he should support Republican Administration initiatives unless he "had deep reservations." Initially, he had "serious reservations" about FAP, especially in regard to including the "working poor." However, Byrnes had also reached the conclusion they had to increase federal control over AFDC, and that this would require centralizing administrative operations and procedures along the lines suggested in the Nixon plan. In 1970 he defended the President's bill before the House Rules Committee on grounds that there,

> would be much less concern with the costs under this new program, because here we put some restraints, we put some ceilings, on how far the Federal Government will go. We don't give them the blank check that the present system does; we don't say that whatever the state does, we will match it between 50 and 80 percent, depending upon the area that is involved and the income that is involved.
>
> The present system is completely open-ended. The Congress and the Federal Government are at the mercy of the states. You have, for instance, a couple of states—New Jersey is one—that are above the poverty level. Now there is no cutoff in present law, so the number of people that are involved, the families that are involved, and the costs that are involved, are unlimited. The new system, however, would put limitations on these items.[36]

In response to the question, "Why he, a conservative, was willing to support federalizing welfare," he said,

> Hell, we can't trust the states, We can't depend upon them to carry out the philosophy of our program—to enforce the work and training requirements. Look at what has happened to the WIN program, how few states have participated in the program since 1967 and attempted to implement the general philosophy of the program.

Byrnes firmly believed most of the people on AFDC "want to get off, want to be able to work, want to have some independence as far as their economic means are concerned," and that what they need most is a welfare program that encourages and assists them to become "self-sustaining." To him this was the philosophy and objective of the present AFDC program. He was concerned because, as he saw it, many of the states, especially those with the largest AFDC populations, were not following this philosophy as demonstrated by their unwillingness to enforce work and training programs enacted in the 1967 Welfare Amendments. And, under the present federal-state administrative structure, there was little that he or the Federal Government could do to force them to comply with his understanding of existing federal regulations. He supported H.R.1 because he believed it was "work and family oriented," and, although he was aware that you "can't legislate proper administration," he was convinced that it would establish a more efficient and effective administrative structure and provide the members of Ways and Means greater influence in the operations of welfare programs.

As discussed earlier, on one critical issue he was adamant: he did not want and would not support a provision *requiring* the states to supplement the federal benefits provided in H.R.1. He said he was tired of state and local officials complaining "about the Federal Government's forcing them to spend money on federal programs." Furthermore, a supplemental program financed by both the state and Federal Government would be like the existing AFDC program, and would probably produce the same inefficiencies, inconsistencies, and problems of regulation they were at that very moment trying to eliminate.

Mills and Byrnes are "pragmatic conservatives."[37] In principle they are committed to a free enterprise economic system, a limited Federal Government, state's rights, a balanced budget, individualism, the work ethic, and slow, cautious, incremental policy change. However, in 1970 and 1971, it looked to them like drastic changes were required to "prevent the collapse" of what in their opinion was "a very basic function of government, . . . namely, assisting its poorer citizens to a better life."[38] Faced with such a situation, they are, in operation, pragmatic problem solvers. Mills has remarked that, in the Committee process of solving problems and designing public policy,

> there is no place for just the idealist because we're dealing with very practical matters. We're living in a very practical world, we have to find practical answers; generally those answers have to be a compromise of the judgment of the 25 men on the committee and the 435 members of the House. . . .[39]

Byrnes said in an interview,

> A major problem in developing a good program is that on this issue, and some other issues, you always have two extremes. On one side are those who don't want any welfare program. They say that if you don't have a welfare program the people will find jobs. This is a totally irresponsible position but many hold it—there seem to be more in the Senate than here. Most of the public seems to agree with this position. Primarily they are not willing to pay any more taxes for welfare. On the other hand you have the Welfare Rights Organization, social workers, and some recipients who want a minimum level payment of $6,500 or more. Both sides have adherents—more in the Senate than here—and you can't please both of them. Or, to be reasonable, you can't please either because they are extreme positions, neither of them reflect the realities of the problem—neither are responsible positions.

This does not mean that Mills and Byrnes neglect principles or ideology when responding to a failing policy that falls within the Committee's jurisdiction. They simply focus their attention on the problem and possible solutions. Or, the fundamental and overriding principle to which they respond is "the need to do something," and this means finding the best technically, economically, politically feasible solution.

The "welfare crisis," as they saw it, was primarily the result of an outdated, inefficient, and ineffective administrative structure. They supported H.R.1 because it contained what they considered to be necessary changes in the administration of welfare. They believed these changes would rectify the most critical problems with the present programs and, in general, result in a better welfare system, or one more consistent with their understanding of the proper objectives and operations of a welfare system.

The process of building a consensus in the Committee and designing a bill that would be approved by the House dictated the inclusion of a negative tax program for *all* families with children at the insistence of the Administration and Committee-liberals, benefit levels somewhat higher and work requirements somewhat more severe than they would have preferred, and a number of amendments to Social Security, Medicare, and Medicaid, some of which they did not fully appreciate but could live with.

Ways and Means Members: Defeating the Conservative Coalition in Committee

Twenty-two of the 25 Committee members supported H.R.1 in the final Committee vote, and 20 of them voted for the bill when it came before the entire House. The support of Mills, Byrnes, and President Nixon, pressure from state and local officials to increase the federal share of welfare costs (especially in the large urban states), the general agreement among liberal and conservative members that there was a "crisis" situation and that "something had to be done" about welfare, and convergence on the point that the existing federal-state structure provided states too much discretion in administering public assistance, were all important in obtaining Committee approval of H.R.1.

As indicated, the liberals were concerned about welfare payments and administrative procedures in low benefit states like Mississippi. Conservatives worried about the "extraordinary" growth in welfare rolls and blamed high welfare benefits, "bleeding-heart social workers," and "lax welfare bureaucracies" in states like New York. In approving H.R.1 and federalizing welfare, liberals and conservatives agreed to shift future struggles over expanding or restricting welfare from the states to national political institutions.

Furthermore, all those interviewed could identify a specific provision or general feature of H.R.1, and in some cases take credit for its incorporation, which they believed—and had been assured by Mills and Byrnes—

would correct a major problem with the present system. Conservative members said they supported the bill because it would provide greater federal control over welfare costs, encourage work and family stability, and remove the financial incentive for poor people to move from southern rural areas where welfare benefits were low into northern cities and states with higher benefits. A senior conservative Republican member explained,

> When Nixon first announced his proposal on television I was skeptical because welfare is not my thing. But when we got working on the bill itself, with Byrnes supporting it and then when Mills changed his position and supported it, I decided it was the right thing to do.
>
> . . . H.R.1 goes against some of my beliefs like "state's rights," or that the states should be responsible for problems like welfare. However, we've let the states handle it for a long time and it just isn't working out. We needed to get more control over federal expenditures. This is why I wanted the federal share to be limited to $2,100, but $2,400 was the best we could get. . . . I was in favor of the work requirements. I know some people question the extent to which welfare recipients can work or need to be forced to work—but I think the work requirements were a good thing.
>
> . . . I guess the conservatives have dropped my name from their list because I voted for H.R.1—which they think is a far-out bill. We were at a Republican party the other night and H.R. Gross was there. Somebody said, "We don't get together like we used to." And Gross said, "Yes, especially since H.R.1." They (the conservatives) were opposed to the bill because it adds to the number of people already on welfare and because of the cost increases— about $5 billion. Also, some are concerned about what they call the "guaranteed income" that it contains. I tell them that all welfare programs have some kind of an income level which if you are above it you won't get benefits and if you are below it you will— call it a guaranteed income or whatever—in principle we have the same thing in the present program as we do in H.R.1. The main problem is that they just won't listen—they don't want to. I guess I was that way when I first got here; but you soon learn that the extremists will never come up with legislation. Mills said this is a good bill because it has the middle-of-the-roaders voting for it and the extremists opposing it.

A Committee staff member said one thing people should understand is that "since Mills has been chairman, Ways and Means bills have been as liberal as was possible." In the case of H.R.1, Committee liberals agreed with this observation. Corman said, "Hugh Carey and I could have written a better bill, or one that we preferred, but we could never get it approved by the Committee or the House." Liberal members supported the bill because it provided benefits for the "working poor," it raised the benefit levels in some states, and it provided some financial savings for the large urban states.

Liberals Carey, Vanik, Green, and Corman filed "additional views" in the Committee report in which they indicated their support for the basic features and general direction of the bill, but their dissatisfaction with the low benefit levels for families, the lack of a provision mandating state supplementation with federal financial support, and the requirement that mothers with preschool children register for work.

Ullman, Burleson, and Waggonner, who voted against the bill in Committee, were joined in opposing the programs for families on the House floor by Committee Republicans Broyhill of Virginia and Duncan of Tennessee. In an interview, Ullman said he voted against H.R.1 because

> the bill is a mess, Whatever you call it, it's a guaranteed income. The Federal Government looks at people according to three variables: income, number of children, and assets, and then gives them money on the basis of these three variables. The government can't keep track of these and it's ridiculous to trust the people. We're just opening the Federal Treasury to them. . . . They took the idea of dividing the employables and unemployables from my proposal but not the substance of my program because they still left the employables in the welfare system.

Burleson said he opposed H.R.1 because it

> just piles one federal bureaucracy on top of another. I'm not blaming the bureaucrats—it's easy for us who make the laws to criticize those who have to crank the handles. But I think this is an area where the local units of government should handle the job. I have a bill which would change the trend toward centralization of government here in Washington. Also, I'm opposed to a guaranteed income in principle. I know that the Administration and the bill's supporters say it isn't a guaranteed income. We do have provisions which create training programs, but we already have training programs on every corner and they aren't solving our problems— I just don't think the ones in this bill will either.

Joe D. Waggonner said that although he thought welfare should be handled by the state and local governments, he voted against the bill primarily because "the work requirements were too vague."

> The past performance of HEW and the Department of Labor indicates just what they will do under this bill. They will change

the intent of the Committee to meet their own notions—we needed to make the work requirements very strict and very clear—they are too broad and vague. I would have voted for the bill if my amendment requiring a doctor's statement before a person is excused from the work requirement had been incorporated. I announced this in the Committee, but it was defeated 15 to 6.

It appeared to be the intensity of their concern that poor people would not work if guaranteed an income of $2,400 a year that distinguished the Committee members who opposed H.R.1 from the other members. Mills and Byrnes worked hard to convince their conservative colleagues that "the biggest mistake we can make is to assume that a majority of these people don't want to help themselves."[40] In enough cases they were successful in generating at least a modicum of faith in the poor and H.R.1.

Defeating the Conservative Coalition
on the Floor

The first of two key votes on H.R.1 was on June 21 when the House approved a motion 200 to 172 to bring the bill to the floor under a modified closed rule. This rule prohibited amendments but allowed a separate recorded vote on a motion from the floor to strike Title IV from the bill, or to delete that part of H.R.1 that would replace AFDC with the new guaranteed income program (FAP and OFF) for poor families with children. The second critical vote was on the motion offered by Committee member Al Ullman to delete the family programs. The Ullman motion to strike Title IV from the bill was defeated 234 to 187.[41] Information presented in Tables 6-2 and 6-3 show that there was not a stable majority which supported the bill on both votes. House approval of H.R.1 required the engineering of two somewhat different majorities.

As shown in Table 6-2, urban and suburban congressmen were more likely than those from rural districts to support H.R.1 on the Title IV vote but less likely on the earlier modified closed rule motion. Moderates were fairly consistent in their support for H.R.1, but there was a significant amount of shifting among liberals and conservatives on the two key votes. Fifty-three percent of the liberals supported the bill on the rule vote as compared to 77 percent on the Title IV vote; and 43 percent of the conservatives voted in favor of the modified closed rule but only 29 percent voted in favor of retaining Title IV.

Table 6-3 divides House members according to the relative impact of H.R.1 on state welfare costs, caseloads, and current AFDC payment levels. [42] This information, combined with the data in Table 6-2, indicates that moderates and liberals from states that would be the least affected by H.R.1—in terms of the amount of change it would produce in state welfare costs,

Table 6-2.   House Votes on H.R.1: (1) The Modified Closed Rule Motion, and (2) Ullman's Motion to Delete the Programs for Families (Title IV)

	Modified Closed Rule			Retain Title IV		
	Yes (percent)	No (percent)	N	Yes (percent)	No (percent)	N
Party						
Democrats	58.7	41.3	(230)	57.6	42.4	(245)
Republicans	46.7	53.3	(167)	52.8	47.2	(176)
Congressional Districts[a]						
Urban	48.0	52.0	(102)	52.3	47.7	(107)
Suburban	53.4	46.6	(178)	65.6	34.4	(186)
Rural	59.0	41.0	(117)	43.8	56.3	(128)
General Policy Orientation[b]						
Liberals	52.8	47.2	(142)	77.3	22.7	(150)
Moderates	75.9	24.1	(87)	72.5	27.5	(91)
Conservatives	43.4	56.6	(166)	29.2	70.8	(178)

Source: U.S., Department of Commerce, Census Bureau, *Congressional District Data, Districts of the 92nd Congress* (Washington, D.C.: Government Printing Office, 1971); *Congressional Quarterly Weekly Report* (Washington, D.C.: Congressional Quarterly Service, January 15, 1972), pp. 74–80.

[a]Same as note (a), Table 6-1.

[b]General Policy Orientation is based on the *Congressional Quarterly*'s Conservative Coalition Opposition Score defined in note (b), Table 6-1. Congressmen with scores of 50% or higher were classified as *liberals*; those with scores of 20% to 49% as *moderates*; those with scores below 20% as *conservatives*.

number of welfare recipients and present AFDC payment levels—were the most receptive to Mills, Byrnes, and the Administration in their efforts to mobilize support for radical welfare reform. These were representatives from states where welfare costs, caseloads, and payment levels were the highest under current law, and the House members who were under the most pressure from state and local officials to support any measure that would reduce state welfare expenditures.

Most of the opposition came from conservatives representing states with the lowest welfare costs and payment levels under existing programs: states that would experience the greatest change under H.R.1 in terms of a large increase in welfare recipients and benefit levels and a large decrease in state welfare costs. As indicated in Table 6–4, these were primarily southern and border states.

It was Democratic congressmen, as shown in Tables 6–5 and 6–6, who were doing most of the switching on the two key votes. A number of

Table 6-3. House Votes on H.R.1: (1) The Modified Closed Rule
Motion, and (2) Ullman's Motion to Delete the Programs for
Families (Title IV)

Policy Consequences of H.R.1	Modified Closed Rule			Retain Title IV		
	Yes (percent)	No (percent)	N	Yes (percent)	No (percent)	N
Welfare Recipients[a] Percent State Increase						
High	52.9	47.1	(121)	36.9	63.1	(130)
Moderate	47.0	53.0	(134)	55.9	44.1	(136)
Low	60.6	39.4	(142)	71.0	29.0	(155)
Welfare Costs[b] Percent State Increase						
High	48.3	51.7	(145)	36.6	63.4	(153)
Moderate	54.8	45.2	(146)	65.4	34.6	(159)
Low	59.4	40.6	(106)	67.9	32.1	(109)
Welfare Benefits[c] $2,400 as a percent of AFDC benefits						
High	47.4	52.6	(116)	31.5	68.5	(124)
Moderate	48.5	51.5	(130)	57.5	42.5	(134)
Low	62.9	37.1	(151)	72.4	27.6	(163)

[a]This classification of House members is based on the information presented in Table 5-5 (Chapter 5), in which states are grouped according to the percent increase in welfare recipients that would occur under H.R.1. Congressmen from states that would experience 0 to 49% increase were classified in the *low* category; 50 to 99% in the *moderate* category; and 100% and above in the *high* category.

[b]This classification is based on information presented in Table 6-4 in which states are grouped according to the percent decrease in welfare costs under H.R.1. Congressmen from states that would experience less than a 20% decrease in welfare costs were classified as *low*; 21 to 40% as *moderate*; and 41% and above as *high*.

[c]This classification is based on information presented in Table 5-7 (Chapter 5), where states are grouped according to the percentage increase in payments to families that would occur under H.R.1. Congressmen from states in which $2,400 was equal to 75% or less of the March 1971 AFDC maximum payment were classified as *low*; 76 to 109% as *moderate*; and 110% and above as *high*.

liberal urban and suburban Democrats voted against the Ways and Means Committee position on the rule vote, then switched on the second vote and supported Title IV. In contrast, some southern conservative Democrats supported the Committee on the rule vote (enough to make up for defecting liberals), then voted to delete Title IV.

It is possible that some of the liberals who were dissatisfied with

Table 6-4.   Estimated States' Savings in 1973 Welfare Expenditures Under H.R.1

Percent Decrease in State Costs Under H.R.1	Number of States	States
0–20	12	Maine, Wash., Vt., N.H., Pa., N.Dak., Idaho, Mass., Mo., Calif., Minn., Nebr.
21–41	20	Alaska, Del., Mich., Ill., N.J., N.Y., R.I., Va., Ind., Nev., Colo., Conn., Utah, Hawaii, S.Dak., Wyo., Ky., Kans., Mont., Oreg.
41–60	5	N.Mex., Ohio, Iowa, Tex., Wis.
61–80	6	Md., Okla., Ariz., N.C., Ala., Tenn.
81–100	7	Ga., W.Va., La., Fla., Ark., Miss., S.C.

Source: Percentages were derived from information presented in U.S., Congress, House, Social Security Amendments of 1971, House Ways and Means Committee Report on H.R.1, 92nd Congress, 1st sess., 1971, p. 216.

Table 6-5.   Vote Switching on the Modified Closed Rule Motion and the Motion to Strike Title IV

	Yes: Rule Yes: Title IV (percent)	No: Rule Yes: Title IV (percent)	Yes: Rule No: Title IV (percent)	No: Rule No: Title IV (percent)
Party				
Democrats	59.6	62.7	68.2	47.9
Republicans	40.4	37.3	31.8	52.1
Congressional Districts[a]				
Urban	21.7	29.3	22.7	29.4
Suburban	50.9	54.7	27.3	37.8
Rural	27.3	16.0	50.0	32.8
General Policy Orientation[b]				
Liberals	42.2	66.7	10.6	22.7
Moderates	31.7	20.0	22.7	8.4
Conservatives	26.1	13.3	66.7	68.9

[a]Same as note (a), Table 6-1.
[b]Same as note (b), Table 6-2.

the low benefits, the strict work requirements, and the lack of required state supplementation voted against the modified closed rule in hopes that, if defeated, H.R.1 would be debated under an open rule and they would be able to eliminate some of its defects through amendments. However, Mills would not have allowed the bill brought to the floor under an open rule. Some liberals

Table 6-6. Vote Switching on the Modified Closed Rule Motion and the Motion to Strike Title IV

Policy Consequences of H.R.1	Yes: Rule Yes: Title IV (percent)	No: Rule Yes: Title IV (percent)	Yes: Rule No: Title IV (percent)	No: Rule No: Title IV (percent)
Welfare Recipients[a] Percent State Increase				
High	23.0	14.7	50.0	41.2
Moderate	31.1	34.7	21.2	38.7
Low	46.0	50.7	28.8	20.2
Welfare Costs[b] Percent State Decrease				
High	24.8	21.3	53.0	52.1
Moderate	43.5	48.0	25.8	30.3
Low	31.7	30.7	21.2	17.6
Welfare Benefits[c] $2,400 as a percent of AFDC Benefits				
High	18.0	13.3	48.5	44.5
Moderate	29.8	38.7	25.8	33.6
Low	52.2	48.0	25.8	21.8

[a]Same as note (a), Table 6-3.
[b]Same as note (b), Table 6-3.
[c]Same as note (c), Table 6-3.

who were under pressure from state and local officials, party leaders, and Mills to support the bill and from liberal, welfare oriented groups to oppose it possibly decided that switching positions on the two votes was a compromise. Others, those with the strongest reservations about the bill, hoped it could be defeated on the less visible rule vote.

Probably the best answer as to why 20 to 30 southern conservative, antiwelfare Democrats, who voted against Title IV, voted in support of the rule motion is that, because of liberal defections, this was the precise number of votes Mills needed. A few days before the House votes on H.R.1, Mills reassured members of the League of Women Voters who were worried about liberal defections, "we will get more Southerners to go along this time—because I've been working harder."

Widespread dissatisfaction with existing welfare programs, lobbying of state and local officials, and Presidential sponsorship were important conditions in explaining why H.R.1 and the policy innovations it contained were approved by Ways and Means and the House. An equally important condition was the presence and support of knowledgeable and powerful congressional leaders like Mills and Byrnes, who had sufficient leverage to shift the attention of other legislators to this innovative course of action, to maintain Committee and House attention and deliberations focused on this policy alternative, and, in one way or another, to deliver the votes in committee and on the floor.

Chapter Seven

Welfare Policy and Process: The Senate

*As I gather it, I don't see a person around this table who is satisfied
with H.R.1. We are all concerned about it. Now it may be that all
of us together can come up with some amendments to this program.
Perhaps we can't, but I think we ought to give it a try, Mr. Chairman.*

> —Senator Abraham Ribicoff, Senate
> Finance Committee Hearings,
> August 1971

*The reason Congress has found it difficult to find a plan that
provides universal benefits at a level regarded as reasonable, that
preserves work incentives, and that is not vastly more expensive
than President Nixon's proposal is that no such plan exists or can
be devised: These objectives are mutually inconsistent.*

> —Henry J. Aaron, "Why Is Welfare
> So Hard to Reform?" 1973

In October 1972, sixteen months after House passage of H.R.1, there were
four alternative proposals pertaining to the reform of AFDC before the Senate:

1. Title IV of H.R.1 (the OFF and FAP programs for families) as approved
   by the House in 1971—which had the official support of President Nixon.
2. A liberalized version of the family programs in H.R.1 that would increase
   the minimum payment to $2,600 for a family of four, mandate state sup-
   plementation of federal payments, and liberalize work requirements—
   sponsored by Senator Abraham Ribicoff of Connecticut.
3. A "workfare" plan that would make all ablebodied family heads, male
   or female, ineligible for welfare (removing approximately 1.2 million from
   the welfare rolls) and require them to take federally guaranteed jobs—

which had been approved by the Senate Finance Committee and was
sponsored by Committee Chairman Russell Long of Louisiana.
4.   A proposal to provide $400 million a year for a two- to-four-year test of
the family programs in H.R.1, Senator Ribicoff's liberalized Family Assistance Plan, and Senator Long's "workfare" program—sponsored by Senator
William Roth of Delaware and Senator Harry Byrd of Virginia.

Unable to organize a majority in support of either of the proposed new programs, by a vote of 46 to 41 the Senate approved the Roth-Byrd motion to
test the three alternative welfare plans.

For the second time in three years, the Senate did not approve a
proposal to replace AFDC with a negative tax program for families with children
that had been passed in the House. However, the Senate did approve the new
federal guaranteed income for the aged, blind, and disabled (the Supplemental
Security Income program) developed in the House Ways and Means Committee.
This chapter describes the decision making process and conditions associated
with the Senate's welfare actions in 1971-1972 and the major changes in U.S.
welfare programs after almost four years of policy analysis and debate over
radical welfare reform.

DECISION PROCESS

Senate Finance Committee

Senate counterpart of the House Ways and Means Committee is
the Senate Finance Committee. The similarity of the two committees, however,
is virtually limited to a common responsibility for the trade, tax, and welfare
proposals that come before their respective chambers. Differences in membership and policy making style of the two committees are important in explaining the decision making process and outcome of Senate welfare deliberations
in 1971 and 1972.

Regarding membership, of the eight states with the highest state
and local expenditures for public assistance in fiscal 1972 (New York, California, Illinois, Pennsylvania, Michigan, Massachusetts, New Jersey, and Ohio [1]),
all but New Jersey had a representative on Ways and Means and all but Massachusetts and New Jersey had two congressmen on the House Committee in
1971. Thirteen of the 25 members of Ways and Means were from the eight
states with the highest welfare costs, largest welfare populations and whose
governors, mayors, and other public officials were exerting the greatest amount
of pressure on national legislators to support measures that would reduce state
welfare expenditures.

In contrast, as indicated in Table 7-1 only one of these states had
a Senator on the Finance Committee. This was Senator Robert Griffin from

Table 7-1. Members of the Senate Finance Committee, 92nd Congress: State and Conservative Coalition Opposition Scores for 1971

Members	*State*	*Conservative Coalition Opposition Score*[a]
Democrats		
Russell B. Long	La.	14
Clinton P. Anderson	N. Mex.	28
Herman E. Talmadge	Ga.	08
Vance Hartke	Ind.	65
J.W. Fulbright	Ark.	63
Abraham Ribicoff	Conn.	71
Fred R. Harris	Okla.	44
Harry F. Byrd	Va.	07
Gaylord Nelson	Wisc.	91
Republicans		
Wallace F. Bennett	Utah	02
Carl T. Curtis	Neb.	02
Jack Miller	Iowa	10
Len B. Jordon	Idaho	05
Paul J. Fannin	Ariz.	01
Clifford P. Hansen	Wyo.	01
Robert P. Griffin	Mich.	16

Source: Congressional Quarterly Weekly Report (Washington, D.C.: Congressional Quarterly Service, January 15, 1971), pp. 74–80.
[a]Same as note (b), Table 6–1 (Chapter 6).

Michigan who was the newest Republican member, appointed in 1971, and whose interest in welfare reform was drastically reduced by a tough reelection campaign. Reflecting the influence of conservative business interests in the recruitment of Senate Finance Committee members, especially the oil lobbies, in 1971-72 its membership was less urban and more conservative and generally more antiwelfare than Ways and Means, the House, or the full Senate.[2]

Whereas liberal and conservative congressmen appointed to Ways and Means tend to be pragmatic in policy making and amenable to a Committee style characterized by exhaustive, patient pursuit of technically sound, consensus legislation that is assured passage on the House floor, the Finance Committee operates with limited concern for agreement within the Committee or passage of Committee bills on the Senate floor.[3] Based on interviews with Finance Committee members, Fenno describes a policy style that is oriented toward helping interest groups that appeal for redress from House decisions, and is characterized by vigorous advocacy of individual policy positions in concert with whatever allies can be found inside or outside the Committee or the Senate.[4] Most important, Senator Long, the Committee Chairman, and

Senator Bennett, the ranking Republican, did not provide the leadership in Committee and Senate deliberations—the attention directing and preference shifting leverage—exercised by Mills and Byrnes in the House.

Reflecting the individualistic policy style of the members and the absence of effective leadership, the major participants in the Senate welfare deliberations were unable to arrive at a common agenda of problems and possible solutions in reforming AFDC. Finance Committee conservatives, Senate liberals, and the Administration pursued three different courses of action which were revealed in the first few days of public hearings on H.R.1 beginning July 27, 1971.

The Senate's Welfare Agenda

On the first day of hearings Senator Long provided the new Secretary of HEW, Elliot Richardson, the following example of a "fundamental problem" with the existing AFDC program which he did not think the new family programs in H.R.1 would alleviate.

> Let us take the typical example of the man-in-the-house situation. Here is a man with three children who look exactly like him. He lives in the house every night with Mama. He has an income of $6,000. Mama is drawing welfare payment of $5,000 a year for the benefit of herself and those children. Combined total income, $11,000. They are not in poverty. The Supreme Court has held that we cannot assume that 5 cents of that $6,000 of Papa's income is available for the support of that mother and those three children who are his. There is nothing in this bill that would even give Mama the first cash incentive to sue Papa. As a practical matter, the evidence is entirely within the possession of mother and father that that money is in fact available to that family unit and he is spending every night there, but you cannot presume that he is willing to pay 5 cents to support his own children.
>
> Now, that $5,000 welfare payment is a subsidy on illegitimacy, it is a cash bonus not to marry, and it creates the height of resentment on his neighbor next door, who has married the woman who is the mother of his children, and who is bringing his $6,000 home to help support those children. Until we do the first simple thing about that, how can you call this a welfare reform bill?[5]

The Chairman was convinced that "fifty percent of the people on the welfare rolls are benefiting in one respect or another because of this kind of corruption," which he labeled "legalized fraud."[6]

Long and the other conservatives on the Committee, which included the seven Republicans and at least three of the nine Democrats (Long, Talmadge, and Byrd), believed that the major problems with AFDC included the high incidence of welfare cheating, the lax if not corrupt administrators who refused to enforce the existing work requirement, the incentives for illegitimacy and disincentives for work, and the uncontrollable expansion in costs and caseloads. They were opposed to the new family programs in H.R.1 because to them FAP (and OFF) appeared to intensify rather than alleviate most of these problems. From their perspective H.R.1 was the opposite of "welfare reform" because it would double rather than reduce the number of welfare recipients and, most significant, because they were convinced a guaranteed income would completely undermine the already deteriorating "work ethic" among the poor. Republican Senator Carl Curtis of Nebraska told Secretary Richardson that H.R.1 was not "welfare reform": it was "a guaranteed annual income under the name of welfare reform."[7] And Long predicted in an interview that the $2,400 "guaranteed wage for not working . . . would destroy this country." Under H.R.1,

> people have it entirely within their power to get the money without doing any work at all. And I don't see why anybody is going to work for that money if he's never worked before anyway, and he can get just as much without working.[8]

Senator Hanson, Republican from Wyoming, could not support H.R.1 because it would shift welfare

> from the idea of . . . being something that a nation and a people with big hearts want to do for those less fortunate, in a direction and down a road that indicates not a willingness on the part of others to share what we have with those less fortunate but the assertion of the right of people to welfare and to increasing amounts of support from all the taxpayers, and this seems to me to be a very, very important new direction from the one we have been pursuing.[9]

The conservative majority on the Finance Committee wanted to abolish AFDC, but they did not want to replace it with a guaranteed income for families with children. They preferred a program based on the principles that "you are not eligible for welfare to begin with," and "you are not eligible for welfare so long as there are jobs available"; a program which would pay nothing to a "mother if she refused to identify the father so he could be made to contribute to the support of his own children."[10] On the eve of Finance Committee hearings on welfare, Long told reporters,

> The majority of the committee is ready to vote for a workfare program rather than a welfare expansion program, a program that provides a guaranteed work opportunity rather than the guaranteed income that the administration bill would provide for doing nothing at all.[11]

Liberals on the Committee, particularly Senator Ribicoff and Senator Harris of Oklahoma, understood as well if not better than Senator Hansen and other conservatives the conceptual changes H.R.1 represented, and they supported the "new direction" in welfare contained in the legislation. Ribicoff praised President Nixon for initiating a proposal which represented "substantial reform of our nation's inadequate, inefficient, and degrading welfare system" and which had the "potential" for reducing or even eliminating poverty in the U.S. Essentially, liberals objected to H.R.1 because the family programs as designed by Ways and Means and approved by the House did not extend far enough the logic and implications of the conceptual shifts in welfare policy it would introduce.

For example, Ribicoff found it "heartless" and "cynical" to talk about reducing poverty by providing "direct cash assistance," public service employment, and financial work incentives and then to enact a program which excluded poor childless couples and single individuals, provided $2,400 for a family of four (without mandatory state supplementation) when the poverty level was $3,900, required 2.6 million people to register for work and provided only 200,000 public service jobs and 412,000 training slots, and forced people to take jobs paying $1.20 per hour or a yearly wage of $2,496 which was $1,400 less than the prevailing poverty level. Harris commended the Administration for supporting a new program which would guarantee an aged, blind, or disabled couple at least a poverty level annual income. But he could not "justify paying $2,400 to an aged couple and only the same $2,400 to a family of four."[12]

Ribicoff and Harris were as anxious as the conservatives to abolish AFDC and replace it with a more effective welfare program. To them this meant a program which focused on alleviating income poverty by providing all poor people, those with incomes below the poverty level, "direct cash payments with no strings attached."[13] H.R.1 was an unexpected large step in this direction, but it needed "substantial improvement." Specifically, the liberals wanted to increase the federal minimum payment to families, mandate state supplementation of the federal benefits up to current payment levels, simplify eligibility determination procedures, insure adequate protection of recipients' rights, increase the financial work incentives, and expand the number of public service jobs provided in the legislation approved by the House.

During the second day of public hearings Senator Ribicoff told Secretary of Labor James Hodgson and Assistant Secretary of Labor Jerome Rosow, who were testifying at the time, that the Administration had "to make a choice," whether to "go for the philosophy of Senator Long or Senator Ribicoff, that is the decision that has to be made."[14] Throughout the hearings, however, Administration spokesmen attempted to shift the attention of the members and the agenda of the Committee to that of finding a middle ground between liberal and conservative concerns and reaching a compromise. Secretary Hodgson told the members he

> was confident that we will find a consensus of what to do about the welfare crisis, wholly within the American sense of fair play and justice, and my purpose in being here is to work for that consensus.[15]

The Administration's position was that H.R.1 reflected the concerns and problems with AFDC articulated by both Senator Long and Senator Ribicoff and represented a middle ground or compromise proposal. It would take the elderly and disabled out of poverty, provide cash supplements for working poor families, and assistance for all poor children in the U.S. On the other hand, H.R.1 would tighten up the administration of welfare and, with the work requirement and financial work incentives, encourage the work efforts of welfare recipients. Secretary Richardson told the Committee he was ready to work with them "toward any better solution than we have been able to produce." But he predicted that if the Committee seriously attempted to resolve and compromise differences between liberals and conservatives and write a program that could be enacted, as he hoped they would, they would end up with a package that looked "quite a lot like this (H.R.1) because there just are not that many ways of doing it."[16] In the Senate, however, the Administration did not have Wilbur Mills or John Byrnes to help them direct the attention of the members, establish a common agenda, and engineer a compromise bill.

Program Design: Senate Liberals
On October 28, 1971, Senator Ribicoff and Republican Governor Francis Sargent of Massachusetts announced the "formation of a coalition to support welfare reform" and unveiled an alternative to the family programs in H.R.1 which had been developed by "a bipartisan group of senators, governors under the leadership of Governor Francis Sargent of Massachusetts, mayors, county leaders, and welfare administrators."[17] The Ribicoff-Sargent proposal would provide a yearly federal payment of $3,000 for a family of four with no other income. This would be increased each year until reaching the Census Bureau defined poverty level in 1976. States would have to supplement the federal payment up to current benefit levels including the value of food stamps with the Federal Government financing 30 percent of the supplemental payments. State supplementation payments and costs would be phased out over a five-year period so that by 1976 public assistance would be completely federalized.

Recipients would be allowed to keep the first $720 of their earnings plus 40 percent of the remainder without loss of benefits, 300,000 public service jobs would be authorized, mothers with children under age six would not be required to register for work, and no recipient could be forced to take a job paying less than the prevailing federal minimum wage. Single individuals and childless couples would be eligible for benefits, and eligibility determination would be streamlined, assuring recipients due process and other procedural rights.

By January the proposal had the endorsement of 22 Senators, 15 governors,[18] the National League of Cities, U.S. Conference of Mayors, National Association of Counties, League of Women Voters, Common Cause, AFL-CIO, United Auto Workers, American Federation of State County and Municipal Employees, National Association of Social Workers, American Public Welfare Association, American Jewish Committee, American Association of University Women, Council for Community Action, B'Nai Brith Women, Americans for Democratic Action, and the National Conference of Catholic Charities.

Estimated federal welfare costs in 1973 under the Ribicoff-Sargent plan, H.R.1 as approved by the House, and existing public assistance programs are shown in Table 7–2. These figures were submitted by Senator Ribicoff when he announced the Ribicoff-Sargent plan in October 1971. According to Ribicoff's figures, his proposal would cost the Federal Government approximately $22.4 billion in 1973 and approximately 30 million people would be eligible for benefits. In January 1972 HEW produced figures estimating

Table 7–2.   Total Federal Welfare Costs Under Existing Public Assistance Programs, H.R.1, and the Ribicoff-Sargent Proposal, Fiscal 1973
(billions of dollars)

Program	Existing Programs	H.R.1	Ribicoff-Sargent Proposal
Family Payments	$3.9	$ 6.5	$11.3
Childless Couples and Singles	—	—	1.0
Adult Categories	2.2	4.1	4.1
Food Programs	2.4	1.0	1.0
Child Care Services	.3	.7	1.5
Child Care Facilities Construction	—	.05	.1
Supportive Services	—	.1	.1
Manpower Training	.2	.54	1.0
Public Service Jobs	—	.8	1.2
Equal Employment Compliance Activities	—	—	.01
Administration	.4	1.1	1.1
Miscellaneous Costs	—	.7	—
Total	$9.4	$15.6	$22.41

Source: U.S., *Congressional Record,* October 29, 1971, p. S17118.

that by 1977 upwards of 72 million persons would be eligible for cash benefits under the Ribicoff-Sargent program and that federal costs could go as high as $42 billion. These HEW cost and caseload projections were revealed by Republican Senator Curtis—before Ribicoff had seen them or was even aware of their existence—during Governor Sargent's testimony before the Finance Committee on behalf of the Ribicoff-Sargent proposal. According to Ribicoff's legislative assistant Geoffrey Peterson,

> the HEW cost estimates given to Curtis shocked Ribicoff. The Senate is totally dependent on HEW cost estimates and there was no way for our office to check their accuracy. The Senate Finance Committee, who doesn't trust HEW, hired Myers to do estimates. But he was doing them for Long, so who could the liberals trust? If we got into an argument over costs and caseloads with HEW we would be at a total loss. We didn't have the resources to argue with their computer experts.

On January 25 Senator Ribicoff received a letter from Stephen Kurzman, Assistant Secretary of HEW, containing the projections Curtis had disclosed a few days earlier. Kurzman explained in the letter that the estimates had been requested by the Finance Committee staff and it was due to an "oversight" in his office that Ribicoff did not receive them the same time they were delivered to the Committee staff. Ribicoff remained convinced that the White House had planned the embarrassing disclosure of the figures; that it was a deliberate move aimed at undermining his efforts to obtain Senate passage of a guaranteed income for families.

Senator Ribicoff had experienced some important changes in his thinking about welfare policy since 1962 when he was one of the principal advocates of the social service and rehabilitation approach to poverty. His faith in the effectiveness of social services was diminished. His attention had shifted from the problem of people who were poor because they were unable to work to the problem of income poverty, which included all persons, employable or unemployable, working or nonworking, with incomes below the poverty level. He now believed direct cash assistance was the most effective and probably the most efficient way for the Federal Government to assist the poor. During the Committee hearings on H.R.1 he suggested that the Administration and Congress should seriously consider eliminating many if not most of the existing service and in-kind welfare programs and using the money saved to establish a national income maintenance program that would assure a yearly income at or above the poverty level for all Americans.[19]

However, the Senator was sensitive about the promises and results of the Social Service Amendments he sponsored as Secretary of HEW under President Kennedy, especially the assurances he gave Senators and Congressmen in 1962 that an increase in social workers and service programs would eventually produce a decrease in welfare costs and recipients. As a result, he was somewhat reluctant to enact a major change in welfare policy with unpredictable results, especially one bearing his name, which had not been pretested to the extent possible. During the 1970 Senate debate over Nixon's Family Assistance Plan he proposed that a "series of pretests and evaluations of the major reform provisions" in the President's proposal be undertaken before they were implemented. In explaining his proposed pretests in August 1970, he said he believed FAP was "a major step in the direction of progressive welfare reform," but he had become

> increasingly concerned over the difficulties encountered by social legislation enacted in Congress. Laws that have been approved in legislative Chambers and acclaimed as social milestones, have not passed muster in the field. The bureaucratic tangles and massive cost overruns of many of these measures have come as a profound shock to Congress and the country.[20]

The large expansion in federal welfare costs and recipients under the Ribicoff-Sargent program projected by HEW heightened Ribicoff's concern about possible undesirable fiscal and political consequences of a poverty level guaranteed income. Reflecting this concern and his anger with the Administration for the manner in which the estimates had been revealed, Ribicoff surprised his staff, cosponsors, and the Administration with an announcement during Committee hearings on January 28, 1972 that he wanted to test any new program for the "working poor" before putting it into effect.

When Ribicoff announced this unexpected decision he said he was convinced the President no longer wanted FAP and that in sponsoring pretests of some of the proposed changes he was "trying to salvage something" out of the two-year debate. "The idea is good," he said, "but the President doesn't really believe in it."[21] In a letter sent the following day to cosponsors of the Ribicoff-Sargent proposal he explained:

> I intend . . . to continue to seek the enactment of my amendments which you have supported. I am, however, going to propose the establishment of substantial programs to test the working poor provisions.
>
>   From discussion with welfare experts I am convinced that to fold millions of additional people into a new and untested welfare system would be unmanageable and might lead to the failure of the entire reform program.

Organizations supporting the Ribicoff-Sargent plan and liberal newspapers that favored some kind of a national guaranteed income for fami-

lies accused the Senator of "running out" on welfare reform. They urged him
to reverse his decision and to continue to fight for immediate enactment and
implementation of a liberalized version of the family programs in H.R.1. An
editorial in the *New York Times* read:

> For two years Mr. Ribicoff has provided valiant leadership to
> Senate liberals in their efforts to improve upon President Nixon's
> basic blueprint for a guaranteed federal floor under family income.
> Now, on the lame excuse that the Administration is not fighting
> hard enough for its own program, he embraces that favorite dodge
> of the program's enemies—a time-wasting period of demonstration
> projects in the practicality of income guarantees.[22]

On January 31 President Nixon called Ribicoff to personally reaffirm his support
for FAP. John Ehrlichman, Presidential Assistant on Domestic Affairs, and
Secretary Richardson met with the senator the morning of February 2. That
afternoon Nixon had Daniel Moynihan fly down from Cambridge to discuss
Ribicoff's ideas on pretesting and urge him to continue to support welfare reform. Moynihan told Ribicoff that Nixon still supported FAP and that this
program would "do more than all the Kennedy and Johnson antipoverty programs put together—that it was a landmark, historic proposal."

These discussions resulted in a "compromise." The White House
agreed to a series of pretests between the enactment and implementation of
any negative tax program that included "working poor" families, and Ribicoff
agreed to an "automatic trigger provision" under which the program would
automatically go into effect on a certain date unless rejected by *either* House
of Congress as a result of information produced by the tests. An assistant to
Ribicoff explained,

> What Ribicoff really wanted was a pilot program of the President's
> proposal. Then they would look at the results and design a pro-
> gram on the basis of these results. The Administration opposed
> this—they wanted an automatic trigger if a pilot program was put
> into effect. Ribicoff opposed an automatic trigger but the liberal
> welfare groups persuaded him to support a trigger. They were
> infuriated when he announced his decision to test the program
> in the first place. He was sensitive about the results of the Social
> Service amendments he sponsored as Secretary of HEW and wanted
> a pilot program before he did anything else in welfare. But he was
> frozen into his position by the supporters of the proposal worked out
> with Sargent.

A new version of the Ribicoff-Sargent welfare proposal was distributed by Ribicoff's office on April 28, 1972. The only change in the original

plan was that it now included a provision establishing a series of demonstration projects to test provisions pertaining to "working poor" families before they automatically went into effect on a certain date unless rejected by a majority vote of *both* Houses of Congress.

Program Design: Senate Finance

An election year is a good time to support a Social Security increase but not a guaranteed income for families with children. Senator Long knew President Nixon and supporters in the Senate would not want to be fighting for the Family Assistance Plan during the peak of the 1972 presidential and senatorial campaigns and that FAP's chances would grow slimmer as November drew closer. Consequently, anticipating the Senate would not approve the kind of reforms preferred by a majority of the Finance Committee and preferring AFDC to the new family programs in H.R.1, Long's strategy was to delay Senate action on welfare until as late into the 1972 election year as possible.

President Nixon's anti-inflation measures announced August 15, 1971 included a one year postponement of the House approved starting dates for the new adult and family programs in H.R.1. Supporters and opponents of H.R.1 interpreted this delay as evidence the President was backing away from welfare reform. Ribicoff said he "was dismayed" that the President had "undercut the chances for welfare reform by postponing its implementation" and he rejected any economic arguments for this delay.[23] Long, however, remarked that he welcomed the postponement because "it would give the Finance Committee an opportunity to study some alternatives."[24] He would not say when the Committee would report a welfare bill and it was obvious the delay had reduced the pressure on him to expedite Committee action on H.R.1.

In October, four months after House passage of H.R.1, Ribicoff threatened to offer the Ribicoff-Sargent program as a floor amendment to either a pending tax bill or Social Security increase if the Finance Committee did not begin deliberations on the House bill. Long told reporters that if Ribicoff attached his welfare proposal to either of the bills, "you'll see the fight of your life. . . . We'll still be fighting that measure when you're up to your knees in snow and we might be here till spring."[25] Meetings in October between Majority Leader Mike Mansfield, Administration officials, Ribicoff, and Long produced what Secretary Richardson and Senator Ribicoff thought was a commitment from Long to get welfare reform to the Senate floor by March of 1972. On March 27, 1972 President Nixon sent a "strongly worded" message to Congress prodding the Committee to speed up action on welfare reform. Senator Long replied, "I suggest that the Administration folks keep their britches on long enough for us to act. . . . We're moving along as fast as we know how."[26]

From March until June 13, 1972 the Finance Committee conservatives toiled away on a welfare reform package. To the amazement of Senate
liberals and pro-welfare organizations and news reporters, the Committee's
alternative to FAP got progressively worse and, when finally completed, they
summarily dismissed it as "an abomination." In March, in order to prevent a
person from receiving more than one welfare check by applying under different
names and furnishing Social Security cards issued in those names, the Committee voted to require that Social Security numbers be issued to every child
upon entering the first grade, to all immigrants upon entry into the country,
and to all welfare applicants who do not already have a number. In April, the
following provisions were approved:

1. To encourage state and local officials to prosecute cases of welfare fraud
   more vigorously, those units of government would be allowed to retain
   a larger share of recovered money.
2. A mother seeking AFDC benefits would have to agree to cooperate in trying
   to locate the father of dependent children as a condition of eligibility.
3. AFDC mothers afraid to seek child support payments from the fathers of
   their children would be required to assign their rights to institute action
   in such cases to law enforcement officials.
4. A portion of child support payments received by AFDC families from the
   father of the children would be disregarded in calculating welfare benefits.
5. The use of federal funds for welfare suits against the Federal Government
   without specific authorization by the Attorney General was prohibited.

On April 28, by a vote of 10 to 4, with Ribicoff, Hartke, Harris, and Nelson
opposing the motion, the Committee replaced the FAP and OFF programs
for families in H.R.1 with a new "Guaranteed Employment Opportunity
Program." Under this "workfare" program, families headed by ablebodied
fathers or ablebodied mothers (with no child under six years of age) would
be ineligible for AFDC benefits. It was estimated that this would remove about
1.2 million current recipients from the AFDC rolls. These families would be
eligible to participate in an employment program providing a "guaranteed
job opportunity" at a wage of $1.20 an hour or $2,400 a year. Employed
heads of families working for at least $1.20 an hour would be provided a
"wage supplement" of three-fourths the difference between their pay and the
minimum wage of $1.60 an hour. Family heads employed in jobs covered by
the Social Security or Railroad Retirement programs would receive a "work
bonus" equal to 10 percent of their wage income up to $4,000. Single indi-
viduals and childless couples would not be eligible to participate in these "workfare" programs.

In May the Committee voted to cut federal welfare grants to
states in which over 3 percent of the AFDC recipients were found to be either

underpaid, overpaid, or ineligible. Measures were approved making the federal "locater" service available in tracking down "runaway fathers" who fail to support their children, and instructing HEW to establish regional laboratories for blood typing to help establish paternity in a case in which a male denies he is the father of a child.

In June they voted to cut off federal welfare payments to drug addicts and alcoholics who were not undergoing treatment; to authorize states to drop families from welfare in cases where a man, although not the legal father, had by his presence in the home over a period of time "placed himself in the long term position of head of the household"; and to penalize states that failed to provide birth control counseling and devices for the poor. The work requirement approved in April was modified so that a mother with school-age children who refused to accept available work would continue to receive full welfare payment for one month. After a month, payments covering the children's needs would be made to a third party—a relative or "landlord."

On June 13, 1972, a year after House passage of H.R.1, Senate Finance announced tentative approval of a welfare reform bill. Along with the provisions pertaining to cash assistance programs for families described above, the bill prohibited states from reducing AFDC benefits below $2,400 for a family of four; required states to establish a three-month residency requirement; and required recipients to allow case workers to enter their homes.

At this point the Committee had dropped the new federal program for the aged, blind, and disabled that had been approved by the House. Under the legislation tentatively approved by the Committee in June, the existing federal-state public assistance programs would be maintained. However, the federal share of costs for aged, blind, and disabled programs would be increased and national minimum payment standards of $130 a month for an individual recipient and $195 for a couple would be established. The bill also proposed a 10 percent increase in Social Security payments retroactive to June 1972— twice the increase authorized by the House in H.R.1.

Shown in Table 7-3, two sets of cost estimates for the family programs in the Finance Committee bill and the House-approved H.R.1 were produced: one prepared by HEW and the other by Robert Myers, consultant to the Finance Committee and former Chief Actuary of the Social Security Administration. HEW estimated that in 1974, federal costs for family programs in H.R.1 would be about $9.5 billion and that the Guaranteed Employment Opportunity program for families in the Committee bill would cost $18 billion (HEW estimated the family programs in the Ribicoff-Sargent plan would cost approximately $17 billion in 1974). Myers's estimates showed the programs for families in H.R.1 and the Committee bill costing the same: $11.5 billion in 1974, an increase of $4.5 billion over existing public assistance programs.

Table 7-3. Cost Estimates of Family Programs in H.R.1 and Senate
Finance Committee Bill by HEW and Myers, Fiscal 1974
(billions of dollars)

Program Components	H.R.1		Finance Bill	
	HEW Estimate	Myers Estimate	HEW Estimate	Myers Estimate
Government employment	$–	$ –	$ 5.7	$ 2.6
Wage supplement	–	–	1.7	.3
Children's allowance	–	–	.5	–
10% work bonus	–	–	1.1	1.2
Welfare payments	5.1	7.1	3.2	3.7
Cost of cashing out food stamps	1.5	1.5	1.8	1.8
Child care:	.8	.8	1.5	.8
Additional included in gov't employment				(0.4)
Public service jobs	.8	.8	–	–
Services, training	.6	.6	.8	.4
Administration:	.7	.7	1.7	.7
Additional included in gov't employment				(0.4)
Total	$9.5	$11.5	$18.0	$11.5
Total Cost Under Existing Programs	$7.0	$ 7.0	$ 7.0	$ 7.0
Net Increased Cost	$2.5	$ 4.5	$11.0	$ 4.5

Source: U.S., Senate, Finance Committee, *Staff Data On H.R.1: Analysis of Cost of Committee Bill,* 92nd Congress, 2nd sess., June 12, 1972, p. 11.

Program Design: The Administration

President Nixon would not support a proposal for reforming AFDC
as expensive as either the Ribicoff-Sargent plan or, according to HEW estimates,
the family programs developed in the Finance Committee. Furthermore, he
opposed the "Federal Government as employer of last resort" concept underlying the Committee's "workfare" program. In 1972, three courses of action
were debated within the White House by those aware of Nixon's dissatisfaction
with the two principal alternatives to FAP developed in the Senate. John D.
Ehrlichman, Assistant to the President for Domestic Affairs and executive
director of the President's Domestic Council, maintained that H.R.1 represented
a middle ground between the Ribicoff and Long proposals and that the Administration should continue to support only the House-approved family
programs. Secretary of HEW Richardson, Undersecretary Veneman, and Labor
Secretary Hodgson wanted to create a center-left majority in the Senate by
negotiating a compromise with Ribicoff. Clark MacGregor, counsel to the
President for congressional relations, Presidential Assistant William E. Timmons,

and Tom C. Korologos, deputy presidential assistant for congressional relations and former administrative assistant to Senator Wallace Bennett, the ranking Republican on Senate Finance, argued that the best course of action would be to develop a center-right majority by working out a compromise bill with Senators Long and Bennett.

The debate between Nixon's advisers took place within a White House welfare reform working group, which was chaired by Ehrlichman and included Richardson, Veneman, Hodgson, MacGregor, Korologos, Treasury Secretary George P. Schultz, Director of OMB Caspar Weinberger, and Deputy HEW Undersecretary Richard P. Nathan. Discussing the welfare reform working group, Ehrlichman explained to a reporter,

> the President is charting the course here . . . so that it (the welfare reform working group) isn't a debating society. It is a forum for deciding how to get done that which the President wants done. He's calling the shots.[27]

Shortly after the episode over the disclosure of HEW costs estimates of the Ribicoff-Sargent plan and after agreement was reached on Ribicoff's proposed pilot programs, negotiations between Richardson and Ribicoff were approved by the President and Ehrlichman. Weekly meetings were instituted between Geoffrey Peterson, legislative assistant to Ribicoff, James Edwards from HEW, and Paul Barton representing Labor, with Mitchell Ginsberg, dean of Columbia University's School of Social Work and former New York City Human Resources administrator, and Leonard Lesser, counsel for the Center for Community Change, serving as consultants for both Ribicoff and HEW. The meetings were closely monitored by Ribicoff and Richardson, but it was not clear the extent to which Richardson could speak for the President in these negotiations or how much, if any, direct communication he had with him on the issues being discussed.

While these negotiations were going on between Ribicoff and HEW, Korologos, MacGregor, and others, under direction from Ehrlichman, were monitoring the Senate Finance Committee deliberations and attempting to move the Committee's final product closer to H.R.1. When Senate Finance announced its "guaranteed job opportunity" program near the end of April, Richardson and Hodgson called a press conference and denounced it as "a $9 billion step backward, backward into the leaf-raking schemes of the 1930s."[28] MacGregor and Korologos, however, were still holding out for a possible compromise with the Committee, and in late May Ehrlichman said,

> We are talking to the Republicans of the Senate Finance Committee about the Chairman's proposal and we're finding out that it is not yet crystallized. There's quite a lot of flexibility regarding certain principles.[29]

By May Secretary Richardson and Senator Ribicoff, on the basis of polls taken by both their offices, were convinced there were not enough votes for either H.R.1 or the Ribicoff-Sargent proposal. Ribicoff called a meeting of the senators who had endorsed his bill to ask their support for a series of compromises his staff was discussing with HEW. Those present made it clear they would approve a compromise only if it contained significant improvements in H.R.1: they preferred the existing AFDC program to the new family programs in H.R.1.

Richardson, convinced an acceptable compromise with Senate Finance was impossible, intensified his efforts to obtain Administration support for an accommodation with Ribicoff. Throughout May he tried in vain to see Nixon personally to explain details of the compromises under discussion. His requests for a meeting were turned down on grounds that the President was busy preparing for his trip to Moscow and Richardson was compelled to make his arguments to the President through Ehrlichman. At the urging of Senators and groups supporting the Ribicoff bill, Moynihan tried unsuccessfully in May to reach Nixon by telephone in hopes of persuading him to agree to a compromise with Senate liberals. He finally wrote him a letter.

On June 16, a month after his initial request, Richardson met with Nixon in a meeting also attended by Ehrlichman, Weinberger, Korologos, and MacGregor. The day before this meeting Nixon received a letter signed by 19 Republican senators urging him to work out a compromise with Ribicoff.[30] At the meeting Richardson argued that some kind of a compromise between H.R.1 and the Ribicoff proposal was the only welfare program that could pass the Senate, and he recommended that the President immediately announce his support for a Ribicoff-Administration compromise position. According to a *National Journal* report on the meeting, Ehrlichman and Korologos countered the Republican letter and Richardson's recommendation with the warning that,

> a hasty move would only offend the Republican members of the Finance Committee whose support the President needed on such key votes as general revenue sharing and ratification of the SALT agreement. . . .
> Ehrlichman questioned the wisdom of President Nixon's closing ranks with many of Ribicoff's Democratic cosponsors, some of whom had been abusive of the President in the past three years and whose commitment to the President was suspect in an election year. He also noted that Ribicoff himself was a key adviser in McGovern's campaign and could not be counted on to support the President if such support might embarrass McGovern.[31]

By this time, June 1972, a welfare reform plan supported by Democratic Presidential candidate George McGovern had become a campaign issue. In January, in a speech at Iowa State University, Senator McGovern proposed that existing welfare programs be replaced with some form of a demo-grant system under which "every man, woman and child" would "receive from the Federal Government an annual payment."[32] As one of three illustra-tions used to explain the principle of demogrants, he proposed the Federal Government pay every person, rich or poor, $1,000 a year and thereby provide a poverty level minimum income of $4,000 for a family of four with no other income. The McGovern proposal received national publicity during the Califor-nia presidential primary election in May, when in a nationally televised debate Senator Hubert Humphrey charged that the $1,000-a-person program proposed by McGovern could cost upwards of $210 billion, and McGovern indicated he did not know exactly how much his proposal might cost.[33]

In light of the strong negative reaction to the McGovern proposal following the televised debates, it was obvious to everyone including Richardson and Ribicoff that, at this point, politically it was more advantageous for Nixon to publicize and oppose his opponent's guaranteed income plan than to ener-getically seek and possibly obtain enactment of his own. During a news confer-ence on June 22 Nixon was asked "how badly" he wanted a welfare bill to pass Congress and "how much" he was "willing to compromise either on the principle or the price tag of H.R.1." In response, Nixon said he wanted welfare reform and, referring to the family programs in H.R.1, that he support-ed the "position that has been overwhelmingly approved by the House. . . ."

> It provides for welfare for those who need it. It provides also for those incentives that will move people from welfare rolls to jobs, and it does so at a cost we can afford.

Repeating Ehrlichman's contention that H.R.1 was a middle position between Ribicoff and Long, Nixon added,

> My own present intention . . . is to stay by our middle position. I think it is the right position and I believe that it is a position that can get through this Congress.[34]

The next day Ribicoff revealed the major features of the compro-mise program worked out with Richardson, which had been implicitly rejected by Nixon in the news conference statement. Under the Ribicoff-Richardson compromise, the basic federal payment was $2,600 for a family of four, as compared to $2,400 under H.R.1 and $3,000 in the Ribicoff-Sargent proposal. This basic federal benefit would be increased to $3,000 by 1978 and states were required to supplement up to current public assistance levels. Supplemen-tation costs exceeding a state's 1971 welfare expenditures would be paid by the Federal Government.

There would be simplified eligibility determination procedures, work registration for mothers of preschool-age children would be optional, and no one would be required to take a job paying less than the federal minimum wage. Federal costs under this program for the first full year of operation were estimated to be about $12 billion.

Although Nixon also rejected the Senate Finance Committee's guaranteed employment program in his news conference statement, members of the Committee were not disappointed with the position he had taken. Senator Bennett said,

> I'm very pleased with the President's position. If he is neutral, he is neutral for us. And I hope, as it develops, he will move more in our direction.[35]

On June 27 the President had what was described as "a very relaxed meeting" with Republican members of the Finance Committee. According to a White House aide, Nixon told the senators,

> he wanted welfare reform very badly. That's why he did not come down with them, nor did he come down with Ribicoff. He told them, 'I don't agree with Ribicoff and I'm not going to agree with you guys. I want H.R.1.'[36]

Policy Alternatives and Choice

By midsummer no one was optimistic about the passage of legislation reforming AFDC. The Administration maintained a public posture of being "committed to the cause of welfare reform."[37] And, according to Ribicoff, Richardson continued to talk about a compromise. "I stopped taking his calls in the last days," Ribicoff said.

> It grew embarrassing. I never questioned his intent, his determination. But in the Nixon Administration it had become apparent the Cabinet doesn't amount to a tinker's damn.[38]

Long was still stalling. At one point Senator Ribicoff considered the possibility of working out a compromise with Long. Ribicoff's legislative assistant Geoffrey Peterson explained,

> It is amazing how close some essential parts of the Long "workfare" proposal were to our bill—or the Richardson-Ribicoff compromise. For example, our definition of employability was the same. The liberal groups—League of Women Voters, Common Cause, labor unions, the welfare groups, the *Post* and the *Times*— however, prevented us from working on a compromise with Long.

The name Mike Stern (Senate Finance Committee staff member) frightens them to death. Without them I think we would have worked out a compromise with Long. Ribicoff asked me to identify all the points on which we agreed with Long. But Ribicoff didn't want to be accused of 'selling out the poor' by the *Washington Post* or the *New York Times*, or by Senate liberals like Kennedy. He was frozen into a 'more liberal than Nixon' position by these groups. In the first place, welfare is not a popular issue. Second, if he compromised with Long they would have accused him of selling out the poor. All he could do was lose at both ends. His best position, similar to Nixon's was to stick with his proposal.

Finally, on September 26, 1972, fifteen months after the House passed H.R.1, Senate Finance reported a welfare reform bill. The Committee had replaced the FAP and OFF programs for families approved by the House with the Guaranteed Job Opportunity program described above. By this time, however, the Committee had reversed its earlier position and approved the federal guaranteed income program for the aged, blind, and disabled (SSI) developed by Ways and Means. A Senate staff member said,

> The Committee looked at the new program for aged and disabled adults early in the proceedings and they voted to change H.R.1 so the adult programs would remain under state administration. This motion was advocated by the "states' rights types" on the Committee. It took a big lobbying job by HEW to get the federal program approved by the House back into the Committee's bill.

With three weeks remaining before Congress was to adjourn, the debate over radical welfare reform moved to the Senate floor.

On September 28 Senator Ribicoff offered an amendment to the Committee bill on the Senate floor that would replace the guaranteed job program for families with the compromise program he had worked out with Secretary Richardson. He labeled his amendment the "Ribicoff-Administration compromise proposal." Before he had finished explaining the provisions of the program a courier from HEW arrived in the Senate press gallery with a news release from Secretary Richardson denying Administration support of the Ribicoff amendment. In the press release Richardson accused Ribicoff of having

> mistakenly labeled his new welfare proposal a "Ribicoff-Administration" compromise. The Senator knows very well that the Administration has consistently supported the House-passed version of H.R.1, and only that.

I am encouraged, however, to find that the Senator's amendments move a considerable distance away from his original position and toward the President's program. It is a sign, I believe, that those who are seriously interested in seeing reform enacted this year are coming to recognize that the President's H.R.1 proposals are the best welfare reform alternative available. The Senate may now be ready to engage in a serious and constructive debate on the welfare crisis, and to attempt seriously to deal with it. I hope so.

A copy of the news release with a note asking him to comment was sent to Ribicoff on the Senate floor by newspaper reporters Marjorie Hunter of the *New York Times* and Vincent Burke of the *Los Angeles Times.* On the back of the release Ribicoff scribbled, "More Administration doubletalk. It is time for Richardson to show the courage of his convictions."

Speaking to a nearly empty Senate chamber, Ribicoff questioned the President's commitment to welfare reform and said that in refusing to compromise Nixon had "run away from his own child." Nixon's commitment to FAP was also questioned by Senator Long, who responded to Ribicoff by saying,

> it was not the President who dreamed up the guaranteed income plan. The probabilities are if President Nixon were on the (Finance) Committee he would have voted the same way the other Republicans did.[39]

Senator Harry F. Byrd, Independent from Virginia, offered an amendment on September 30 that would replace most of the provisions pertaining to families in the Finance bill with a plan to test through a series of pilot programs the FAP and OFF programs approved by the House, Ribicoff's liberalized version of FAP, and the Finance Committee's guaranteed job program. Support for the motion to test the rival plans increased under threats of a filibuster by conservatives if it appeared as though either the House-approved family programs or the Ribicoff amendment might pass, and as it became apparent there were not enough votes to pass any of the proposed new programs for poor families.

On October 3 Senator Long said he was, "willing to stay here until Christmas, if necessary, to educate the Senate on the dangers of this idea of a guaranteed annual income."[40] However, in order to end the impasse, he said he was prepared to vote for the motion to test alternative welfare programs, which had been reintroduced by Republican Senator William Roth of Delaware. That same day the Ribicoff proposal was defeated when a motion by Long to table the Ribicoff amendment was approved 52 to 34.

The following day Senator Bennett, ranking Republican on Finance, said he would support the Roth-Byrd test proposal. He explained that he

> would have preferred to see the committee's so-called "workfare" program remain in the bill and become law. However, I realize that under the circumstances this is not possible. And under those circumstances I am delighted that the Senator from Delaware has offered his proposal, which should be fair to all of us who advocated different programs to solve the problem. . . . I am happy to join with the distinguished chairman of the Committee in supporting the amendment of the Senator from Delaware. I hope that all of our colleagues will also support it so that we can lay at rest once and for all the differences that exist with respect to the proper way to approach this problem. I certainly hope that the Senator's amendment is agreed to by the Senate. [41]

With the support of the Finance Committee Chairman and ranking Republican, and no word of opposition or support from the President, the Roth-Byrd amendment was adopted on October 4 by a vote of 46 to 41. Twelve of the sixteen members of the Finance Committee supported the motion.

Following approval of the Roth-Byrd plan, Democratic Senator Adlai Stevenson III of Illinois offered an amendment that proposed a program for families with provisions almost identical to those approved by the House in H.R.1, including a $2,400 minimum payment for a family of four. His motion was defeated 51 to 35.

Information presented in Tables 7-4 and 7-5 indicate fairly stable and predictable voting blocs on the Ribicoff, Roth-Byrd, and Stevenson proposals pertaining to the reform of AFDC. As shown in Table 7-4, a majority of both parties voted against the Ribicoff and Stevenson programs on recommittal motions and voted in support of the Roth-Byrd plan to test alternative programs. Over seventy-five percent of the liberal senators voted in support of the Ribicoff and Stevenson reform programs and against the Roth-Byrd pilot program proposal. In contrast, 94 percent of the conservatives voted against the Ribicoff program, 85 percent voted against the Stevenson program, and 82 percent supported the motion to test the rival welfare plans.

Information in Table 7-5 shows that support for the liberal position on the three votes generally came from senators representing states where the negative tax plan for families approved by the House in H.R.1 would have the least impact in terms of increasing the number of welfare recipients and decreasing state welfare costs. Senators supporting the conservative position on the votes were from states that would experience a moderate to large increase in welfare caseloads and moderate to large decrease in welfare costs under such a program.[42] As in the House roll call votes examined in Chapter

Table 7-4. Senate Votes on the Ribicoff, Roth-Byrd, and Stevenson Amendments

	Recommit Ribicoff Proposal			Approve Roth-Byrd Test Proposal			Recommit Stevenson Proposal		
	Yes (percent)	No (percent)	N	Yes (percent)	No (percent)	N	Yes (percent)	No (percent)	N
Party									
Democrats	59.6	40.4	(47)	51.5	48.9	(47)	58.7	41.3	(46)
Republicans	61.5	38.5	(39)	55.0	45.0	(40)	60.0	40.0	(40)
General Policy Orientation[a]									
Liberals	22.6	77.4	(31)	21.9	78.1	(32)	23.3	76.7	(30)
Moderates	63.6	36.4	(22)	52.4	47.6	(21)	68.2	31.8	(22)
Conservatives	93.9	6.1	(33)	82.4	17.6	(34)	85.3	14.7	(34)

Source: Congressional Quarterly Weekly Report (Washington, D.C.: Congressional Quarterly Service, January 15, 1972), pp. 74–80.
[a]Same as note (b), Table 6–2, Chapter 6.

Table 7-5.   Senate Votes on the Ribicoff, Roth-Byrd, and Stevenson Amendments

Policy Consequences of H.R.1	Recommit Ribicoff Proposal			Approve Roth-Byrd Test Proposal			Recommit Stevenson Proposal		
	Yes (percent)	No (percent)	N	Yes (percent)	No (percent)	N	Yes (percent)	No (percent)	N
Recipients[a]									
Percent state increase									
High	83.3	16.7	(30)	64.3	35.7	(28)	79.3	20.7	(29)
Moderate	60.0	40.0	(35)	54.1	45.9	(37)	54.1	45.9	(37)
Low	28.6	71.4	(21)	36.4	63.6	(22)	40.0	60.0	(20)
Welfare Costs[b]									
Percent state increase									
High	87.1	12.9	(31)	67.7	32.3	(31)	78.1	21.9	(32)
Moderate	51.5	48.5	(33)	50.0	50.0	(34)	54.5	45.5	(33)
Low	36.4	63.6	(22)	36.4	63.6	(22)	38.1	61.9	(21)

[a]Same as note (a), Table 6-3, Chapter 6.
[b]Same as note (b), Table 6-3, Chapter 6.

Six, liberals and conservatives and senators from states that would experience the greatest and least amount of change in welfare under H.R.1 were generally in opposition on Senate roll call votes pertaining to the reform of AFDC. The crucial difference, and the reason radical reform of AFDC passed in the House but failed in the Senate, was that whereas a majority of moderate congressmen consistently voted in support of replacing AFDC with the negative tax plan in H.R.1, a majority of moderate senators consistently voted against similar proposals.

The Senate completed action on the welfare bill and House and Senate conferees began meeting to work out the differences between House passed H.R.1 and the Senate legislation just ten days before Congress was scheduled to adjourn. Unable to reach agreement in the short time remaining, the conferees dropped both the FAP and OFF programs for families in the House-passed bill and the Roth-Byrd pilot plan and remaining "workfare" provisions in the Senate legislation. On October 17, the day before the session ended, the Senate and House approved the conference report, which contained the new Supplemental Security Income Program for aged, blind, and disabled adults, but left the existing public assistance program for families—AFDC— unchanged.

DECISION CONDITIONS

The Supplemental Security Income Program (SSI) encompassed the same conceptual shifts—including a federal guaranteed income—that produced intense opposition to the Family Assistance Plan proposed by Nixon in 1969 and the modified version of this negative tax program for families with children approved by the House in 1971. SSI, however, was approved by the Senate because needy blind, aged, and disabled adults were seen as more deserving of help than poor families, because it did not cost as much or add as many new recipients to welfare rolls, and, most important, because the attention of the Senate was focused almost completely on the proposed programs for families. Describing action on the Senate floor, Ribicoff's legislative assistant said,

> people were so concerned about Title IV (the family provisions) that no one paid any attention to Title III (provisions pertaining to aged, blind, and disabled adults). If SSI had been on its own it never would have made it. Also, it passed because it looked like peanuts next to the family programs.

A Senate Finance Committee staff member told a reporter that "During conference, the SSI barely captured the conferees' attention."[43]

The preceding chapter explained House approval of a federal guaranteed income for families with children by identifying several conditions conducive to legislative approval of radical welfare change: the failure of existing programs, the existence of an innovative course of action sponsored by the President, and the presence and support of effective congressional leaders. An explanation of why a negative tax program for families was not approved by the Senate in 1972 is offered in the following paragraphs in terms of identifying important changes in these conditions.

Welfare 1972: A Diminishing Crisis

After three years of unprecedented growth, public assistance costs and caseloads appeared to have stabilized or leveled off by mid 1971 and throughout 1972. News accounts and HEW reports indicated this new stability in public assistance, especially AFDC, was largely a result of "welfare cutbacks" or "welfare tightening" measures undertaken by state and local governments.

The *New York Times* reported in July 1971, a month after the House approved H.R.1, that a "confidential" HEW survey found "welfare cutbacks" had been approved and would be in effect in 10 states by the end of the year. Twelve more states were considering similar actions and legislative attempts to reduce payments had failed in four states. The reported "cutbacks" included the dropping of 6,000 families from AFDC rolls in Alabama, elimination of the unemployed parent program (AFDC-UP) in Maine, a 20 percent cut in maintenance payments in Kansas, a 10 percent reduction in AFDC benefits in South Dakota, and a 10 percent reduction in the New York City AFDC payment standard which would decrease payments to 85 percent of all families receiving AFDC in the state.[44] An updated HEW report, which Senator Ribicoff inserted in the *Congressional Record* on October 20, 1971, showed that from July 1970 to September 1971 twenty states had reduced their AFDC payments through legislative or administrative changes.[45]

On August 2, 1971, the third day of Senate Finance Committee hearings on H.R.1, the *Washington Post* reported,

> welfare tightening in at least six states has contributed to the smallest monthly increase in two years for the nation's major relief program.[46]

HEW statistics released the end of August, and reported in a front page story in the *Washington Post* on August 26, showed the nation's public assistance caseload had dropped by .3 percent in April 1971. This was the first decrease in three years.[47] In September, Jule M. Sugarman, Human Resources Administrator for New York City, announced the fourth straight month without a significant increase in welfare recipients and said the growth in New York City's welfare rolls appeared to have "reached a plateau."[48]

Reports of monthly decreases in the number of public assistance recipients and substantial reductions in the annual growth rate of the programs continued throughout 1972.[49] In October 1972, when the Senate was debating alternative AFDC reform programs, the latest figures showed a 6 percent yearly increase in AFDC recipients and a 4 percent increase in total public assistance recipients, as compared to a 20 to 35 percent increase in AFDC and a 14 to 20 percent increase in all programs in each of the previous three years.[50] The day before the vote on Ribicoff's alternative to the "workfare" programs in the Senate Finance legislation, Senator Harry F. Byrd, Jr. told the Senate,

> Today's *New York Times,* in column 8 on page 1, states that a dramatic decrease in welfare case load persons and expenditures for July is to be announced by the (New York City) Human Resources Administration.
>
> That is good news. Finally the people themselves, the taxpayers, are waking up to the fact that the politicians and the administrators have been squandering and wasting their money and putting people on welfare rolls who have no right to be there and, in many cases, as has been brought out a number of times by the Senator from Louisiana [Mr. Long] where the same person has drawn four, five, or six welfare checks. So I think it is very important that the administrators tighten up on the administration of the laws. It is good to know that New York State at long last is beginning to do this.[51]

To many Senators the rapid increase in AFDC costs and caseloads during the past several years appeared to be the essence of the "welfare crisis." For them, the apparent stability if not decline in welfare recipients attributed to state cutbacks and attempts to "tighten up welfare" removed the primary incentive to radically change the present system.

Other developments that to some conservative Senators appeared to further reduce the need for drastic reform of AFDC included passage in December 1971 of a revised Work Incentive Plan sponsored by Senate Finance member Herman Talmadge of Georgia. This legislation incorporated a number of work related provisions in H.R.1 including a more stringent and less discretionary work requirement for AFDC recipients, the creation of public service jobs to provide employment for welfare recipients, and authorization of $750 million to expand day care and other child services for welfare mothers. Congressman John Byrnes said he "reluctantly" voted for this legislation when it was before the House, not because he opposed tougher work requirements, but because he was concerned it would hurt the chances for Senate passage of H.R.1 "by taking away what some consider the sweetener."[52]

A primary objective of those in the Administration who designed the original Family Assistance Plan was to provide benefits for "working poor" families ineligible for federal welfare benefits in most states. Many liberals in the House who voted for the FAP and OFF programs in H.R.1 did so mainly

because "working poor" families would be better off under these programs.
However, by mid 1972 food stamps were available to all persons with incomes
below a certain level—including "working poor" families—in almost all parts
of the country. The value of food stamp allotments had been increased substantially and the number of recipients had grown from 2 million in 1969 to 11
million in 1972.[53] The Senate Select Committee on Nutrition reported in
March 1972 that, because of provisions in H.R.1 as approved by the House
of Representatives prohibiting cash recipients from receiving food stamps,
"working poor" families in 42 states were likely to receive lower total welfare
benefits than they were currently eligible for under the expanded food stamp
program.[54]

In other words, because of the expansion of food stamps since
FAP was first introduced, and because of changes made by the Ways and
Means Committee prohibiting cash recipients from receiving food stamps,
the enactment of the family programs in H.R.1 would have reduced the total
amount of cash and in-kind benefits many "working poor" families could
receive under existing programs. This reduced the enthusiasm of some members
of the Administration and the incentive for liberal Senators to support the
family programs in H.R.1. According to Richard Nathan, Deputy Undersecretary of HEW in 1972, the expansion of the food stamp program was "a
basic reason why FAP failed" in the Senate in 1972.[55]

Administration officials and members of Congress agreed that
the financial pressures on some state and local governments partially due to
increasing welfare costs, and the lobbying of state and local officials in support
of welfare legislation that would provide fiscal relief, were crucial in obtaining
Nixon's support for, and House approval of, radical welfare change. The pressure
on some Senators to support H.R.1 was reduced when the House passed Nixon's
revenue sharing bill on June 22, 1972—the same day Nixon announced his
decision not to compromise with Ribicoff on welfare reform. At this point
governors, mayors, and other state and local officials shifted their attention
and lobbying efforts in the Senate from welfare reform to revenue sharing
because it would provide state and local governments more money than H.R.1
and they would receive it sooner. Furthermore, by the summer of 1972 few
expected welfare reform to pass; but, with Congressmen Mills and Byrnes,
Senate leaders Mansfield, Scott, Long, and Bennett supporting revenue sharing,
everyone expected it to become law before the end of the congressional session.

Policy developments and administrative modifications, in other
words, appeared to have slowed down if not stopped the increases in AFDC
recipients, eased the financial problems of states, established a firmer and more
enforceable work requirement, and increased the resources of poor people,
especially "working poor" families. Problems constituting the "welfare crisis"
as perceived by conservatives and liberals had to some extent been mitigated

by 1972. Consequently, there was less of an incentive for Senators to support expensive and radical welfare changes with unpredictable results.

Equally important, the attention of the President and at least one-third of the Senate had shifted to a competing domestic problem: the 1972 elections. Referring to the family programs in H.R.1, a White House aide told an interviewer in 1972,

> This particular bit of legislation is a delicate flower, and delicate flowers don't grow in hailstorms. . . . This far into the election year, we're in a hailstorm. What you need is an oak, such as increasing Social Security cash benefits—a perfect example of a bill that will pass with a Republican President and a Democratic Congress in a presidential election year.[56]

Senator Hubert Humphrey's attacks on the McGovern welfare plan during the televised California primary election debates brought radical welfare change to the public's attention and made welfare reform more useful to Nixon as a campaign issue than an accomplishment. The support of some Senators for radical reform was withdrawn or weakened because they were not sure their constitutents would distinguish between McGovern's proposal to guarantee every family $1,000 per person, Ribicoff's plan to provide every poor family of four $750 per person, or the programs in H.R.1 that would pay every poor four-member family $600 per person. Ribicoff's legislative assistant said that by June of 1972, after the California primary election debates were televised, the McGovern proposal "became the major welfare issue."

> When the McGovern bill became public, and McGovern told Humphrey he did not know how much it would cost, our office and the Senate Finance Committee were deluged with letters and telegrams regarding the McGovern bill. . . . McGovern's proposal made all welfare reform suspect—made people look at the costs and caseloads. It scared senators from doing anything about welfare. When Nixon refused to accept the Ribicoff-Richardson compromise we decided to wait until it came up on the floor. We dropped the minimum level from $2,800 to $2,600 and I wanted to demonstrate that this would bring us more support. But I called a lot of offices for cosponsors and most of them wouldn't touch it—particularly those up for election. . . . A good number of those who had supported our earlier, more liberal proposal would not cosponsor the more conservative one after the McGovern proposal. So we decided to go without sponsors because a drop would look bad. We had anticipated more, not fewer, sponsors.

In sum, one reason radical reform of AFDC was not approved by the Senate was because the severity and relative importance of the "welfare crisis," as perceived by conservative and liberal Senators and the President, were significantly diminished by mid 1972.

Reduced Presidential Resolve

The personal involvement that characterized President Nixon's activities in behalf of his welfare reform plan in 1970 and early 1971 was missing in 1972: the kind of personal and energetic involvement conducive to congressional approval of radical welfare change. In regard to FAP and other welfare issues he met several times with Wilbur Mills and John Byrnes and held special breakfasts in the White House for Republican congressmen in 1970 and early 1971. He addressed the National Governors Conference in Washington in February 1970, spoke to the 50th annual convention of the Junior Chamber of Commerce in St. Louis in June, met with key Finance Committee members at San Clemente in August, met with other congressional leaders and visited the Washington headquarters of the Retail Clerks International Association in November—all in behalf of welfare reform.[57] Ehrlichman acknowledged that the President was spending less "personal time" on welfare in 1972 than he had previously. He explained,

> there simply has not been that much for him to do. . . . That ground has been pretty well plowed, and we know what his position is on most of the alternatives and derivatives that are possible.[58]

The Family Assistance Plan was not approved by the Senate in 1972 in large part because Nixon did not want the programs in H.R.1 or a compromise with liberals: not enough to expend the time and energy required, make the phone calls, personal visits, and requests necessary to shift enough votes to H.R.1 or some other version of FAP. An important difference between Senate votes on welfare reform in 1972 and House votes in 1971 was that in the House most "moderate" congressmen voted in support of the negative tax program for families in H.R.1, whereas in the Senate moderates generally voted against similar proposals (compare information in Table 6–2 and Table 7–4). Moderates in both Houses were less likely than liberals or conservatives to be ideologically committed or have firm policy positions on the issue of welfare. They were probably the most receptive to cues and requests from the President and House leaders in House votes on H.R.1 and would have responded to similar leadership in the Senate if it had been forthcoming. It was not.

In May 1972, after Secretary of HEW Richardson and Labor Secretary Hodgson denounced the "workfare" program developed by the

Finance Committee, Senator Long told an interviewer that the Committee relied on HEW for statistical work and advice, but that there was "no attempt to resolve basic differences in approaching welfare reform." The White House, however, was a different matter. Long said:

> I just haven't seen any indication from the White House that they are against what we are trying to achieve. I am talking about the President. I am talking about Mr. Ehrlichman, Mr. Korologos, or just anybody at the White House who has asked to talk to me about the problems of the President.[59]

Before the Senate voted on the Stevenson $2,400 minimum benefit program similar to the family provisions in H.R.1, Ribicoff appealed from the Senate floor for support from the Administration,

> the time has come to ask the President of the United States and the Secretary of Health, Education, and Welfare, Mr. Richardson, to come out of hiding. . . .
> Here is a proposal introduced by two Republicans and one Democrat which calls for $2,400, which is the figure originally proposed by the President and passed by the House. I ask you, President Nixon, wherever you may be, . . . will you tell the American people, do you support welfare reform? . . . Come to the Congress of the United States, call the Republican members of the U.S. Senate and tell them you still support a payment level of $2,400. This is the chance for the President of the United States and the Secretary of Health, Education, and Welfare to tell the American people whether they are for welfare reform.[60]

Senate Minority Leader Hugh Scott, Republican from Pennsylvania, acknowledged his approval of the Stevenson plan after Ribicoff made his plea for some word from the President. When Senator Long asked Scott if President Nixon supported the proposal, Scott said he was,

> not able to say that the President of the United States supports the proposal. The President has not said to me that he wishes me to make any statement against the proposal. If he wished to support the proposal, I assume he would send information to one or another Senator on that. I am speaking personally, . . . I have wrestled with this, and I am satisfied that I must support it.[61]

Long said he asked the question because he had been told by "two of the President's most well-regarded liaison people," and "not some Under Secretary of the Department of Health, Education, and Welfare, or some person in that agency who might even have been held over from the Roosevelt administration," that the President opposed the Stevenson proposal. "I think we ought to understand that this is not something that the President is for." [62]

Nixon's personal involvement in the 1972 Senate welfare debate was limited because his interest in welfare had declined: his attention and concerns had shifted to other problems and policy areas that were perceived as more pressing or promising. In late 1971 and throughout 1972 his major domestic concerns included inflation and the success of his new economic policy announced August 15, 1971, the upcoming presidential election and, after it received the support of Wilbur Mills, the passage of revenue sharing. Along with the election, Nixon was most interested in and personally occupied with Viet Nam, his trips to China, Russia, and other foreign affairs, and defense related matters.

According to Moynihan, during the development of FAP and the debate over radical welfare reform within the Administration in 1969 he had an "intangible but unmistakable advantage" over Arthur Burns because he operated out of the White House and Burns's office was next door in the Executive Office Building. [63] Nixon's personal involvement in welfare reform waned in 1971 and 1972 largely because, by this time, among those who had the greatest access to the President and the most influence in directing his attention and structuring his perceptions, interpretations, and preferences there was no one intensely committed to radical welfare change. At the end of 1970 Moynihan returned to Harvard. Finch had lost both interest in welfare and influence in the White House. A former Administration official who had been involved in the development of FAP said the President's interest and involvement in welfare reform was reduced in 1972 because,

> the people who supported the bill—especially Moynihan and
> Schultz—had left. Schultz moved to Treasury from OMB and was
> no longer in the welfare pipeline—was not in the decision loop
> for welfare. He didn't get the welfare memos. Moynihan, Schultz,
> and myself were replaced by Ehrlichman, who was sort of neutral
> on FAP initially, and guys like Buchanan and Huston, who were
> opposed to FAP. Another important change was replacing Cowen
> (White House liaison officer responsible for contacts with the
> Senate Finance Committee) with Korologos—who was Senator
> Bennett's former Administrative Assistant. Korologos was death
> on FAP. This surprised us. Before he moved to the White House,
> when we would go in to see Bennett he usually wouldn't come
> into the meetings and we felt he was either for the bill or didn't
> care. But he was opposed. So, Moynihan and others were replaced
> with a group opposed to FAP.

A Senate staff member said,

Tom Korologos, who was an assistant to Bennett and had moved over to the White House, was a major force in the White House against the Ribicoff compromise. He told the President not to lock himself into a Ribicoff compromise; that he should wait to see what the Finance Committee came up with. Korologos told the President he would have to work with Long and Bennett on other matters like the debt ceiling, which was coming up soon, and revenue sharing, and that he should try to work out a compromise with them or at least stick with H.R.1. This is a hell of a persuasive argument.

Secretary of HEW Richardson, Undersecretary Veneman, Secretary of Labor Hodgson, and others within the Administration most supportive of the family programs in H.R.1 faced the problem of limited support for FAP from the President's most consistent allies in the Senate and no support from the Republicans on the Finance Committee. There was no one to help them mobilize moderate and conservative Republican support as John Byrnes had done in the House. Senator Bennett, ranking Republican on Finance, supported FAP in 1970 but switched his position and, according to a Senate staff member, was "a strong force in opposition to H.R.1 in 1972." Senate proponents of radical welfare reform were liberal Republicans and Democrats, and Nixon was not used to siding with Ribicoff and liberal Republicans like Percy in opposition to normal allies like Senator Bennett. An HEW official said Nixon "was uncomfortable with this ideological grouping."

However, the basic problem Richardson, Veneman, and other supporters of FAP faced was limited access to Nixon. It took Richardson over a month to obtain a meeting with the President so he could personally explain the agreements worked out with Ribicoff. By the time the meeting was finally held the McGovern plan had received national publicity and opposition to a guaranteed income and expanding welfare costs had become a Republican campaign issue. Senator Ribicoff said Richardson was "an ardent and eloquent spokesman" for welfare reform.

But, as was soon demonstrated, he did not have the access to the President which Moynihan had had; there was no one in the White House to fight day-by-day for FAP. The long, slow process of defusing support for FAP began in the White House. The Ehrlichmans and Haldemans were now fully in control of domestic policy and did not have to deal with the liberal gadfly—Pat Moynihan.[64]

The Lack of Senate Leadership

Senate Republican leader Hugh Scott supported H.R.1 and favored liberalization of the House-passed family provisions. Senate Majority Leader Mike Mansfield, however, had doubts about H.R.1 and the concept of a guaranteed income. Senate liberals complained that Mansfield had failed to put sufficient pressure on the Finance Committee to speed up action on welfare even though he did attempt to get a commitment from Long to have H.R.1 out by March 1972. Other formal leaders, Senator Long and Senator Bennett, the chairman and ranking minority member of the committee responsible for welfare, opposed the family programs in H.R.1. In the Senate as well as the House, deference is granted the Chairman and ranking member and their opposition generally means defeat for a bill reported by their Committee.

However, even if the Senate leadership had favored FAP in 1972, there was no one among the formal leaders with the attention directing and preference shifting leverage exercised by Mills and Byrnes in the House—the kind of influence necessary to obtain legislative approval of radical change in welfare policy, especially in the absence of energetic Presidential support. There have been powerful Senate leaders in the past. The Senate is susceptible to this type of leadership as demonstrated by the direction and influence Lyndon Johnson exercised when he was Majority Leader.[65] If Ribicoff had had the help of a Majority Leader like Johnson, a version of FAP might have been approved despite limited support from the White House.

Because effective leadership was lacking in the Senate, welfare deliberations and attempts to design a reform program for families in 1972 were fragmented. What one Senate staff member called the "leadership vacuum" was filled in part by interest groups. Separate groups of senators supported by different interest groups went in opposite directions. Long and Bennett with encouragement from the Chamber of Commerce and other conservative interest groups developed their "workfare" proposal. Ribicoff with assistance and support from liberal welfare groups designed his liberalized version of FAP. Similar proposals supported by the same groups were put forward in the House but never made the Ways and Means or House welfare agenda.

The following excerpts from letters written by the Ad Hoc Committee Against Bogus Federal Welfare Reform, following private meetings with Senators Edward Brooke and Edward Kennedy, suggest how some liberal groups proceeded in their attempts to structure the attention, perceptions, and behavior of certain senators during the H.R.1 debate. The letter to Senator Brooke said:

> We are writing to review the areas of agreement we reached with you during our appointment on April 14. Before doing that, we want to convey the group's feeling that it was a good meeting, both because we felt you heard our deep concern over the dangers

of H.R.1 seriously eroding the rights of welfare recipients and because we, in turn, heard your awareness of and sensitivity to this issue.

We appreciated an opportunity to discuss possible strategies for dealing with the fact that the Ribicoff amendments are not an answer to this problem, since they have virtually no chance of surviving the Joint-Conference process and, even if they did, do not sufficiently alter the basic framework of H.R.1 to remove our objections.

In view of this, we urged you to publicly state you would vote against H.R.1 and the Ribicoff amendments. You felt that since there was some chance the bill might never come out of the Senate Finance Committee, you were more comfortable with a strategy which would keep your options open. You agreed to meet with us for further discussion if the bill comes out of committee.

To recapitulate the areas of agreement: You agreed that we could quote you as saying you are "against H.R.1 in its present form." Further, that you "are very doubtful of the possibility of the survival of any amendments." You stated that you are "very disturbed about the rights issues." You agreed to raise and discuss with some of your colleagues the threat the violation of the rights of *any* part of the citizenry poses to the rights of *all* of us. More specifically, you agreed to make clear to your fellow senators the areas in H.R.1 that threaten recipients: lack of due process, forced work at less than minimum wage, no options on child care facilities, etc. It was agreed that the goal would be to have your colleagues participate in an endeavor to educate the public as to the real nature of H.R.1—not a reform bill, but a bill that seeks to control the poor.

In response to our statements that we need you to give voice to these concerns and offer the public information, interpretation, and leadership, you agreed to make public statements and/or speeches helping Americans to understand what is wrong with H.R.1 and why it is not reform legislation.

To Senator Kennedy they wrote:

Reviewing our meeting with you on April 3, we all agreed that while we really never had any serious doubts that you would give leadership to the struggle to defeat H.R.1, it was very reassuring to get that commitment from you.

As we explained, the idea that H.R.1 is a welfare "reform" bill is firmly fixed in most people's minds and the need is urgent for interpretation that the bill is repressive—dangerous to *all* citizens because it is a threat to the rights of *some* citizens. This is the reason we stressed the urgency of your finding occasions to speak publicly on this subject. It was our understanding that you were responsive to this need, leading us to look forward to statements from you that will enlighten the public.

We felt it was very helpful that we were able to clarify together that a down vote on H.R.1 is no real threat to Titles I, II, and III since we all agreed—with the helpful insights of Mr. Manning of the Council of Older Americans—that these titles could easily pass as a separate bill once H.R.1 is defeated.

Your statement that you would vote against H.R.1 was consistent with your speech of January 17 that the bill was "primitive in philosophy, pitiless in substance, and punitive in practice." The discussion about the Ribicoff amendments has so muddied the waters that it was relieving to hear you agree that you "do not stand in a different place" from our view that on top of not correcting H.R.1's basic flaws, the amendments clearly don't have a chance in Joint-Conference.

The influence of interest groups in the Senate welfare deliberations was indicated in Senator Ribicoff's rejection late in 1972 of the possibility of working on a compromise with Long. Ribicoff decided against approaching Long because he felt "frozen into a more-liberal-than-Nixon position by the liberal groups," not because he was convinced a Ribicoff-Long compromise that represented improvements in AFDC was unattainable.

In sum, there were no Senate leaders who could bridge the ideological and communication gap between the liberals and conservatives and between Congress and the Executive branch, or with the leverage to keep attention and welfare deliberations focused on designing a proposal which the President would support and was likely to pass on the Senate floor.

STATE OF WELFARE 1974

The perceived "crisis" in welfare, lobbying of state and local officials, energetic sponsorship by the President, and the support of powerful House leaders were identified in Chapter Six as conditions conducive to House approval of radical welfare reform in 1971. Radical reform of AFDC failed in the Senate in 1972 because by this time policy developments had reduced pressure for reform, upcoming elections diverted attention of policy makers away from welfare, support in the White House for such a move had diminished significantly, and, in the Senate, a guaranteed income for families was not supported by powerful Congressional leaders. In the 1973 State of the Union Message on Human Resources, three and one-half years after the Administration's welfare reform plan was first announced over national television, President Nixon formally abandoned further attempts to obtain congressional approval of FAP. At a press conference on March 2, he told reporters:

. . . with regard to Family Assistance, I thought at the time that I
approved it—and this view has not changed—that it was the best
solution to what I have termed, and many others have termed
before me, the "welfare mess." I believe that it is essential that
we develop a new program and a new approach to welfare in
which there is a bonus not for welfare but a bonus, if there is
to be one, for work. . . . The Family Assistance Program I thought
then, and I think now, is the best answer.

Now, there are many who object to it, and because of those objections there is no chance—and we have checked this out. . . .
There is no chance that we can get it through the Senate because
of the objections, on the one side, to any Family Assistance Program at all, on principle, and to objections, on the other side,
if we put up the program to raise the price tag so high that we
could not possibly afford it.

So we have to find a different way. . . . The family assistance
may be part of that answer, but I know we are going to have to
change it in order to get a vote. . . .[66]

Although the Family Assistance Plan or a version of FAP—the
"cornerstone" of the Administration's new "income" approach to welfare—
had not been enacted, several changes in U.S. welfare programs were in effect
by 1974, largely as a result of the issues raised and the policy review and debate initiated by the Nixon welfare reforms proposed in 1969. The most
significant of these changes included the implementation of the new Supplemental Security Income (SSI) program, the stabilization of AFDC costs and
caseloads, and the modification and expansion of the food stamp program.

Assistance for the Aged, Blind and Disabled

The most dramatic policy shift directly related to the FAP debate
occurred with the implementation of SSI in January 1974. By the time SSI
actually replaced existing federal-state public assistance programs for the
aged, blind, and disabled (OAA, AB and APTD) a number of modifications
had been made in this new program approved in October 1972. In order to
protect OAA, AB, and APTD recipients from a reduction in benefits when
SSI went into effect, legislation was enacted in July 1973 requiring the states
to supplement federal SSI payments up to the December 1973 public assistance payment levels. States that failed to comply with this requirement would
lose federal matching funds for Medicaid.

In December 1973, less than a month before the first SSI checks
were to be mailed, the basic federal payments were increased to $140 per
month for an individual and $210 for a couple as of January 1, 1974—or date
of implementation. Further increases to $146 for a single person and $219

for a couple, effective July 1974 were also approved. The prohibition enacted
in 1972 against SSI recipients participating in the food stamp program was
repealed, except in those states where the state supplemental payments included the value of food stamps received before implementation of SSI.
The essential provisions of SSI as of January 1, 1974 were:

1. A *national uniform federal benefit,* which guaranteed a minimum yearly
    income of $1,680 to all needy aged, blind and disabled individuals and
    $2,520 for couples.
2. *Nationally uniform eligibility requirements,* including level and type of
    resources allowed and definitions of disability and blindness.
3. *State supplementation* of the basic federal cash benefit and *food stamp
    and Medicaid eligibility* for most SSI recipients to protect individuals
    from a reduction in benefits received before the implementation of the
    SSI program.
4. *Federal administration* of the basic benefit and incentives for federal ad-
    ministration of the state supplemental payment.[67]

      An estimated 2.8 million needy, aged, blind, and disabled individuals
were eligible for cash assistance under SSI who would not have been eligible
under existing public assistance programs in 1974, with the largest increase
occurring among aged persons. Over 4 million, or one out of every five Americans
over 65, were eligible for benefits under SSI as compared to 2 million under
public assistance.[68] It was initially estimated that the SSI program would
increase federal expenditures from $2.2 billion to $4.1 billion. More recent
projections show SSI costing the Federal Government $5.2 billion the first
full year of operation as compared to $2.6 billion for aid to needy aged, blind,
and disabled persons under public assistance.[69]

Cash Assistance for Families

      Table 7-6 shows the amount of federal and state expenditures for
AFDC and the number of recipients in June of each year from 1968 to 1973.
As indicated, from June 1969 to June 1971 the number of AFDC recipients
increased at a yearly rate of over 20 percent and expenditures at a rate exceeding 30 percent. However, between June 1971 and June 1972 the number of
recipients increased by only 7 percent and there was a small reduction in recipients between 1972 and 1973. The annual rate of increase in AFDC expenditures dropped to 12 percent between 1971 and 1972 and to 4 percent by June
1973. The stabilization in AFDC costs and recipients that became apparent in
late 1971 noticeably reduced the saliency of the program and the public concern and controversy AFDC generated during the years of rapid growth.

      A number of explanations have been offered for the stability in
AFDC since 1971, including the decline in unemployment in 1971 and 1972

Table 7-6. Number of AFDC Recipients and Federal and State
AFDC Expenditures as of June 1968 to 1973

Year	Number of Recipients (millions)	Percent Increase	Monthly Expenditures (thousands)	Percent Increase
1968	5.6		$234.7	
1969	6.6	17	288.3	23
1970	8.3	26	391.2	36
1971	10.2	23	509.7	30
1972	10.919	7	569.5	12
1973	10.912	0	591.3	4

Source: U.S., Department of Health, Education, and Welfare, *Public Assistance Statistics* (Washington, D.C.: Government Printing Office, October 1970, 1971, 1972 & 1973).

and the possibility that nearly everyone eligible for AFDC benefits was participating in the program by 1971. However, the reduced growth rate appeared to be due primarily to the efforts of state and local governments, with encouragement in the form of administrative directives from HEW, to "tighten up" welfare. Actions taken by different state and local governments with the objective of reducing AFDC recipients and expenditures included reducing AFDC benefit levels, using more restrictive eligibility determination standards and more stringent enforcement of the existing work requirement, reinstating residency requirements, and establishing new procedures for investigating cases of overpayment, ineligibility, and fraud.[70]

Richard Nathan, who was involved in the development of FAP and served as Deputy Undersecretary of HEW in 1972, related these restrictions and reductions in AFDC to the FAP debate:

> ... the discussion of a "crisis" in welfare—which in part the Administration generated; we had to talk about the problems of the present system if we were calling for reforms like FAP—produced some self-correction at the state and national level. The states and counties began to tighten up administration of AFDC on their own in hopes of reducing state costs. The moves in HEW to tighten up welfare during the 1971–72 Senate debate over FAP were, in part, strategic in nature.
>
> I firmly believed that HEW should be moving in the direction of better management of welfare talked about in FAP and H.R.1. John Veneman (Undersecretary of HEW in 1972) and I disagreed on this matter. The HEW bureaucrats were also opposed to administrative changes aimed at "tightening up." I felt we would get into trouble with the Republicans on Senate Finance if we were advocating a more "firm and fair" administrative procedure in H.R.1 but at the same time were not doing what was in our power

to do under existing law to move in this direction. . . . [T] he discussion of the "welfare crisis," uncontrollable costs, lax administration produced this kind of a self-corrective reaction.

In-Kind Assistance for Families
Modifications in the food stamp program were enacted in1971
and 1973 which substantially increased the number of food stamp recipients.
These changes reflected some of the issues and concerns—assisting the "working poor," establishing national eligibility and benefit standards—that were
raised to the agenda of national politics by the FAP debate.

Specific changes approved in 1971 and implemented in 1972 included: (1) the establishment of uniform national eligibility standards for
food stamps; (2) an increase in the value of food stamps allotted to a family
considered sufficient to purchase a nutritionally adequate diet; (3) the provision of free food stamps for the lowest income households and the requirement
that payments for food stamps were not to exceed 30 percent of a family's
income; (4) a requirement that the value of the food stamp allotment be ad-
justed annually to reflect changes in the prices of food published by the Bureau
of Labor Statistics; and (5) establishment of a work registration requirement.
A provision enacted in 1973 required *every* political subdivision in *all* states
to implement the food stamp program by July 1, 1974; and the requirement of
an annual price-of-food adjustment in food stamp allotments was changed
to provide for semiannual adjustments.

These changes resulted in the development of a nationwide federal,
income in-kind type of negative tax program for all needy Americans including "working poor" families. As of July 1, 1974 all four member families
in the U.S. with an annual income of $6,000 or less were eligible for a yearly
food stamp coupon allotment of $1,800. As a family's income went down
the cost of $1,800 worth of food stamps decreased. For example, a family of
four with an annual income of $6,000 paid $1,512 for $1,800 worth of stamps;
a family with an income of $4,000 paid $1,140; a family with an income of
$2,000 paid $492; a family with an income of $1,000 paid $228; and a four
member family with a yearly income below $360 was eligible for $1,800 worth
of stamps at no cost. It was estimated that 12.5 million Americans would
receive food stamps in 1974 at a cost of over $2.5 billion; as compared to
fewer than 8 million recipients in 1970 and 2 million in 1968.[71]

Federal Welfare Programs and
Expenditures in 1974
The establishment of a federal guaranteed income for the aged,
blind, and disabled under SSI and an income in-kind type of guaranteed income
for all needy individuals and families under an expanded food stamp program
represented significant innovations in U.S. welfare programs. These innovations

increased the resources of many poor Americans, but they did not eliminate income poverty in the U.S. In 1974 there was still a large number of individuals and families with yearly incomes below the poverty level because the "working poor" were generally ineligible for AFDC and in many states AFDC benefit levels were below the Census Bureau poverty line.

Estimates of federal expenditures for major welfare programs in fiscal 1974 are shown in Table 7-7. These figures suggest that the general distribution of welfare benefits in 1974 had changed very little since 1972. (see Tables 2-5 and 2-6). Three-fourths of the $110.0 billion federal expenditures for major programs in 1974, about $85.0 billion, went for direct cash programs. Most of this money went to aged and disabled persons, many of whom were not poor, under non-means tested programs like Social Security. About one-quarter of the 1974 welfare expenditures, approximately $25.0 billion, was for income in-kind and service programs. Most of the benefits provided under these programs went to the poor, or those with incomes below the poverty level.

Table 7-7. Federal Outlays for Major Cash and In-Kind Welfare Programs in 1974
(billions of dollars)

Programs		Estimated 1974 Outlays	Percent of Total
Cash Benefits			
Social Security (OASDI)		$53.2	48.2
Federal employee benefit		10.7	9.7
Veterans benefits		6.3	5.7
Public assistance—AFDC & SSI		6.9	6.3
Unemployment insurance		4.6	4.2
Railroad retirement		2.5	2.3
Other programs		1.1	1.0
Total		$85.3	77.4
Income In-Kind Benefits			
Food stamps & food commodities		$ 3.9	3.5
Health care		16.7	15.1
Medicare	($11.7)		
Medicaid	($ 5.0)		
Housing		2.0	1.8
Social services—including WIN		2.4	2.2
Total		$25.0	22.6
Grand Total		$110.3	100.0

Source: U.S., Executive Office of the President, *Budget of the United States Government 1974: Special Analysis* (Washington, D.C.: Government Printing Office, 1973).

Chapter Eight

Substance and Process in Policy Change: Theory Increments

The normal incremental mode of policy making is broken in enough instances . . . and these instances are such important departures in policy, that more attention is due to the reasons why federal institutions take new paths in policy making and do not simply rest content with marginal adjustments in the status quo. For basic policy decisions that significantly extend the scope of federal involvement in American life (e.g., federal aid to education), that transform existing policies (e.g., disengagement from Vietnam), and that alter arrangements among governmental units (e.g., tax sharing), a model of "abnormal decision making" is needed.

—John F. Manley

. . . political change is limited by the speed at which people can change their ideas of the world they live in, their expectations of it, and their willingness to accept its expectations of them. . . .

—Sir Geoffrey Vickers

In this chapter the policy decisions and decision making processes and conditions associated with White House and congressional welfare actions discussed in previous chapters are compared with the "normal incremental mode" of decision making and policy change described by Simon, March, and Lindblom.[1] The purpose of this comparison is to organize and make more explicit certain theoretical propositions pertaining to political decision making and policy change drawn from the preceding examination of FAP and SSI.

165

POLICY DECISIONS: SMALL AND
LARGE CHANGES

The essence of "incrementalism" as applied to political change is that "democracies change their policies almost entirely through incremental adjustments. Policy does not move in leaps and bounds."[2] As a model of political decision making, it predicts that the normal outcome of the decision making processes through which political institutions develop solutions for public problems is the design and approval of small, marginal, or incremental changes in existing policies that will result in small, marginal, or incremental alterations in existing social states. "It is decision making through small or incremental moves on particular problems rather than through a comprehensive reform program."[3]

The theoretical utility of the incremental model is severely limited by the lack of a reliable definition of what constitutes a "small" or incremental, as distinguished from a "large" or radical, decision outcome or policy change.[4] Lindblom and Braybrooke suggest that "the introduction through public policy of what is considered to be a new and important element (in the combination of elements to which people refer in explaining important social change)" would be a "large or nonincremental change." And, "a somewhat greater or reduced use of an existing social technique or a somewhat higher or lower level of attainment of some existing values is a small or incremental change."[5] They acknowledge, however, that nothing is entirely without some identifiable precedent. Consequently, the originality of a "new" policy element, to some extent, is always a matter of judgment. And the importance of a "new" policy element depends on the value attached to the new element or the policy in general and this can vary from person to person.[6]

Given the complex and multidimensional nature of public policies and the subjective quality of individual perceptions and evaluations of any particular policy, Lindblom appears willing to leave the definition of incremental and nonincremental policy change to the judgment of every individual analyst.

> For any analyst, therefore, a policy is incremental if, given the variables he considers consequential to his analysis and given his evaluations, the policy affects few of them and alters them only by small magnitudes. Clearly, a choice can be incremental with respect to some values and nonincremental with respect to others, as well as incremental to one analyst and nonincremental to another.[7]

The identification of FAP and SSI in preceding chapters as representing "radical" change in U.S. welfare programs is based on the conceptualization of public policy and interpretation of policy innovation suggested earlier. In Chapter One policy is defined in terms of three general components: *conceptual* (problem identification, policy objectives); *technical* (administrative arrangements and procedures); and *consequential* (costs, intended and unintended results). Policy innovation refers to identifiable alterations or shifts in one or more of these components of a particular policy or program. Logically, the more comprehensive a policy decision or proposal in terms of policy components affected, and fundamental in terms of basic elements altered, the larger or more radical the change it represents.

Together FAP and SSI represented radical change because they entailed major shifts in conceptual, technical, and consequential dimensions of existing public assistance programs for families (AFDC) and adults (OAA, AB, APTD). They would redefine the objective of federal cash assistance programs from combating economic dependency to reducing income poverty (conceptual dimension), restructure the federal-state administrative and fiscal arrangements for providing cash assistance (technical dimension) and substantially expand costs and recipients of federal cash welfare benefits (consequential dimension).[8] The enactment and implementation of the SSI program produced radical (i.e., comprehensive and fundamental) change in federal cash assistance programs for aged, blind, and disabled Americans.

The provisonal distinction suggested in this analysis is that radical change entails the transformation of an existing policy or program in that fundamental elements in all components, and particularly conceptual dimensions, are significantly altered. In contrast, incremental change would be a decision or proposal limited to minor adjustments of essentially technical (e.g., administrative procedures) or consequential (e.g., yearly expenditures) dimension of a policy.

DECISION MAKING PROCESSES:
SMALL AND LARGE CHANGES

Incremental policy decisions are the outcome of a decision process with the following essential elements:

1. The search for a solution to a policy problem begins with decision makers looking at existing solutions to "old" problems.
2. The attention of the policy makers involved in the search remains focused on existing precedents and policy alternatives that constitute no more than incremental changes in existing policies. That is, attention remains focused on marginal adjustments in primarily technical or consequential dimensions of existing policies.
3. Even if proposals for radical change (i.e., the transformation of existing policy through major shifts in fundamental conceptual, technical, and consequential dimensions) come to the attention of some policy makers,

the process of policy analysis, choice, and design within the political institution is restricted to incremental alternatives.

Incremental decision making is not as mechanical or predictable as this might imply. In the first place, invariably there are many more public problems than there are public resources—including the time, energy, and interest of policy makers. An important question for students of public policy and political decision making is why some problems come to the attention of Presidents and other policy makers, or make it onto the national agenda, and others do not; or why some are given higher priority than others. Furthermore, policy makers will not inevitably perceive or interpret a particular problem or set of problems in the same way or relate a "new" problem to the same "old" problem or existing policies.

In other words, in the process of incremental decision making, the perceptions, attention frames, and policy orientations of the policy makers involved will determine how a "new" problem is defined, what precedents will be followed or what incremental alternatives will be considered. For example, given the widespread discontent with welfare policy in 1969 it was quite predictable that both President Nixon and Congress would consider and approve incremental changes in AFDC. It was less predictable, however, whether they would approve incremental modifications in the direction of the 1967 welfare amendments which required AFDC recipients to accept work or training and placed a ceiling on federal expenditures; or, whether they would support liberal adjustments in public assistance like instituting national standards and increasing federal financial participation in the programs as recommended by the Nathan task force.

If the President and Congress had approved incremental changes, the decision process within the different institutions would have included: (1) the activities which directed attention to the problem of welfare and that influenced the interpretation of the welfare problems perceived; (2) the selection or choice between alternative incremental changes; and (3) the design of a legislative proposal containing marginal adjustments in welfare policy.

In other words, analytically the process of incremental decision making involves the same stages or functional activities as the process that yielded FAP and SSI. The essential difference is that, during the process of attention directing, choice, and design that yields a radical policy decision like FAP, the attention and preferences of enough policy makers shift to radically innovative policy alternatives. Most important, a decision to support a radical policy alternative means that a significant number of policy makers and especially the policy leaders within an institution (the President, key presidential assistants, committee chairmen, ranking minority members of committees and others with attention directing and preference shifting leverage) have revised or replaced, temporarily or permanently, some of the perceptions, assumptions, and expectations they previously associated with the policy or problem under consideration—as, for example, Senator Abraham Ribicoff and Congressman John Byrnes acknowledged they had done in explaining their support for radical welfare reform.

DECISION CONDITIONS: SMALL AND LARGE CHANGES

There are logical and empirically verifiable explanations of why political decision making, problem solving, and policy change in modern democratic countries is generally incremental in nature. In the first place, most of what policy makers know about the nature of a particular problem and how to deal with it is based on past experience with existing policies and programs.

New interpretations of a problem and radically innovative courses of action are not always available or visible to policy makers. When a proposal for radical change is presented to policy makers they are seldom interested because the economic, social, and political consequences of comprehensive and fundamental innovation are less predictable than the effects of small or incremental changes. Consequently, large changes generally present a significant risk to the policy makers, whereas incremental decisions tend to maximize security by continuing in a well known direction with more predictable results.

Furthermore, serious consideration of radical innovation is likely to produce an unusually comprehensive and extensive examination of the problem and existing policies, which tends to magnify fundamental policy or ideological disagreements among participating decision makers. As a result, the process of selecting, designing, and mobilizing support for a proposal entailing radical change is generally more arduous, disruptive, and uncertain than incremental decision making.

Political institutions do make radical policy decisions, however. Large changes do occur. In the case of President Nixon's decision to sponsor FAP and House approval of H.R.1 (and to a lesser extent Senate passage of SSI), the normal incremental mode of decision making was broken: approval of comprehensive and fundamental change in public assistance programs, as opposed to incremental modifications, emerged from welfare deliberations in executive and legislative institutions.

Circumstances conducive to the consideration and approval of radical innovation suggested in the preceding examination of FAP are summarized here as conditions associated with the incentive and opportunity to innovate.

The Incentive to Innovate
Widespread discontent among public officials and the general public with the results of a particular policy or program provides an incentive for

policy makers to investigate the problems articulated and initiate reforms. The case of FAP and H.R.1 suggests that, in their search for an appropriate course of action, policy makers will be more receptive to proposals constituting radical change in present policy under certain conditions:

1. If repeated attempts in the past to modify the policy or program in response to similar complaints have failed and, consequently, doubts are articulated by many as to the effectiveness of further incremental alterations.
2. If some of the most salient consequences of the current program, or indicators of policy performance (e.g., increases in program costs and caseloads in public relief policy), are highly erratic and unpredictable, and appear to some policy makers to be uncontrollable as the policy or program is presently constituted.
3. If it appears to decision makers that the distribution of costs and benefits associated with a particular policy is flagrantly inequitable; or, that the unintended effects of the policy are intolerably inconsistent with fundamental or widely accepted values such as the solvency of government (national, state or local), general economic and political stability, family stability, personal safety, the welfare of children, basic parental prerogative, etc.
4. If recognized policy experts support radical innovation, agree on at least the general nature and direction of the changes that should be made, and have information by which they and the policy makers can predict important consequences of comprehensive innovation (e.g., probable costs and caseloads in welfare policy).
5. If influential individuals and groups support or appear amenable to drastic change, and public discontent with existing policies is sufficiently widespread and intense that drastic change appears politically possible, necessary, or advantageous.

The Opportunity to Innovate

Radical decision making occurs when a proposal specifying radical innovation in existing policy is formulated and approved by a policy making institution. Or, it occurs when, in searching for a solution to a public problem, the *attention and preferences* of enough of the decision makers in an institution shift to a radically innovative course of action because radical change appears economically and politically feasible and promises to distribute costs and benefits more equitably than current policy, provide greater control over salient policy consequences than existing programs, or produce results more consistent than current policy with generally accepted values and newly formed conceptions of the problem and how to deal with it.

When there is widespread discontent with a current policy or program and a radical course of action supported by recognized policy experts is available, it is most likely to be approved and sponsored by the White House:

1. Shortly after the election of a new President in an area in which he has a special interest, or about which he had some concern before inauguration.
2. When there are presidential advisers with continual access to the President who are committed to reforming current programs, capable of designing and defending substantively and politically a proposal entailing radical innovations, and willing to energetically attempt to persuade the President to sponsor drastic change.

Providing the incentive for reform exists, congressional institutions are most likely to approve an available proposal entailing comprehensive and fundamental change:

1. When the President initiates such a proposal and energetically attempts to obtain Congressional approval.
2. When Congressional leaders (e.g., committee chairmen, party leaders) support the President's proposal (or a modified version of it) and have sufficient leverage to shift the attention and preferences of enough of the members to the radical changes sponsored by the White House.
3. When influential interest groups and individuals (e.g., mayors and governors) favor and lobby in support of the proposed radical change.

CONCLUSION

Policy innovation involves a complex series of conditions, activities and events occurring outside as well as within political institutions. Analytically, the process of policy change can be divided into (1) the *predecisional phase*—the genesis, development, and diffusion of new policy related problems, ideas and techniques; (2) the *decision making phase*—the entry of public problems, innovative policy ideas, and courses of action into the political system, and the consideration, design, and enactment of specific policy changes; and (3) the *postenactment phase*—the implementation, impact, and review of new policies and programs.[9] This study of the Family Assistance Plan and the Supplemental Security Income program focused on activities and events comprising the decision making phase of innovation in U.S. welfare policy. This included the shift in attention of executive and legislative welfare policy makers to problem perceptions, objectives, and administrative structures associated with policy alternatives to public assistance like a negative tax plan and other guaranteed income programs; the formulation of legislative proposals that would replace public assistance programs for families and adults with negative tax programs; and the attempts to mobilize support for these proposals and final enactment of a guaranteed income for aged, blind, and disabled adults.

It is not inevitable that the remaining federal-state public assistance program for families (AFDC) will eventually be replaced with some form of a federal guaranteed income like FAP. But it is probable, because the initial and fundamental developments in the decision making stage of radical change in AFDC have occurred as a result of the four-year debate over the Family Assistance Plan. That is, the attention of policy makers influential in welfare policy has shifted to the specific problem of the "working poor," the general problem of "income poverty," and the objective of a nationwide income floor that would provide a minimum level of income for all poor families. Support for replacing AFDC with a federally administered and financed cash assistance program with nationally uniform eligibility and payment standards has increased. A number of federal income guarantee programs that would replace AFDC have been designed and an important precedent has been established in the replacement of OAA, AB, and APTD with a federal negative tax program for the aged, blind, and disabled.

Notes

NOTES TO CHAPTER 1

1. Quotes are from President Nixon's August 11, 1969 Message to Congress on Welfare Reform, reprinted in U.S., Congress, House, *Social Security and Welfare Proposals, Hearings* before House Committee on Ways and Means, 91st Congress, 1st sess., 1969, pp. 103–109.

2. Gilbert Y. Steiner, *The State of Welfare* (Washington, D.C.: Brookings Institution, 1971), p. 31.

3. John Osborne, *The First Two Years of the Nixon Watch* (New York: Liveright, 1971), chap. 19, p. 100.

4. *1970 Congressional Quarterly Almanac* (Washington, D.C.: Congressional Quarterly Service, 1971), p. 1030; *1971 Congressional Quarterly Almanac* (Washington, D.C.: Congressional Quarterly Service, 1972), p. 520.

5. He repeated this in several public speeches and during my interview with him. See, for example, U.S., Congress, House, Committee on Ways and Means, "Remarks of Congressman Wilbur D. Mills to the Joint Session of the Tennessee General Assembly" (mimeographed Committee print, 1971).

6. Herbert Simon, *Administrative Behavior* (2nd ed.) (New York: MacMillan, 1957); James G. March and Herbert Simon, *Organizations* (New York: Wiley, 1958), especially pp. 173–210; Richard C. Snyder, "A Decision-Making Approach to the Study of Political Phenomena," in *Approaches to the Study of Politics,* ed. Roland Young (Evanston, Ill.: Northwestern University Press, 1958), pp. 2–38; James N. Rosenau, "The Premises and Promise of Decision-Making Analysis," and James Robinson and R. Roger Majak, "The Theory of Decision-Making," in *Contemporary Political Analysis,* ed. James C. Charlesworth (New York: Free Press, 1967), pp. 175–211; David Braybrooke and Charles Lindblom, *A Strategy of Decision* (New York: Free

Press, 1963); Sir Geoffrey Vickers, *The Art of Judgment* (New York: Basic Books, 1965).

7. Rosenau, "Decision-Making Analysis," p. 194.

8. *Ibid.*, p. 195.

9. Herbert A. Simon, "Political Research: The Decision-Making Framework," in *Varieties of Political Theory,* ed. David Easton (Englewood Cliffs, N.J.: Prentice-Hall, 1966), p. 21. See also, Harold D. Lasswell, "The Decision Process: Seven Categories of Functional Analysis," in *Politics and Social Life,* ed. Nelson W. Polsby, et al. (Boston: Houghton Mifflin, 1963), p. 93; Harold D. Lasswell, *A Preview of Policy Sciences* (New York: American Elsevier, 1971), pp. 14–33; Charles O. Jones, *An Introduction to the Study of Public Policy* (Belmont, Calif.: Wadsworth, 1970).

10. For definitions of policy, see Harold D. Lasswell and Abraham Kaplan, *Power and Society* (New Haven, Conn.: Yale University Press, 1950), p. 71; Austin Ranney, "The Study of Policy Content: A Framework for Choice," Robert H. Salisbury, "The Analysis of Public Policy: A Search for Theories and Roles"; James N. Rosenau, "Moral Fervor, Systematic Analysis, and Scientific Consciousness in Foreign Policy Research"; and James Davis, Jr. and Kenneth Dolbeare, "Selective Service and Military Manpower," in *Political Science and Public Policy,* ed. Austin Ranney (Chicago: Markham, 1968), pp. 7, 115, 152–153, 211–215; H. Hugh Heclo, "Review Article; Policy Analysis," *British Journal of Politics,* 2 (Winter 1972): 84–85; Ira Sharkansky, "Environment, Policy, Output, and Impact: Problems of Theory and Method in the Analysis of Public Policy," in *Policy Analysis in Political Science,* ed. Ira Sharkansky (Chicago: Markham, 1970), pp. 61–80.

11. See Lewis Anthony Dexter, "Toward a Sociological Analysis of Policy" (paper presented at the 66th Annual Meeting of the American Political Science Association, Los Angeles, Calif., September 7–12, 1970), p. 14.

12. Administration officials interviewed included the following: Paul Barton (Department of Labor); James Edwards, Glen Frederick, Charles Hawkins, Thomas Joe, Michael Mahoney, John C. Montgomery, Robert Patricelli, John Veneman (Department of Health, Education, and Welfare); Richard Nathan (Office of Management and Budget); John Price (Domestic Council, Assistant to Daniel Moynihan).

Ways and Means members interviewed included: (Democrats) Wilbur Mills, Al Ullman, Martha Griffiths, Dan Rostenkowski, Phil Landrum, Richard Fulton, Omar Burleson, James Corman, William Green, Sam Gibbons, Joe D. Waggonner; (Republicans) John Byrnes, Jackson Betts, Herman Schneebeli, Barber Conable, and Jerry Pettis. Interviews were also held with Senator Abraham Ribicoff and two of his legislative assistants, Geoffrey Peterson and Taggert Adams.

NOTES TO CHAPTER 2

1. "The Social Security Revolution," *Congressional Quarterly Congress and the Nation* 1 (1965): 1225. At one point during the Rules Committee Hearings on the Family Assistance Plan in 1970, Congressman Madden reminded those present of the resistance to this legislation and the changes it entailed. "I remember many a member down there on the [House] floor who used to get up in the 1940s and condemn Social Security as being socialistic. You remember that, Mr. Chairman." Quoted in U.S., Congress, House, *The Family Assistance Act of 1970, Hearings* before the House Rules Committee on H.R. 16311, 91st Congress, 2nd sess., 1970, p. 121.

2. U.S., Congress, Senate, Committee on Finance, *Information on Federal Programs to Aid the Poor,* 92nd Congress, 2nd sess., Feb. 15, 1972.

3. "The Social Security Revolution," p. 1225.

4. U.S., Department of Health, Education, and Welfare, *Social Security Programs in the United States* (Washington, D.C.: Government Printing Office, 1971), p. 1.

5. Lawrence M. Friedman, "Social Welfare Legislation: An Introduction," Institute for Research on Poverty Discussion Paper (Madison, Wisc.: University of Wisconsin, 1968), p. 28.

6. As discussed in Chap. One, in January 1974 the SSI program replaced OAA, AB and APTD. AFDC, however, remained a federal-state program.

7. Robert J. Lampman, "Nixon's Family Assistance Plan," Institute for Research on Poverty Discussion Paper (Madison, Wisc.: University of Wisconsin, 1969), p. 7.

8. Gilbert Y. Steiner, *Social Insecurity* (Chicago: Rand McNally, 1966), pp. 18–47.

9. Lampman, "Nixon's Family Assistance Plan," p. 7.

10. This is still the case with AFDC, which was not affected by the SSI program.

11. U.S., Department of Health, Education, and Welfare, *Public Assistance Programs: Standards for Basic Needs, July 1972* (Washington, D.C.: Government Printing Office, May 14, 1973), Tables 2 and 6.

12. U.S., Department of Health, Education, and Welfare, *Source of Funds Expended for Public Assistance Payments: Fiscal Year Ended June 30, 1972* (Washington, D.C.: Government Printing Office, March 15, 1973), Tables 4, 5, 6, and 7.

13. U.S., Department of Health, Education, and Welfare, *Trend Report: Public Assistance and Related Data, 1971* (Washington, D.C.: Government Printing Office, October 6, 1972), p. 15.

14. Gilbert Y. Steiner, *The State of Welfare* (Washington, D.C.: Brookings Institution, 1971), p. 31.

15. See President's Commission on Income Maintenance Programs, *Background Papers* (Washington, D.C.: Government Printing Office, 1970), p. 11.

16. See Joel F. Handler, *Reforming the Poor: Welfare Policy, Federalism and*

Morality (New York: Basic Books, 1972); Joel F. Handler and Ellen Jane Hollingsworth, *The 'Deserving Poor': A Study of Welfare Administration* (Chicago: Markham, 1971); Francis F. Piven and Richard A. Cloward, *Regulating the Poor: The Functions of Public Welfare* (New York: Pantheon, 1971).

17. Nick Kotz, *Let Them Eat Promises* (Garden City: Doubleday Anchor, 1971); A Report by the Citizens' Board of Inquiry into Hunger and Malnutrition in the United States, *Hunger U.S.A.* (Boston: Beacon Press, 1968).

18. See comments in U.S., Congress, House, Committee on Ways and Means, *The Family Assistance Act of 1970*. Report of the House Ways and Means Committee, 91st Congress, 2nd sess., 1970, p. 30.

19. Steiner, *Social Insecurity*, p. 258.

20. Martin Rein, Social Policy: *Issues of Choice and Change*, (New York: Random House, 1970), p. 312.

21. *Ibid.*

22. Steiner, *The State of Welfare*, p. 33.

23. Rein, *Social Policy*, p. 305.

24. James L. Sundquist, "Jobs, Training, and Welfare for the Underclass," in *Agenda for the Nation*, ed. Kermit Gordon (Washington, D.C.: Brookings Institution, 1968), p. 53. For a discussion of the war on poverty legislation and programs, see Robert J. Lampman, *Ends and Means of Reducing Income Poverty* (Chicago: Markham, 1971), and Joseph A. Kershaw, *Government Against Poverty* (Chicago: Markham, 1970).

25. Daniel P. Moynihan, "The Crisis in Welfare," *The Public Interest* (Winter 1968): 3.

26. Steiner, *The State of Welfare*, p. 25.

27. Rein, *Social Policy*, pp. 312–313.

28. U.S., Congress, Joint Economic Committee, *Public Income Transfer Programs*, James R. Storey (Washington, D.C.: Government Printing Office, 1972).

29. *Ibid.*

30. U.S., Congress, Senate, Committee on Finance, *Information on Federal Programs to Aid the Poor*, 92nd Congress, 2nd sess., Feb. 15, 1972.

31. *Background Papers*, p. 168.

32. U.S., Department of Commerce, Bureau of the Census, *Characteristics of the Low-Income Population 1970* (Washington, D.C.: Government Printing Office, 1971), p. 1.

33. U.S., Department of Commerce, Bureau of the Census, *Characteristics of the Low-Income Population 1972* (Washington, D.C.: Government Printing Office, 1973).

34. *Characteristics of the Low-Income Population 1970*, p. 10.

35. U.S., Congress, Senate, *Social Security Amendments of 1971, Hearings* before the Senate Finance Committee, 91st Congress, 1st sess., 1971, pp. 189–190.

36. From President John F. Kennedy's 1962 State of the Union Message, quoted in Steiner, *Social Insecurity,* p. 257.
37. Quoted in Steiner, *The State of Welfare,* p. 36.

NOTES TO CHAPTER 3

1. U.S., Congress, House, *Social Security and Welfare Proposals, Hearings* before the House Ways and Means Committee, 91st Congress, 1st sess., 1969, p. 49.
2. Daniel P. Moynihan, "One Step We Must Take," *The Saturday Review* (May 23, 1970), pp. 20–23.
3. See President Nixon's August 11, 1969 Message to Congress on Welfare Reform in *Social Security and Welfare Proposals, Hearings,* pp. 103–109; President Nixon's Televised Speech on Public Welfare, reprinted in *Congressional Quarterly Weekly Report,* August 15, 1969, pp. 1517–1520.
4. From President Nixon's Remarks at the White House Conference on Food, Nutrition, and Health, December 2, 1969 (Washington, D.C.: Government Printing Office, 1969).
5. Moynihan, "One Step We Must Take," p. 21.
6. *Social Security and Welfare Proposals, Hearings,* pp. 50, 121–122.
7. U.S., Congress, Senate, *Family Assistance Act of 1970, Hearings* before Senate Finance Committee, 91st Congress, 2nd sess., 1970, pp. 198–199.
8. *Ibid.*
9. *Social Security and Welfare Proposals, Hearings,* pp. 360.
10. *Ibid.,* p. 52.
11. *Ibid.,* p. 121.
12. *Ibid.,* p. 108.
13. *Ibid.*
14. See Lawrence M. Friedman, "Social Welfare Legislation: An Introduction," Institute for Research on Poverty Discussion Paper (Madison, Wisc.: University of Wisconsin, 1968); and, Gilbert Y. Steiner, *The State of Welfare* (Washington, D.C.: Brookings Institution, 1971), pp. 17–30.
15. Bill Cavala and Aaron Wildavsky, "The Political Feasibility of Income by Right," *Public Policy* (Spring 1970): 336.
16. When he presented FAP to the Rules Committee in 1970, Wilbur Mills, Chairman of the House Ways and Means Committee, pointed out that one of the most significant changes contained in the FAP legislation was that "for the first time" it would define and incorporate "the dollar amounts . . . set for the poverty level" in the Federal Social Security Law. See *The Family Assistance Act of 1970, Hearings,* p. 108.

   An important accomplishment of the "war on poverty" initiated with the enactment of the Economic Opportunity Act of 1964 was the development of two reliable standards by which the success or failure of antipoverty efforts could be evaluated: (1) the number of people below the poverty income line and (2) the size of the poverty-income gap. However, it was only in regard to the performance of education, manpower, and employment opportunity programs that there had been official reference to the rate of change in these two measures. The FAP legislation, for the first time, as pointed out by Mills, would officially link the poverty line and these two performance indicators to federal *cash* assistance programs. See James Tobin, "Raising the Incomes of the Poor," in *Agenda for the Nation,* ed. Kermit Gordon (Washington, D.C.: Brookings Institution, 1968), p. 41; Robert J. Lampman, *Ends and Means of Reducing Income Poverty* (Chicago: Markham, 1971), p. 56.

17. Friedman, "Social Welfare Legislation," p. 17.

18. When the family's outside earnings, minus the earnings disregard of $720 plus 50 percent of the remainder, are equal to or more than the basic $1,600 FAP payment for a family of four they would no longer be eligible for benefits: and, 50 percent of $3,920 minus $720 equals $1,600.

$3,920   (family earnings)
<u>- 720</u>   (initial disregard)

$3,200

$3,200
<u>X   50%</u>(additional disregard)

$1,600   (deductible income)

$1,600   (basic payment)
<u>-1,600</u>   (deductible income)

00   (FAP benefits payable)

19. See Mollie Orshansky, "Counting the Poor," and Martin Rein, "Problems in the Definition and Measurement of Poverty," in *Poverty in America,* ed. Louis Ferman, et al. (Ann Arbor, Mich.: University of Michigan Press, 1969), pp. 67–132.

20. Robert J. Lampman, "Nixon's Family Assistance Plan," Institute for Research on Poverty Discussion Paper (Madison, Wisc.: University of Wisconsin, 1969), p. 7.

21. *Social Security and Welfare Proposals, Hearings,* p. 127. Robert J. Myers, Chief Actuary of the Social Security Administration, defended the Administration's estimated costs of FAP, but with the following caveat: ". . . in a new program such as this, with its many completely new features, it must be recognized that any cost estimates made cannot be too precise or accurate and necessarily contain a possible margin of variation which may be as much as 20% or 25%." This is an important qualification, which applies to cost and caseload estimates in this and subsequent chapters. See Myers's comments in *Social Security and Welfare Proposals, Hearings,* p. 333.

22. Charles L. Schultze, et al., *Setting National Priorities: The 1972 Budget* (Washington, D.C.: Brookings Institution, 1971), p. 177.

23. Robert J. Lampman, "NIT: Welfare-Oriented Negative Rates Plan and Negative Rates Plan for the Working Poor," in *Poverty Policy,* ed. Theodore R. Marmor (Chicago: Aldine, 1971), pp. 108–116; President's Commission on Income Maintenance Programs, *Poverty Amid Plenty* (Washington, D.C.: Government Printing Office, 1969), pp. 57–63.

     FAP differed from many negative tax proposals and other forms of a guaranteed income in several respects which should be noted. First, it excluded ablebodied and childless adults and couples from cash benefits. The payment levels for families were lower than in many of the NIT schemes that have been developed, and most of these proposals would provide the same amount of benefits for adult and family recipients. And, most NIT and other income maintenance schemes have relied on financial incentives to encourage the work efforts of recipients and not work requirements or financial penalties incorporated in FAP.

24. See Robert Haveman and Robert Lampman, "Two Alternatives to FAP's Treatment of the Working Poor," Institute for Research on Poverty Discussion Paper (Madison, Wisc.: University of Wisconsin, 1971).

NOTES TO CHAPTER 4

1. Quoted in Rowland Evans and Robert Novak, *Nixon in the White House* (New York: Random House, 1971), p. 224.

2. The full text of this speech is reprinted in *1968 Congressional Quarterly Almanac* (Washington, D.C.: Congressional Quarterly Service, 1969), pp. 995–998.

3. Quoted in *New York Times,* October 16, 1968, p. 1.

4. These changes had been recommended by the Advisory Council on Public Welfare appointed in 1964, and by the National Advisory Commission on Civil Disorders appointed in 1967. See Theodore R. Marmor, *Poverty Policy* (Chicago: Aldine, 1971), pp. 57–79; and *Report of the National Advisory Commission on Civil Disorders* (New York: Bantam, 1969), pp. 457–466.

5. Gilbert Y. Steiner, *The State of Welfare* (Washington, D.C.: Brookings Institution, 1971), pp. 6–11.

6. *Ibid.,* p. 94.

7. *Gallup Opinion Weekly,* January, 1969, pp. 20–21.

8. Evans and Novak, *Nixon in the White House,* p. 11.

9. Daniel P. Moynihan, *The Politics of a Guaranteed Income* (New York: Random House, 1973), p. 80.

10. *Ibid.,* p. 92.

11. Stephan Hess, review of *The Third Year of the Nixon Watch,* by John Osborne, *Washington Post,* "Book World," June 18, 1972, p. 4.

12. John Osborne, *The First Two Years of the Nixon Watch* (New York: Liveright, 1971), p. 143.

13. *New York Times,* January 12, 1969, p. 68; Steiner, *The State of Welfare,*
       pp. 110–116.
14. Quoted in Franklin D. Raines, "Presidential Policy Development: The Gene-
       sis of the Family Assistance Plan" (senior thesis, Harvard, 1970), p.
       14 (mimeographed); and Moynihan, *Guaranteed Income,* p. 72.
15. Daniel P. Moynihan, "The Crisis in Welfare," *The Public Interest* 10 (Winter
       1968): 4; See also Moynihan, "The Negro Family: The Case for National
       Action," in *The Moynihan Report and the Politics of Controversy,*
       ed. Lee Rainwater and William L. Yancey (Cambridge, Mass.: MIT
       Press, 1970).
16. See Adam Yarmolinsky, "Ideas into Programs," *The Public Interest* (Winter
       1966): 75.
17. Steiner, *The State of Welfare,* p. 114.
18. Raines, "Genesis of the Family Assistance Plan," p. 62.
19. Evans and Novak, *Nixon in the White House,* pp. 225–226.
20. Moynihan, *Guaranteed Income,* pp. 147–148.
21. *Wall Street Journal,* May 29, 1969, p. 38.
22. Quoted in *New York Times,* May 4, 1969, section 4, p. 8.
23. Quoted in *Wall Street Journal,* May 20, 1969, p. 16.
24. *Wall Street Journal,* May 29, 1969, p. 38.
25. Moynihan, "The Crisis in Welfare," p. 3.
26. Quoted in Steiner, *The State of Welfare,* p. 120.
27. See Daniel Schorr, "Behind the Nixon Welfare Showdown," *The New Leader,*
       August 18, 1969, p. 3.
28. Quoted in Schorr, "Behind the Nixon Welfare Showdown," pp. 3–4.
29. The full text of this message is reprinted in *1969 Congressional Quarterly
       Almanac* (Washington, D.C.: Congressional Quarterly Service, 1970),
       pp. 39A–40A.
30. *New York Times,* July 15, 1969, pp. 1, 78.
31. *Ibid.*
32. Thomas C. Schelling, *The Strategy of Conflict* (London: Oxford University
       Press, 1960), pp. 57, 68–69; Jeffrey L. Pressman, *House vs. Senate:
       Conflicts in the Appropriations Process* (New Haven, Conn.: Yale
       University Press, 1966), pp. 71–73.
33. Quoted in *Wall Street Journal,* August 8, 1969, p. 2.
34. On the basis of interviews with members of Congress and Administration
       officials in March 1969, Cavala and Wildavsky concluded that incre-
       mental modifications in public assistance were likely to be proposed
       and enacted, but not radical change in the form of replacing existing
       programs with a guaranteed income. "The President will not support
       it and Congress would not pass it if he did." See Bill Cavala and Aaron
       Wildavsky, "The Political Feasibility of Income by Right," *Public
       Policy* 18 (Spring 1970): 349–350.
35. Steiner, *The State of Welfare,* p. 99.
36. All past Secretaries of the Department of Health, Education, and Welfare
       publicly endorsed FAP after it was introduced.

37. Gilbert Y. Steiner, *Social Insecurity: The Politics of Welfare* (Chicago: Rand McNally, 1966), pp. 140–141.
38. Quoted in James L. Sundquist, *Politics and Policy* (Washington, D.C.: Brookings Institution, 1969), pp. 111–112.
39. See *Report on the National Advisory Commission on Civil Disorders* (New York: Bantam, 1969), pp. 456–466.
40. Full text of the January 4, 1971 televised interview is reprinted in *Congressional Quarterly Weekly,* January 8, 1971, pp. 98–102.
41. See Daniel P. Moynihan, "A Crisis of Confidence," *The Public Interest* 7 (Spring 1967): 3–10.

NOTES TO CHAPTER 5

1. For a discussion of House and Senate 1970 welfare reform deliberations see Daniel Patrick Moynihan, *The Politics of a Guaranteed Income,* (New York: Random House, 1973), pp. 348–543; and *1970 Congressional Quarterly Almanac* (Washington, D.C.: Congressional Quarterly Service, 1969), pp. 1030–1040.
2. U.S., Congress, House, *Social Security Amendments of 1971,* House Ways and Means Committee Report on H.R.1, 92nd Congress, 1st sess., 1971, p. 165.
3. For example, see James L. Sundquist, "Jobs, Training and Welfare for the Underclass," in *Agenda for the Nation,* ed. Kermit Gordon (Washington, D.C.: Brookings Institution, 1968), pp. 60–63, 72–76.
4. According to Administration figures, the composition of the welfare population under H.R.1 would have been the same as that indicated in Table 3–6, Chap. Three.
5. See Table 3–7, Chap. Three.

NOTES TO CHAPTER 6

1. Liberal members interviewed identified a "liberal minority of six": Democrats Burke, Vanik, Corman, Green, Gibbons, and Carey. These were the members who consistently supported the liberal position in Committee. They viewed the rest of the members as moderates or conservatives—mainly the latter.
2. John F. Manley, *The Politics of Finance: The House Committee on Ways and Means* (Boston: Little, Brown, 1970); Manley, "The House Committee on Ways and Means: Conflict Management in a Congressional Committee," *American Political Science Review* LIX (December 1965): 927–939.
3. Manley, *The Politics of Finance,* p. 47.
4. *Ibid.,* p. 57.
5. *Ibid.,* p. 64; Manley, "Committee on Ways and Means," p. 929.
6. Manley, *The Politics of Finance,* pp. 231, 241.
7. *Ibid.,* p. 100. See Murray Seeger, "The Most Powerful Man in Congress,"

Washingtonian (August 1969): 41, 81–82. When there was talk of Mills running for President in 1971, Committee member Sam Gibbons is supposed to have asked him, "Why would you want to become President and lose your grip on the country?"

8. Charles E. Lindblom, *The Policy-Making Process* (Englewood Cliffs, N.J.: Prentice-Hall, 1968), pp. 33–34; Lindblom, *The Intelligence of Democracy* (New York: Free Press, 1965), pp. 3–86.

9. Manley, *The Politics of Finance,* p. 104, 150.

10. *Ibid.,* p. 220.

11. From 1961 to 1968 Ways and Means lost on two roll call votes (see Manley, *The Politics of Finance,* p. 207). The third defeat was on June 29, 1973 when the House rejected a Committee bill increasing the public debt limit (see the *Congressional Record,* June 29, 1973, pp. H 5705–H 5728). The following day, June 30, 1973, the House approved a modified version of the debt ceiling bill. In introducing the revised bill Mills said, "Mr. Speaker, let me say first that perhaps the House made the proper decision last night, although it was somewhat embarrassing to some of us on the Committee. However, I think I can say that it avoided the even greater embarrassment of having a bill from the Committee on Ways and Means bearing my name . . . vetoed by a President. In the years that I have been chairman of the committee, I have never had that experience; I did not want it." *Congressional Record,* June 30, 1973, p. H 5770.

12. Quoted in Frank Fowlkes and Harry Lenhart, Jr., "Congressional Report/ Two Money Committees Wield Power Differently," *National Journal* 3 (April 10, 1971): 783.

13. Quoted in Julius Dusha, "Mighty Mills: The Ways and Means to Power," *Washington Post,* September 12, 1971, p. 3.

14. *U.S. News and World Report,* March 15, 1971, pp. 42–48; *Washington Post,* March 28, 1971, p. 2.

15. *U.S. News & World Report,* March 15, 1971, p. 45.

16. U.S., Congress, House, "Remarks of Congressman Wilbur Mills to the Joint Session of the California State Legislature" (House Ways and Means Committee Mimeographed Print, 1971), p. 1.

17. *Washington Post,* February 11, 1971, p. 1.

18. See their comments in *New York Times,* February 26, 1971, p. 1.

19. See *New York Times,* March 25, 1971, p. 1; *Washington Post,* March 27, 1971, p. 1.

20. *Washington Post,* March 27, 1971, p. 17.

21. *Ibid.*

22. A 10 percent increase in Social Security benefits had been enacted in March. See *Congressional Quarterly Weekly Report,* March 19, 1971, pp. 600–602.

23. See report in *New York Times,* May 18, 1971, p. 1.

24. John F. Manley, "The Family Assistance Plan: An Essay on Incremental and Nonincremental Policy-Making" (paper presented at the Annual Meeting of the American Political Science Association, September 1970, Los Angeles, Calif.), p. 10.

25. Bill Cavala and Aaron Wildavsky, "The Political Feasibility of Income by Right," *Public Policy* 18 (Spring 1970): 321.

26. Manley, "The Family Assistance Plan," p. 8.

27. John F. Manley, *The Politics of Finance: The House Committee on Ways and Means* (Boston: Little Brown, 1970), p. 327.

28. Gilbert Y. Steiner, *The State of Welfare* (Washington, D.C.: Brookings Institution, 1971), pp. 335–336.

29. Manley, "The Family Assistance Plan," p. 13.

30. U.S., Department of Health, Education, and Welfare, "Highlights of Welfare Reform" (Washington, D.C.: Government Printing Office, 1970), p. 8.

31. See the interview with Mills in *U.S. News & World Report,* March 15, 1971, pp. 42–48.

32. U.S., Congress, House, *The Family Assistance Act of 1970, Hearings* before the House Rules Committee on H.R.16311, 91st Congress, 2nd sess., 1970, p. 136.

33. See U.S., Congress, House, Committee on Ways and Means, *Social Security Amendments of 1971,* House Ways and Means Committee Report on H.R.1, 92nd Congress, 1st sess., 1971, p. 188.

34. *Washington Post,* March 9, 1971.

35. There is a mathematical relationship among the three basic features of a negative tax plan: the minimum payment level, the tax rate on earnings, and the cutoff point. The value of any two determines the value of the third. See Christopher Green, *Negative Taxes and the Poverty Problem* (Washington, D.C.: Brookings Institution, 1967).

36. *The Family Assistance Act of 1970, Hearings,* pp. 156–157.

37. Manley, "The Family Assistance Plan," p. 16.

38. This quote is from Mills's statement on the House floor in defense of H.R.1, *Congressional Record,* June 21, 1971, p. H 5537.

39. Manley, *The Politics of Finance,* p. 112.

40. *The Family Assistance Act of 1970, Hearings,* p. 120.

41. H.R.1, the total bill, was subsequently approved 288 to 132.

42. The states can be identified by looking at Tables 5-3, 5-5, and 5-7, Chap. Five.

NOTES TO CHAPTER 7

1. U.S., Department of Health, Education, and Welfare. *Source of Funds Expended for Public Assistance Payments: Fiscal Year Ended June 30, 1972* (Washington, D.C.: Government Printing Office, 1973), Table 3, p. 3.

2. See John F. Manley, *The Politics of Finance: The House Committee on Ways and Means.* (Boston: Little, Brown, 1970), pp. 294–300; Frank V. Fowlkes and Harry Lenhart, Jr., "Congressional Report/Two Money Committees Wield Power Differently," *National Journal,* April 10, 1971, pp. 795–800.

3. Richard F. Fenno, Jr., *Congressmen in Committees* (Boston: Little, Brown, 1973), pp. 182–183.

4. *Ibid.,* pp. 157, 159–160.

5. U.S., Congress, Senate, *Social Security Amendments of 1971, Hearings*
   before the Senate Finance Committee, 91st Congress, 1st sess., 1971,
   p. 48.
6. *Ibid.,* pp. 49–51.
7. *Ibid.,* p. 265.
8. Paul L. Leventhal, "Congressional Report/Revenue Sharing Gains in Senate
   as Drive for Welfare Reform Falters," *National Journal,* August 5,
   1972, p. 1253.
9. *Social Security Amendments of 1971, Hearings,* p. 143.
10. Statements made by Senator Long during hearings, *Ibid.,* p. 3, 180.
11. *Washington Post,* July 27, 1971, p. A6.
12. *Social Security Amendments of 1971, Hearings,* p. 187.
13. *Ibid.,* p. 5.
14. *Ibid.,* p. 159.
15. *Ibid.,* p. 135.
16. *Ibid.,* p. 237.
17. *Congressional Record,* October 29, 1971, pp. S17117–S17125.
18. Cosponsors of the Ribicoff-Sargent proposal included: *Senators* Ribicoff,
    Hartke, Kennedy, Javits, Brooke, Stafford, Muskie, Humphrey,
    Jackson, Hart, Gravel, Mondale, Tunney, Bayh, Metcalf, Pastore,
    Hughes, Cranston, Moss, Williams, Inouye, Hatfield. *Governors*
    Sargent (Mass.), Peterson (N.H.), Davis (Vt.), Curtis (Me.), Licht
    (R.I.), Shapp (Pa.), Mandel (Md.), Gilligan (Ohio), McCall (Ore.),
    Lucey (Wisc.), Andrus (Idaho), Milliken (Mich.), Burns (Hawaii),
    Anderson (Mont.), Egan (Alaska).
19. *Social Security Amendments of 1971, Hearings,* pp. 3–5, 188–190.
20. *Congressional Record,* August 18, 1971, p. 29275.
21. Quoted in *New York Times,* January 29, 1972, pp. 1, 27.
22. *New York Times,* January 31, 1972, p. 40.
23. Quoted in *New York Times,* September 9, 1971, p. 19.
24. Quoted in *New York Times,* August 19, 1971, p. 21.
25. Quoted in *Wall Street Journal,* October 8, 1971, p. 2.
26. Quoted in *New York Times,* March 28, 1972, pp. 1, 28.
27. Paul L. Leventhal, "Welfare Report/Divided Administration, Fragmented
    Senate Threaten Passage of Reform Legislation," *National Journal,*
    June 10, 1972, p. 976.
28. *Ibid.,* p. 980.
29. *Ibid.,* p. 978.
30. The letter was signed by Senators Percy, Pearson, Cook, Schweiker, Brooke,
    Dole, Fong, Packwood, Taft, Beall, Stafford, Saxbe, Javits, Cooper,
    Stevens, Case, Weicker, Mathias, and Hatfield. It read in part:

    ". . . the time has now come when we, together, must fashion a
    humane and decent compromise reform measure that would be
    acceptable to a majority of the Congress and to the Administration.
    Without that compromise and a final effort now by the Administra-
    tion and those members of both parties, certainly including Senator

Ribicoff, who wish to see a successful and acceptable program adopted, we firmly believe welfare reform is almost certain to die."

31. Leventhal, "Congressional Report/Revenue Sharing," p. 1254.
32. Quoted in *New York Times,* July 8, 1972, p. 10.
33. See *New York Times,* May 25, 1972, pp. 1, 18.
34. Quoted in *New York Times,* June 23, 1972, p. 14.
35. Leventhal, "Congressional Report/Revenue Sharing," p. 1252.
36. *Ibid.,* p. 1256.
37. Secretary of HEW Richardson quoted in *New York Times,* September 15, 1972, p. 94.
38. Quoted in Christopher Lydon, "Where You Stand Depends On Where You Sit—Richardson and Justice," *New York Times Magazine,* May 20, 1973, p. 95.
39. Quoted in *New York Times,* September 29, 1972, p. 1, 24.
40. Quoted in *New York Times,* October 4, 1972, p. 24.
41. *Congressional Record,* October 4, 1972, p. S16816.
42. The states can be identified by looking at Tables 5–3 and 5–5, Chap. Five.
43. Karen E. DeWitt, "Welfare Report /Complexities and State Pressures Could Delay Welfare Responsibilities Shift to U.S.," *National Journal,* May 12, 1973, p. 679.
44. *New York Times,* July 9, 1971, pp. 1, 9.
45. *Congressional Record,* October 20, 1971, pp. S16653–S16657.
46. *Washington Post,* August 2, 1971, p. A4.
47. *Washington Post,* August 26, 1971, p. A1.
48. *New York Times,* September 13, 1971, p. 16.
49. See *New York Times,* July 31, 1972, p. 53.
50. See U.S., Department of Health, Education, and Welfare, "Public Assistance Statistics: October 1972" (Washington, D.C.: Government Printing Office, 1972).
51. *Congressional Record,* October 2, 1972, p. S16498.
52. See *New York Times,* December 5, 1971, p. 31; December 15, 1971, pp. 1, 52; December 29, 1971, pp. 1, 15.
53. See U.S., Congress, Joint Economic Committee, *Studies in Public Welfare: Handbook of Public Income Transfer Programs* (Washington, D.C.: Government Printing Office, 1972), pp. 269–281.
54. Reported in *New York Times,* March 5, 1972, p. 42.
55. See Richard P. Nathan, "What Went Wrong With FAP: Should We Give Up" (paper presented at the National Conference on Social Welfare, Atlantic City, N.J., May 28, 1973); Nathan, "Workfare/Welfare," *The New Republic,* February 23, 1973.
56. Leventhal, "Welfare Report/Divided Administration," p. 975.
57. *Ibid.,* p. 979.
58. *Ibid.*
59. *Ibid.,* p. 978.
60. *Congressional Record,* October 4, 1972, p. S16822.
61. *Ibid.,* p. S16823.

62. *Ibid.*
63. Daniel Patrick Moynihan, *The Politics of a Guaranteed Income* (New York: Random, 1973), p. 163.
64. Senator Abraham Ribicoff, "He Left at Half Time," *The New Republic,* February 17, 1973, p. 25.
65. See Ralph K. Huitt, "Democratic Party Leadership in the Senate," *American Political Science Review* 55 (June 1961): 333–344; Rowland Evans and Robert Novak, *Lyndon B. Johnson: The Exercise of Power* (Cleveland: World Publishing, 1966).
66. Full text of the news conference is reprinted in *Congressional Quarterly Weekly Report,* March 10, 1973, pp. 516–517.
67. Thomas Joe, "A Primer on the Supplemental Security Income Program" (New York: McKinsey and Co., staff paper, 1973), p. 15.
68. U.S., Department of Health, Education, and Welfare, *Supplemental Security Income* (Washington, D.C.: Government Printing Office, April, 1973), p. 8.
69. See *Wall Street Journal,* November 26, 1973, p. 10.
70. See "Crackdown on Welfare Begins to Take Hold," *U.S. News and World Report,* February 19, 1973, pp. 37–40.
71. U.S., Department of Agriculture, News Release USDA 908–74.

NOTES TO CHAPTER 8

1. John F. Manley, "The Family Assistance Plan: An Essay on Incremental and Nonincremental Policy-Making" (paper presented at the Annual Meeting of the American Political Science Association, Los Angeles, California, September 7–12, 1970), p. 6; David Braybrooke and Charles Lindblom, *A Strategy of Decision* (New York: Free Press, 1963); Lindblom, "The Science of 'Muddling Through,'" *Public Administration Review* 18 (June 1959): 79–88; Herbert Simon, *Administration Behavior* (2nd ed.) (New York: MacMillan, 1957); James G. March and Herbert Simon, *Organizations* (New York: Wiley, 1958); Richard M. Cyert and James March, *A Behavioral Theory of the Firm* (Englewood Cliffs, N.J.: Prentice-Hall, 1963).
2. Lindblom, "The Science of 'Muddling Through,'" p. 86.
3. Braybrooke and Lindblom, *A Strategy of Decision,* p. 71.
4. Manley, "The Family Assistance Plan: An Essay on Incremental and Nonincremental Policy-Making," n. 5, pp. 19–20.
5. Braybrooke and Lindblom, *A Strategy of Decision,* p. 64.
6. *Ibid.,* pp. 62–65.
7. Charles E. Lindblom, "Policy Analysis," *American Economic Review* 48 (May 1958): 302.
8. Of course there were welfare reform plans that proposed more comprehensive and fundamental, or radical, innovation than FAP and SSI—e.g., the Ribicoff-Sargent proposed liberalized version of H.R.1; Senator George McGovern's $1,000–per–person plan; and the $6,500 mini-

mum guaranteed income proposed by the National Welfare Rights
Organization.

9. See Harold D. Lasswell, "The Decision Process: Seven Categories of Func-
tional Analysis," in *Politics and Social Life,* ed. Nelson W. Polsby, et
al. (Boston: Houghton Mifflin, 1963), p. 93; Lasswell, *A Preview of
Policy Sciences* (New York: American Elsevier, 1971), pp. 14–33;
Charles O. Jones, *An Introduction to the Study of Public Policy*
(Belmont, Calif.: Wadsworth, 1970).

Selected Bibliography

I. U.S. SOCIAL WELFARE POLICY

Books and Articles

Aaron, Henry J. *Why Is Welfare So Hard to Reform?* Washington, D.C.: Brookings Institution, 1973.

Ball, Robert M. "Social Security Amendments of 1972: Summary and Legislative History." *Social Security Bulletin,* March 1973, pp. 3–25.

Citizens' Board of Inquiry into Hunger and Malnutrition in the United States. *Hunger USA.* Boston: Beacon Press, 1968.

Cohen, Wilbur J., and Friedman, Milton. *Social Security: Universal or Selective?* Washington, D.C.: American Enterprise Institute, 1972.

Ferman, Louis; Haber, Alan; and Kornbluh, Joyce, eds. *Poverty in America.* Ann Arbor, Mich.: University of Michigan Press, 1968.

Fried, Edward R., et al. *Setting National Priorities: The 1974 Budget.* Washington, D.C.: Brookings Institution, 1973.

Green, Christopher. *Negative Taxes and the Poverty Problem.* Washington, D.C.: Brookings Institution, 1967.

——. and Lampman, Robert J. "Schemes for Transferring Income to the Poor." *Industrial Relations* 121, 1967.

Handler, Joel F. *Reforming the Poor: Welfare Policy, Federalism and Morality.* New York: Basic Books, 1972.

——. and Hollingsworth, Ellen Jane. *The 'Deserving Poor': A Study of Welfare Administration.* Chicago: Markham, 1971.

Joe, Thomas. "A Primer on the Supplemental Security Income Program." New York: McKinsey & Co., Staff Paper, 1973.

Kershaw, Joseph A. *Government Against Poverty.* Chicago: Markham, 1970.

Lampman, Robert J. *Ends and Means of Reducing Income Poverty.* Chicago: Markham, 1971.

Levitan, Sar A. *Programs in Aid of the Poor for the 1970s.* Baltimore: The Johns Hopkins Press, 1969.

———. et al. *Work and Welfare Go Together.* Baltimore: The Johns Hopkins Press, 1972.

Marmor, Theodore R., ed. *Poverty Policy.* Chicago: Aldine, 1971.

Miller, Herman P. *Rich Man Poor Man.* New York: Crowell, 1971.

Moynihan, Daniel P. "The Negro Family: The Case for National Action." *The Moynihan Report and the Politics of Controversy.* Lee Rainwater and William L. Yancey, eds. Cambridge, Mass.: MIT Press, 1967.

———. "A Crisis of Confidence." *Public Interest* 7 (Spring 1967).

———. "The Crisis in Welfare." *Public Interest* 10 (Winter 1968).

———. *Maximum Feasible Misunderstanding.* New York: Free Press, 1970.

———. "One Step We Must Take." *The Saturday Review,* May 23, 1970.

———. "Policy vs. Program in the '70's." *Public Interest* 20 (Summer 1970).

———. *The Politics of a Guaranteed Income.* New York: Random, 1973.

Nathan, Richard. "Workfare/Welfare." *The New Republic.* February 23, 1973.

Piven, Frances F., and Cloward, Richard A. *Regulating the Poor: The Functions of Public Welfare.* New York: Pantheon, 1971.

Rein, Martin. *Social Policy: Issues of Choice and Change.* New York: Random House, 1970.

Schultze, Charles L., et al. *Setting National Priorities: The 1972 Budget.* Washington, D.C.: Brookings Institution, 1971.

———. *Setting National Priorities: The 1973 Budget.* Washington, D.C.: Brookings Institution, 1972.

Segal, Judith. *Food for the Hungry: The Reluctant Society.* Baltimore: The Johns Hopkins Press, 1970.

Seligman, Ben B. *Permanent Poverty: An American Syndrome.* Chicago: Quadrangle Books, 1968.

Sirkis, Nancy. *One Family.* Boston: Little, Brown, 1971.

Steiner, Gilbert. *Social Insecurity: The Politics of Welfare.* Chicago: Rand McNally, 1966.

———. *The State of Welfare.* Washington, D.C.: Brookings Institution, 1971.

Sundquist, James L. "Jobs, Training, and Welfare for the Underclass." *Agenda for the Nation.* Kermit Gordon, ed. Washington, D.C.: Brookings Institution, 1968.

Tobin, James. "Raising the Incomes of the Poor." *Agenda for the Nation.* Kermit Gordon, ed. Washington, D.C.: Brookings Institution, 1968.

———. and Wallis, W. Allen. *Welfare Programs: An Economic Appraisal.* Washington, D.C.: American Enterprise Institute, 1968.

Public Documents

U.S., Congress, House, Committee on Ways and Means, *Social Security and Welfare Proposals: Hearings,* 91st Congress, 1st sess., 1969.

U.S., Congress, House, Committee on Ways and Means, *The Family Assistance Act of 1970: Report* of the House Ways and Means Committee, 91st Congress, 2nd sess., 1970.

U.S., Congress, House, Rules Committee, *The Family Assistance Act of 1970: Hearings on H.R.16311,* 91st Congress, 2nd sess., 7 April 1970.

U.S., Congress, House, Committee on Ways and Means, *Statistical Information Related to Family Assistance Provisions,* provided by the U.S. Department of Health, Education, and Welfare, 92nd Congress, 1st sess., 24 February 1971.

U.S., Congress, House, Committee on Ways and Means, *Social Security Amendments of 1971: Report to Accompany H.R.1,* 92nd Congress, 1st sess., 26 May 1971.

U.S., Congress, Senate, Finance Committee, *The Family Assistance Act of 1970: Hearings,* 91st Congress, 2nd sess., 1970.

U.S., Congress, Senate, Finance Committee, *Social Security Amendments of 1971: Hearings,* 92nd Congress, 1st sess., 1971.

U.S., Congress, Senate, Finance Committee, *Social Security Amendments of 1973: Report,* 93rd Congress, 1st sess., 1973.

U.S., Congress, Senate, Committee on Finance, *Information on Federal Programs to Aid the Poor,* 92nd Congress, 2nd sess., 15 February 1972.

U.S., Congress, Senate, Finance Committee, *Analysis of Cost of Committee Bill: Staff Data on H.R.1,* 92nd Congress, 2nd sess., 12 June 1972.

U.S., Congress, Senate, Finance Committee, *Staff Data and Materials on Social Services Regulations,* 93rd Congress, 1st sess., 1973.

U.S., Congress, Joint Economic Committee, *Concepts in Welfare Program Design,* 93rd Congress, 1st sess., 1973.

U.S., Congress, Joint Economic Committee, *Handbook of Public Income Transfer Programs,* 92nd Congress, 2nd sess., 1972.

U.S., Congress, Joint Economic Committee, *How Public Welfare Benefits Are Distributed in Low-Income Areas,* 93rd Congress, 1st sess., 1973.

U.S., Congress, Joint Economic Committee, *The New Supplemental Security Income Program–Impact on Current Benefits and Unresolved Issues,* 93rd Congress, 1st sess., 1973.

U.S., Congress, Joint Economic Committee, *Public Income Transfer Programs,* James R. Storey, 20 December 1973.

President's Commission on Income Maintenance Programs. *Poverty Amid Plenty* Washington, D.C.: U.S. Government Printing Office, 1969.

President's Commission on Income Maintenance Programs. *Background Papers.* Washington, D.C.: U.S. Government Printing Office, 1970.

Executive Office of the President. *Budget of the United States Government 1973.* Special Analysis. Washington, D.C.: U.S. Government Printing Office, 1972.

Executive Office of the President. *Budget of the United States Government 1974.* Special Analysis. Washington, D.C.: U.S. Government Printing Office, 1973.

U.S., Department of Commerce, Bureau of the Census, *Characteristics of the Low-Income Population 1970.* Washington, D.C.: U.S. Government Printing Office, 1971.

U.S., Department of Commerce, Bureau of the Census, *Characteristics of the Low-Income Population 1972.* Washington, D.C.: U.S. Government Printing Office, 1973.

U.S., Department of Health, Education, and Welfare, *Public Assistance Programs:*

Standards for Basic Needs, July 1972. Washington, D.C.: U.S. Government Printing Office, 1973.

U.S., Department of Health, Education, and Welfare, *Social Security Programs in the United States.* Washington, D.C.: U.S. Government Printing Office, 1973.

U.S., Department of Health, Education, and Welfare, *Source of Funds Expended for Public Assistance Payments: Fiscal Year Ended June 30, 1972.* Washington, D.C.: U.S. Government Printing Office, 1973.

U.S., Department of Health, Education, and Welfare, *Supplemental Security Income.* Washington, D.C.: U.S. Government Printing Office, April 1973.

U.S., Department of Health, Education, and Welfare, *Trend Report: Graphic Presentation of Public Assistance and Related Data, 1970.* Washington, D.C.: U.S. Government Printing Office, 23 August 1971.

U.S., Department of Health, Education, and Welfare, *Trend Report: Graphic Presentation of Public Assistance and Related Data, 1971.* Washington, D.C.: U.S. Government Printing Office, 6 October 1972.

Other Materials

American Enterprise Institute, *Welfare Reform Proposals.* Legislative Analysis No. 4. Washington, D.C.: May 17, 1971.

Friedman, Lawrence M. "Social Welfare Legislation: An Introduction." Institute for Research on Poverty Discussion Paper. Madison, Wis.: University of Wisconsin Press, 1968.

Haveman, Robert, and Lampman, Robert. "Two Alternatives to FAP's Treatment of the Working Poor." Institute for Research on Poverty Discussion Paper. Madison, Wis.: University of Wisconsin Press, 1971.

Lampman, Robert J. "Nixon's Family Assistance Plan." Institute for Research on Poverty Discussion Paper. Madison, Wis.: University of Wisconsin Press, 1969.

"Social Security Revolution." In *Congress and the Nation,* Vol. 1. Washington, D.C.: Congressional Quarterly Service, 1965.

U.S. News and World Report. "Crackdown on Welfare Begins to Take Hold." February 19, 1973, pp. 37–40.

"Welfare Legislation." In *Congress and the Nation.* Vol. 2. Washington, D.C.: Congressional Quarterly Service, 1969.

"Welfare Reform Deleted from Social Security Bill." *1972 Congressional Quarterly Almanac.* Washington, D.C.: Congressional Quarterly Service, 1973.

THE WELFARE POLICY MAKING PROCESS

Books and Articles

Bauer, Raymond, and Gergen, Kenneth, eds. *The Study of Policy Formation.* New York: Free Press, 1968.

Braybrooke, David, and Lindblom, Charles E. *A Strategy of Decision.* New York: Free Press, 1970.

Cavala, Bill, and Wildavsky, Aaron. "The Political Feasibility of Income by Right." *Public Policy* 18 (3) (Spring 1970).

Chamberlain, Lawrence H. "The Presidency, Congress, and Legislation." *Political Science Quarterly* 61 (1) (March 1946).

Clausen, Aage R., and Cheney, Richard B. "A Comparative Analysis of Senate-House Voting on Economic and Welfare Policy, 1953–1964." *American Political Science Review* 66 (1) (March 1970).

Cleaveland, Frederic N., et al. *Congress and Urban Problems.* Washington, D.C.: Brookings Institution, 1969.

Dewitt, Karen E. "Welfare Report/Complexities and State Pressures Could Delay Welfare Responsibilities Shift to U.S." *National Journal*, May 12, 1973.

Dexter, Lewis Anthony. *The Sociology and Politics of Congress.* Chicago: Rand McNally, 1969.

Donovan, John C. *The Politics of Poverty.* New York: Pegasus, 1967.

Evans, Rowland, and Novak, Robert. *Nixon in the White House.* New York: Random House, 1971.

Fenno, Richard F., Jr. *Congressmen in Committees.* Boston: Little, Brown, 1973.

———. "The Internal Distribution of Influence: The House." *The Congress and America's Future.* David Truman, ed. Englewood Cliffs, N.J.: Prentice-Hall, 1973.

Fowlkes, Frank, and Lenhart, Harry, Jr. "Congressional Report/Two Money Committees Wield Power Differently." *National Journal* 3 (15) (April 10, 1971).

Hinckley, Barbara. *Stability and Change in Congress.* New York: Harper & Row, 1971.

Huitt, Ralph K. "Democratic Party Leadership in the Senate." *Congress: Two Decades of Analysis.* Ralph K. Huitt and Robert L. Peabody, eds. New York: Harper & Row, 1969.

———. "The Internal Distribution of Influence: The Senate." *The Congress and America's Future.* David Truman, ed. Englewood Cliffs, N.J.: Prentice-Hall, 1973.

James, Dorothy B. *Poverty, Politics and Change.* Englewood Cliffs, N.J.: Prentice-Hall, 1972.

Jones, Charles O. *An Introduction to the Study of Public Policy.* Belmont, Calif.: Wadsworth, 1970.

Kotz, Nick. *Let Them Eat Promises.* Garden City, N.Y.: Doubleday Anchor, 1971.

Leventhal, Paul. "Congressional Report/Revenue Sharing Gains in Senate as Drive for Welfare Reform Falters." *National Journal* (August 1972).

———. "Welfare Report: Divided Administration Fragmented Senate Threaten Passage of Reform Legislation." *National Journal* 9 (2) (June 10, 1972).

Lindblom, Charles E. *The Intelligence of Democracy.* New York: Free Press, 1965.

———. *The Policy-Making Process.* Englewood Cliffs, N.J.: Prentice-Hall, 1968.

———. "The Science of 'Muddling Through.'" *Public Administration Review,* (June 1959).

Manley, John F. *The Politics of Finance: The House Committee on Ways and Means.* Boston: Little, Brown, 1970.
March, James G., and Simon, Herbert A. *Organizations.* New York: Wiley, 1958.
Marmor, Theodore R. *The Politics of Medicare.* Chicago: Aldine, 1973.
Matthews, Donald R., and Stimson, James A. "Decision-Making by U.S. Representatives: A Preliminary Model." *Political Decision-Making.* S. Sidney Ulmer, ed. New York: Van Nostrand Reinhold, 1970.
Mayhew, David R. *Party Loyalty Among Congressmen.* Cambridge, Mass.: Harvard University Press, 1966.
Miller, Warren E., and Stokes, Donald E. "Constituency Influence in Congress." *New Perspectives on the House of Representatives.* Robert L. Peabody and Nelson W. Polsby, eds. Chicago: Rand McNally, 1969.
Moynihan, Daniel P. "Annals of Politics: Income By Right." *The New Yorker* 27 (January 1973).
———. *The Politics of a Guaranteed Income.* New York: Random, 1973.
Neustadt, Richard E. *Presidential Power: The Politics of Leadership.* New York: Wiley, 1960.
Osborne, John. *The First Two Years of the Nixon Watch.* New York: Liveright, 1971.
Putnam, Robert D. "Studying Elite Political Cultures: The Case of 'Ideology.'" *American Political Science Review* 65 (September 1971).
Ranney, Austin, ed. *Political Science and Public Policy.* Chicago: Markham, 1968.
Ribicoff, Abraham. "He Left at Half Time." *The New Republic* 17 (February 1973).
Robinson, James A. and Majak, R. Roger. "The Theory of Decision-Making." *Contemporary Political Analysis.* James C. Charlesworth, ed. New York: Free Press, 1967.
Rossiter, Clinton. *The American Presidency.* New York: The New American Library, 1962.
Rourke, Francis E. *Bureaucracy, Politics and Public Policy.* Boston: Little, Brown, 1969.
Saloma, John S. III. *Congress and the New Politics.* Boston: Little, Brown, 1969.
Sharkansky, Ira. *The Routines of Politics.* New York: Van Nostrand, 1970.
Simon, Herbert A. "Political Research: The Decision-Making Framework." *Varieties of Political Theory.* David Easton, ed. Englewood Cliffs, N.J.: Prentice-Hall, 1965.
Snyder, Richard C. "A Decision-Making Approach to the Study of Political Phenomena." *Approaches to the Study of Politics.* Roland Young, ed. Evanston, Ill.: Northwestern University Press, 1958.
Steiner, Gilbert. *Social Insecurity: The Politics of Welfare.* Chicago: Rand McNally, 1966.
———. *The State of Welfare.* Washington, D.C.: Brookings Institution, 1971.
Sundquist, James L. *Politics and Policy.* Washington, D.C.: Brookings, Institution, 1968.
Thompson, Victor A. "Bureaucracy and Innovation." *Administrative Science Quarterly* 10 (June 1965).

Vickers, Sir Geoffrey. *The Art of Judgment: A Study of Policy Making.* New York: Basic Books, 1965.

Welsh, James. "Welfare Reform: Born, August 8, 1969; Died, October 4, 1972." *The New York Times Magazine,* 7 January 1973.

Wildavsky, Aaron. *The Politics of the Budgetary Process.* Boston: Little, Brown, 1964.

——. ed. *The Presidency.* Boston: Little, Brown, 1969.

——. "The Analysis of Issue-Contexts in the Study of Decision-Making." *The Revolt Against the Masses.* New York: Basic Books, 1971.

Yarlominsky, Adam. "Ideas Into Programs." *The Public Interest* (Winter 1966).

Other Materials

Bicker, William E. "Public Attitudes Towards and Opinions of the Current Welfare System and Major Components of the Proposed Family Assistance Plan." Report submitted to John C. Montgomery, Assistant Secretary, U.S. Department of Health, Education, and Welfare, July 24, 1970.

Dexter, Lewis Anthony. "Towards a Sociological Analysis of Policy." Paper delivered at the Annual American Political Science Association Meetings, 8–12 September 1970, Los Angeles, California.

Manley, John F. "The Family Assistance Plan: An Essay on Incremental and Nonincremental Policy-Making." Paper delivered at the Annual Meeting of the American Political Science Association, 7–12 September 1970, Los Angeles, California.

Raines, Franklin D. "Presidential Policy Development: The Genesis of the Family Assistance Program." Senior thesis, Harvard University, 1970. Mimeographed.

"Welfare Proposals Studied: OASDI Benefits Raised." *1969 Congressional Quarterly Almanac.* Washington, D.C.: Congressional Quarterly Service, 1970.

"Welfare Reform: Disappointment for the Administration." *1970 Congressional Quarterly Almanac.* Washington, D.C.: Congressional Quarterly Service, 1971.

"House Passes Welfare Reform, Senate Delays Action." *1971 Congressional Quarterly Almanac.* Washington, D.C.: Congressional Quarterly Service, 1972.

"Welfare Reform Deleted from Social Security Bill." *1972 Congressional Quarterly Almanac.* Washington, D.C.: Congressional Quarterly Service, 1973.

Index

197

About the Author

Dr. Bowler received his B.A. from Stanford University and his Ph.D. from the University of Wisconsin, Madison. As an American Political Science Association Congressional Fellow in 1970 and 1971, he worked for Senator Abraham Ribicoff of Connecticut and Congressman James C. Corman of California. From 1971 to the present he has been a member of the Political Science Department at the University of Maryland Baltimore County where he teaches courses on legislative and executive policy making and the politics of U.S. social welfare policy. He also serves as a legislative consultant on health and welfare policy to U.S. Representative James Corman, a member of the House Ways and Means Committee.